Lobbying for Libraries and the Public's Access to Government Information

An Insider's View

Bernadine E. Abbott-Hoduski

The Scarecrow Press, Inc.
Lanham, Maryland, & Oxford
2003

SCARECROW PRESS, INC.

Published in the United States of America
by Scarecrow Press, Inc.
A Member of the Rowman & Littlefield Publishing Group
4501 Forbes Boulevard, Suite 200
Lanham, Maryland 20706
www.scarecrowpress.com

PO Box 317
Oxford
OX2 9RU, UK

British Library Cataloguing in Publication Information Available

Library of Congress Cataloging-in-Publication Data

Abbott-Hoduski, Bernadine.
  Lobbying for libraries and the public's access to government information : an
insider's view / Bernadine E. Abbott-Hoduski.
    p. cm.
Includes bibliographical references and index.
  ISBN 0-8108-4585-7 (alk. paper)
    1. Libraries and society—United States. 2. Libraries and state—United
  States. 3. Libraries—Political aspects—United States. 4. Information policy—
  United States. 5. Lobbying—United States. I. Title.
  Z716.4.H63 2003
  021.2—dc21   2002012992

♾™ The paper used in this publication meets the minimum requirements
of American National Standard for Information Sciences—Permanence of
Paper for Printed Library Materials, ANSI/NISO Z39.48-1992.
Manufactured in the United States of America.

Preface

Shortly after I retired from the Joint Committee on Printing as the professional staffer for library and distribution services, Norman Horrocks persuaded me to write this book for Scarecrow Press. Norman and Shirley Lambert patiently guided me through the maze of putting a book together, from deciding on the topic to advising me on how to handle difficult issues raised in the book.

My love for libraries began with my mother, Phyllis Deshner Abbott, who introduced me to libraries and taught me how to read. My love of politics, healthy debate, and the courage to hold my own opinions were instilled in me by my father, Bryce Abbott. My parents believed in America as a place of freedom and believed that freedom was guaranteed by the Constitution. My sister, Leal Abbott, is my ongoing source of wise counsel and positive energy; out of her experience as a psychiatric social worker, she provides me with much-needed advice on the quirkiness of human nature. My brother, Anthony Abbott, a former practicing politician and union president, helps me understand the political mind. My brother, John Abbott, fierce lover of freedom, Harleys, the environment, and the working class, keeps me in touch with the real world. My three wonderful sons, Brian, Mark, and Eric Hoduski, and their families make life worth living.

In librarianship I found my second family. I cannot thank all the librarians who have influenced my professional and personal life, but I would like to thank those who have helped me in the writing of this book. Maryellen Trautman, Lois Mills, Connie McKenzie, Elizabeth Morrissette, Jeanne Isacco, Barbara Smith, Anne Heanue, and Mary Martin encouraged me to write about my experiences in the fascinating world of government information. Mary Redmond invited me to speak to librarians in New York, where I auditioned my idea of writing a book on lobbying. Once I agreed to write the book, Justine Honeyman and James Veatch provided me with good advice on putting together an outline and prospectus and gave me advice on how to market the book.

Once I started writing the book, Victoria Buckley became my guardian angel, patiently reading each version and, as a nonlibrarian, asking the right questions and forcing me to clarify my story. Victoria was so circumspect that she did not even let her husband, Francis, read the drafts of the book, although she did ask him some interesting questions about the players in the book. Francis Buckley provided me with the encouragement I needed to keep working.

Once the book was at a stage where constructive criticism was needed, my sister Leal, Joan Goddard, Anne Heanue, Sandra McAninch, Roberta Scull, Deborah Schlesinger, Elizabeth Morrissette, Mary Redmond, and Larry Abbott-Hageman carefully reviewed my work.

During my twenty years at the Congressional Joint Committee on Printing, I found my third family. I owe a special thanks to Faye Padgett, Roy Breimon, Shirley Woodrow, Sara Jones, Rosemary Cribben, Barbara Jones, and Jean Morton. I could not have survived without them.

In reading this book, keep in mind the changing nature of government as events lead to restructuring and the change of personnel. Just as you keep updating your personal address book, update your information on who runs government and other organizations.

1

Lobbying for a Cause
Is Like Creating a Quilt

Lobbying for good public policies that support libraries and the public's access to information is like making a quilt. A quilt can be created by one person, but a quilt created by a community will bring that community together. One person quilting is simple and peaceful, but a community effort requires thought, cooperation, communication, and sometimes struggle. The quilt made by a community belongs to everyone. A community quilt requires the stitches of the policymakers of our society so that this "star" quilt will be hung in a place of honor, not hidden away, unused in a trunk. Identifying who those policymakers are and getting them to the quilting bee is the trick. The policymakers are not only those who write, pass, and implement laws that support and finance libraries, but those in the community who know what policies should be created and are willing to influence others in the shaping and implementing of those policies.

Once the "star" quilt made up of the policies that ensure public access to libraries and information is created, it must be protected by lobbying. The American Indians of the Northern Plains give star quilts to individuals or organizations that deserve honor. These quilts are displayed like flags or banners at family and civic gatherings. In Montana, American Indian leaders often present such a quilt to a public official who has supported policies and programs good for American Indian communities.

Lobbying is an effective way to guarantee that our people will have access to the information they need to participate in democracy. Lobbying is asking for what we want and need. When people lobby, they persuade, influence, urge, promote, push for, talk into, and sometimes even pull strings. Lobbying requires action, getting out and doing something to accomplish a goal. Sometimes when legislative lobbying fails, it means going to court, as librarians did when they went all the way to the Supreme Court to get the Communications Decency Act declared unconstitutional, or taking action, like ten California groups in filing a class action suit arguing that the state had failed its constitutional obligation to provide library access to public school students in minority, low-income, and immigrant neighborhoods.[1]

People use information from libraries and other sources in their public and private lives. They need information for learning, for working, and for cultural and spiritual enrichment. Libraries are key to the public's ability to access that information. Libraries range from the one-room schoolhouse on the high prairie with a few books and an Internet terminal to the "Library on the Hill," the Library of Congress, collector of the world's information. Libraries all over the world cooperate to preserve and provide public access to information. If we don't lobby for libraries and the public's access to information, the money and support will not be there.

Libraries and information systems owned by the public are part of a social infrastructure that underlies true democracy and therefore must be supported by the people. James K. Galbraith, economist and professor at the LBJ School of Public Policy at the University of Texas, put it well in *Created Unequal* when he argued:

> [M]inor reflection shows that the vast bulk of neglected public works in America would be at best tangential to business needs. Advanced, export-oriented American manufacturing enterprise is not seriously hamstrung by infrastructure problems. What it has traditionally needed—roads, rail, electricity, and water service—it has gotten. . . . What is missing is investment in such things as public libraries, parks, city streets and sidewalks, urban mass transit. Big business gets the infrastructure it needs, and for the rest neither demands great improvements nor suffers unduly when spending is cut back. . . . This explains why business interests are not in the forefront of demands for higher infrastructure spending and why these items were the first to fall in the face of conservative opposition in Congress.[2]

Galbraith encouraged lobbying for the public's interest:

> We need to expand investment in cities and schools precisely to provide the equalizing consumption experiences and political expecta-

tions that the private economy is not providing, precisely to defy and not to accommodate the influence of business needs on the social structure. If progressives are interested in these goals, they must find a language in which to defend them for the sake of the people themselves, for the sake of the culture and society and democracy, and for the sake of civilization. Otherwise progressives will continue to find themselves in reliance on disinterested allies; they may be invited to the parley, but they will never be given the gavel. And they will continue to lose the budget battles when the chips are down.[3]

Lobby everyone who has anything to do with the issue that you are interested in shaping, including

- people in and out of government,
- legislative and executive branches of any level of government,
- those who influence officials in the legislative and executive branches of government,
- members of the nonprofit and for-profit sectors,
- members of your own group,
- the media, and
- the public.

The most important person to be lobbied is the person on the inside of whatever group or organization you are lobbying. Get to know the person on the inside who makes decisions or influences the one who makes decisions about your cause. The person on the inside often needs the ideas, pressure, and support of outsiders before he or she can persuade other insiders to support a policy. Outsiders can provide the research, the data, and the reward for the person on the inside. Most policymakers are on the inside because they think they can do good and make their community appreciate them for doing good. Insiders are human beings, and they need appreciation. To pass a bill, implement a regulation, or establish a policy, insiders may have to prove that there is support for the proposal, bill, or draft regulation. Be aware, however, that while you are lobbying the insiders for a cause, they may actually be lobbying *you*.

Don't count on just one insider to promote the cause of libraries and access to information. Just when you think that something substantial is going to happen, the insider you are depending on may have a personal crisis or move to another position, or some other equally key person proves to be more powerful. For example, several members of Congress, who planned on expanding the public's access to government information beyond the paper world through microforms and electronic access, saw their legislative plans unravel because of their personal problems. See chapter 6 to find out how these legislators' plans to revise the laws concerning the printing and dissemination of U.S. government information were changed in unexpected ways.

If you are lobbying an institution, organization, or association, you need to understand its power structure. You need to find out whom and where you must lobby to accomplish what you want. When I joined the United States Congress as a committee professional staffer, I had a head start on understanding the structure of the Congress and the executive and judicial branches of government because I was a professional government documents librarian. I had to understand the structure of government in order to decipher the government's publications so I could serve the information needs of my library's users.

I understood the structure of Congress because I had studied the power structure of a similar organization, the American Library Association (ALA). ALA's policies are established by a council elected by its membership. Fifty of those elected councilors represent ALA's state chapters. ALA has hundreds of membership units and committees that funnel policy issues to the council for adoption. I learned the structure of ALA because the Missouri Library Association Social Responsibilities Round Table (MLA SRRT) wanted to persuade ALA to censure the Missouri State Library Commission for forcing the resignation of Joan Bodger as consultant for children's services at the Missouri State Library. As coordinator of MLA SRRT, I carried that request to my second ALA conference where Joan Goddard, other Missouri librarians, and I were successful in persuading ALA to censure the commission.

In 1969, Bodger wrote a letter to the *Columbia* (Mo.) *Daily Tribune* saying that she would include the *Free Press*, a University of Missouri student newspaper, in a display of student-produced newspapers at the state library. The display was set up so librarians, teachers, ministers, youth leaders, and students could "avail themselves of the historically important, student-produced newspapers that are proliferating throughout this county." The *Free Press* illustrated its opposition to war and support of the free speech movement with a cartoon on the front page showing a policeman raping the Statue of Liberty. Bodger argued for inclusion of the paper, saying, "All over the world children and young people are protesting. They are not only trying to save their lives, but to save life. Nothing these young protestors do or say is as obscene as the death of body and spirit we seek to impose through war, pollution, population explosion, dehumanization and the bomb." She pointed out that the week before she had said basically the same thing while speaking as a hired expert at an administration approved censorship panel at the University of Missouri. Her speech was quoted approvingly in the *Missourian*, the official campus newspaper.[4]

To persuade ALA to censure the library board, I needed to learn ALA's power structure quickly, so I turned to William DeJohn, coordinator of the ALA Social Responsibilities Round Table (SRRT). SRRT was trying to democratize ALA by lobbying for open meetings and a greater voice for members in the development of ALA policies. DeJohn had been urging me to get more involved in ALA, and since he knew the inner workings of ALA, I asked him for advice. He invited me to shadow him during the 1970 conference, promising to teach me ALA's power structure and to introduce me to the power holders, elected and nonelected. With his tutorial, we were able to make Bodger's case a cause célèbre, and the Missouri State Library Commission was censured by ALA.

Joan Goddard and Carolyn Forsman (founding members of SRRT) showed me how understanding the structure, by-laws, and constitutions of groups affects the members' of those groups ability to influence policy. Norman Horrocks, Arthur Curley, and Eric Moon taught me that mastering parliamentary procedure and willingness to debate other members of an association on issues is an effective way to influence policies. As members of the ALA Council, they understood that what some people consider boring—the analysis of the documents establishing an organization—can give you the tools needed to influence that organization. So if you don't know the rules and the structure of an organization, find people who do and are willing to share that knowledge with you.

I used my knowledge of ALA's power structure to accomplish my next goal, which was a membership voice in ALA for government documents librarians. Most of them did not belong to ALA because they believed they had no home in ALA and no power to affect ALA's policies and activities. In 1970, I convinced the Social Responsibilities Round Table to start the Task Force on Cataloging-in-Publication (CIP) with the primary purpose of convincing the Library of Congress to include government documents in CIP. We then asked that the Library of Congress add the superintendent of documents classification numbers to its catalog cards.[5] In June 1971, the Library of Congress informed us that it would add the number to the catalog cards.[6] Its plans to include government documents in CIP were still in the works by the time we decided in the summer of 1971 to expand our scope and become the SRRT Task Force on Government Publications. We realized that our concerns about government documents went beyond CIP, and we needed a vehicle to attract many more documents librarians to our cause. Although there was an ALA Reference and Adult Services Division/Resources and Technical Services Division/Association of State Library Agencies Interdivisional Committee on Public Documents, we wanted an active membership group, not an appointed committee.

By the fall of 1971, we decided that we needed a round table devoted to government documents issues so we could attract librarians from all types of institutions. Geneva Finn, Candace Morgan, and Mary Redmond at the Illinois State Library; Lois Mills at Western Illinois University; and I started collecting signatures of ALA members on a petition in December 1971 asking ALA to establish the Government Documents Round Table (GODORT). We mailed a flyer and petition form to every federal depository library, asking them to return it to me by the end of the month. We came to the ALA meeting in January 1972 with over three hundred signatures, prepared to persuade the power structure of ALA to give us what we wanted— and they did.

Thanks to DeJohn's tutorial, we knew that we had to lobby two committees, the governing ALA Council and the ALA Executive Board, to authorize the establishment of GODORT. By the end of the week, we were in business and agreed to meet that spring at the Saint Louis Public Library to write the constitution, set up task forces, and prepare a slate of officers.[7] We were ready at the ALA conference in the summer of 1972 for our first membership meeting and were surprised when some 450 documents enthusiasts turned out and we had to move to a bigger room.

To summarize the points of these real-life experiences, if you need to move an entire institution to support your cause, you must

- understand the structure of that institution,
- identify who within that structure has the power to do what you want, and
- lobby those people.

NOTES

1. "Suit Cites Lack of Library Access," *American Libraries* 31, no. 7 (August 2000): 22.

2. James K. Galbraith, *Created Unequal: The Crisis in American Pay* (New York: Free Press, 1998), 207.

3. Galbraith, *Created Unequal*, 209.

4. A Statement of Position from Joan Bodger, consultant, Children's Services, State Library of Missouri, April 7, 1969.

5. Bernadine E. Hoduski, "C.I.P.—A Basic Social Responsibility," *Choice* (December 1970): 1355–56.

6. Letter from C. Sumner Spaulding, assistant director for cataloging, Library of Congress, to Bernadine E. Hoduski, chair, SRRT Task Force on Cataloging in Publication, June 3, 1971.

7. Those in attendance at that meeting were Bernadine Abbott Hoduski, Clare Beck, Marion Carroll, Geneva Finn, Deanne Holzberlein, Lois Mills, Bill Smith, and Maryellen Trautman.

2

The Cause/Quilt Must Be Decided on and Designed

To persuade policymakers to participate in creating library and information access quilts, the community must take a number of steps. The first step is knowing what the community wants. Almost all successful lobbying flows from that knowledge. Arriving at knowing what the community wants is often a painful process. A quilt must be designed and planned before the actual sewing can begin.

Richard Harass in his book *The Power to Persuade* gives advice on how to be effective in government, the public sector, or any unruly organization and cautions that "The political world is characterized— indeed, defined by—a diffusion of power and authority: you can accomplish very little alone. Consequently persuasion is the key to effectiveness. But you cannot persuade independent centers of power if you are not first in control of yourself. You must determine what you want to accomplish and prepare yourself, then proceed with discipline."[1]

Getting from an idea to a law or a program takes many steps. Most policymakers will not take an idea and immediately make it a law or a policy. They feel more comfortable going through a number of steps because this assures them that their constituents support the idea. Policymakers like consensus or at least as little vocal opposition as possible. The time required to complete the steps may cover the tenure of a number of legislators or regulators.

For example, librarians in the 1970s knew that for the public to be well served, electronic government information had to be part of the Federal Depository Library Program. Merely presenting the idea to members of Congress was not enough. After intensive lobbying from librarians, users, and even congressional staff, the Congressional Joint Committee on Printing (JCP) supported a number of initiatives to provide the public with electronic access to government information:

- Senator Charles McC. Mathias Jr. (R-Md.), chair of JCP, established the Ad Hoc Committee on Depository Library Access to Federal Automated Data Bases in May 1983.
- The ad hoc committee issued its report *Provision of Federal Government Publications in Electronic Format to Depository Libraries*[2] in December 1984.
- JCP held an open forum to discuss the report in June 1985.[3]
- JCP passed a resolution in April 1987 authorizing a series of pilot projects to test the feasibility and practicality of disseminating government publications to depository libraries in electronic formats.
- JCP called for proposals for pilot projects from federal publishing agencies.
- JCP and the Government Printing Office (GPO) selected five agency pilots out of sixteen proposals that would answer a number of policy and technical concerns.
- GPO, in consultation with JCP, produced a plan entitled *Dissemination of Information in Electronic Format to Federal Depository Libraries: Proposed Project Descriptions* in June 1988, which JCP accepted on June 29, 1988, and distributed for public comment.
- GPO, working with the publishing agencies, and JCP administered the pilots from 1988 through 1991.
- JCP requested and accepted studies on how best to use electronic technologies to support agency publishers and depository libraries by the Office of Technology Assessment and the General Accounting Office in 1988.
- Hearings on the implementation of the pilot projects were held by Senate and House Appropriations Committees.
- The General Counsel of GPO issued a legal opinion on March 25, 1991, stating that depository libraries could not be asked to pay a fee for access to government publications and that publishing agencies and GPO are responsible for the costs of providing depository libraries with access to electronic publications.
- JCP held hearings in April 1991 entitled "Government Information as a Public Asset" and in June and July of 1991 on "New Technology and the Government Printing Office."

- Two bills were introduced, H.R. 2772, the GPO Wide Information Network for Data Online Act of 1991, and S. 2813, the GPO Gateway to Government Act of 1992, to make online electronic government information a formal part of the Federal Depository Library Program.
- The Committee on House Administration and the Senate Committee on Rules and Administration held joint hearings on the bills on July 23, 1992.
- A mysterious senator put a silent hold on the Senate bill, which killed the bills for 1992.
- The GPO Electronic Information Access Enhancement Act of 1993 (PL 103-40) was introduced and passed early in 1993.
- The appropriations committees held hearings on how much money the Congress should appropriate for the GPO Access program.
- Finally, the statute was implemented by the Government Printing Office in 1994.

Goals may be positive or negative. Positive goals include getting a bill, a policy, or a regulation adopted by policymakers. Negative goals include blocking a bill or a policy that you believe will change an existing law or policy to your cause's detriment. For example, librarians worked to prevent various versions of the Paperwork Reduction Act (PRA) from being enacted until the bill was changed to meet some of their concerns. Librarians feared that the proposed bill would give the Office of Management and Budget (OMB) too much power over the production and dissemination of government information and would promote privatization of government information, taking it out of the public domain and therefore eliminating free public access.

You can work to defeat a bill in a number of ways. One of the lesser-known methods used in the U.S. Senate is the silent hold. A *silent hold* is when a senator writes the leadership of the Senate asking that a bill not be voted on until the senator's concerns are addressed. Leadership attempts to resolve the concern with the bill's sponsoring senator. Sometimes several senators will employ what is known as a *rolling hold*, in which as soon as one issue is resolved, another concern is raised until time runs out for a vote. Only the leadership of the Senate knows the identity of the senator asking for the hold. Most legislative bodies have similar methods to keep legislation from being adopted through consensus.

Two documents librarians, Barbara Smith and Lois Mills,[4] spent their October 1989 weekend at the beach and the last hours of the 102nd Congress calling Senators Paul Simon (D-Ill.) and William Roth (R-Del.), asking them to put a hold on the reauthorization of the Paperwork Reduction Act. They learned about the silent hold from me, and I had learned about it at lunch that Friday with a lobbyist supporting the bill. He informed me that I had lost and he had won because Congress was adjourning over the weekend and that the only thing that could stop the PRA bill at that late hour was a hold by a senator. He realized right away that he should not have tipped his hand and that I just might be able to use the information against the bill. I suspect that there were other opponents of the bill who also called their senators that weekend, but Smith and Mills's calls certainly helped kill the bill.

As of the 106th Congress, holds are not as silent as before, but they are still a tactic to be used by those who want to kill a bill. Many bills at the end of a Congress pass the Senate only if there is a consensus among senators, and it only takes one senator to put a hold on a bill. Prior to the 106th Congress, only the majority leader of the Senate knew which senators had holds on bills, making it difficult to lobby the senator with the hold. Since then, the unwritten rule has been changed to require that the senator putting a hold on the bill notify the sponsor of the bill and the committee responsible for the bill as well as the majority and minority leaders of the Senate.

Be aware that it may take a long time to reach your goal. It took from 1974 to 1993 to pass the GPO Access Act giving depository libraries online access to electronic government information. If your goal is not rooted in your basic beliefs and philosophy, you may get discouraged long before it is achieved. You must also understand your opponents' basic beliefs and philosophy in order to understand the obstacles in your way. Take the initiative in the associations and institutions to which you belong, and advocate a position or a solution. Most people are reluctant to assert their own position but may end up agreeing with yours if you present and argue for it. Only by arguing your position and convincing others to support it will you be able to lobby with the weight of numbers and the authority of leadership.

Spend your energy and time on what is most important to achieve your goal. Make sure your goal is one that will influence policy and is not just of fleeting concern. Do not let others distract you and dissipate your energy. Stop and think about what you are doing. Will it further your goal? If not, do not do it.

Think in cycles: the two-year cycle of Congress and the cycle of the executive branch, which is four years in the federal government and in most states. If you are working on the state or local level, find out what their cycle is and gear your planning and work to fit into the policymakers' cycle. For-profit and nonprofit organizations and associations also have cycles and deadlines for establishing policies, deciding on lobbying priorities, and taking public positions. Remember your high school and college days when you had to meet deadlines or your work was for naught. It is the same in government and other organizations. Timing is important when it comes to legislation, regulations, and the budget process. Do your lobbying close to the time that the decisions will be made. Most policymakers are responsible for a number of quilt squares and cannot think about or work on all of them at once.

NOTES

1. Richard N. Harass, *The Power to Persuade* (Boston: Houghton Mifflin, 1994).

2. U.S. Congress, Joint Committee on Printing, Ad Hoc Committee on Depository Library Access to Federal Automated Data Bases, *Provision of Federal Government Publications in Electronic Format to Depository Libraries*, S. Prt. 98–260 (Washington, D.C.: U.S. Government Printing Office, December 1984).

3. U.S. Congress, Joint Committee on Printing, *An Open Forum on the Provision of Electronic Federal Information to Depository Libraries: Report of the Staff of the Joint Committee on Printing to the Chairman of the Joint Committee on Printing*, S. Rpt. 99-84 (Washington, D.C.: U.S. Government Printing Office, 1985).

4. Barbara Smith was the government documents librarian at the Skidmore College Library, Saratoga Springs, New York, and Lois Mills was the government publications and legal reference librarian at Western Illinois University in Macomb.

3

How to Lobby

MAKE IT PERSONAL

Personal contact is the most effective form of lobbying. It includes face-to-face discussions between a policymaker and an individual, testifying at a legislative or regulatory hearing, speaking up at a public meeting, and engaging in other direct communications. It includes interaction between groups of people and policymakers, such as inviting a member of Congress to address your group and then having a discussion with that member about an issue. I include the legislative process, such as designing a bill and attending hearings, under personal contact because this process involves extensive personal interaction with many people and groups of people.

Work as an Individual

Once you decide on your goal, you must be there every step of the way, whether you are lobbying for a bill, a regulation, a change in policy, or more money. Make sure that the people you are trying to influence know that you are there. Attend public hearings, commission and board meetings, and other meetings where public officials will be in attendance. Be there often enough that they recognize you when you walk into the room or they hear your name. That kind of recognition takes time and persistence.

If you see your legislator, policymaker, officer holder, or a candidate for those offices at church, in an airport, train station, grocery store, or even on the street, walk up and say hello and put in a quick word for libraries. Make friends with legislators, office holders, and politicians. You do not have to buy them lunch, dinner, or drinks. You can be a bit more subtle by frequenting the eating places they frequent such as local restaurants, the cafeteria, or carry-out in the Capitol or government building. Hang out at the bar where politicians go after work. Attend political dinners and receptions. Make sure you say hello to the politicians and office holders and their spouses and other family members. Just attending the dinner to support a candidate is not enough; you should walk up and introduce yourself. There is no sense in going to a reception to talk to your fellow lobbyists. I have gone to many congressional receptions where the host group almost ignored the legislators. Legislators and their top staff do not go to receptions to eat and drink; they go there to show a group that they are willing to listen to their position on issues. Don't waste their time and yours by ignoring them.

Lois Mills, government publications and legal reference librarian at Western Illinois University in Macomb, was very good at influencing local, state, and national elected officials to support policies good for libraries. She got some of that power by persuading good people to run for public office, working in their campaigns, and earning their respect. She not only attended political gatherings, she served as a party precinct committeewoman and, on the McDonough County Democratic Coalition, got people out to vote, held fund-raisers, and even ran for office herself. She ran for the school board, and the local newspaper called her "that woman." She could call a member of the U.S. Congress and actually get to speak to the member. She was not handed off to a staff person because the staff knew that she had a personal working relationship with the senator or representative and a lot of influence back home. Those elected officials who do not hire staff familiar with who is who back home or staff willing to learn who is who often regret it when its time for constituents to vote.

When Lois came to Washington, D.C., to lobby, she introduced me, a congressional staffer, to the staff of the members whom she had helped get elected. She knew the staff and the families of elected officials. Once the wife of a senator took us to lunch in the senators' private dining room in the Capitol. Having lunch with the senator's wife in a restaurant limited to senators and their special guests enhanced Lois's power with the senator's personal and committee staff. It meant that staff would treat her concerns and phone calls as important. Including me in the luncheon enhanced my power with her senator's staff. It also let the staff on my committee know that when we needed help that I could call on an influential constituent of a high-ranking senator.

I understood the symbolic importance of lunch in the senator's dining room because when I started at the JCP, the Republican minority staff director told me that I would never be allowed to eat there unless I was with someone important like himself, the staff director, or the chair of the JCP. I had lunch in the Capitol dining room with the staff director my first week on the job and remember sitting under the stained glass window of George Washington and being awed by the chandeliers, original portrait of Abraham Lincoln, and senators at other tables. I also remember having lunch there years later and telling the hostess that the guy she was ignoring because he looked like a lost teenager was actually a senator—Senator Paul Wellstone (D-Minn.)—newly elected to the Senate.

Get to know the lobbyists on the other side. Learn as much as possible about their positions and arguments, so you know what they are telling policymakers in order to better refute those arguments. Stay friendly. You may have some positions and goals in common and may be able to help each other out. For example, in the early 1970s, librarians and publishers were on opposite sides when it came to micropublishing government publications. Librarians supported the plans by the Government Printing Office to micropublish, whereas the Information Industry Association (IIA) opposed it, arguing that librarians should buy microform copies from private publishers. IIA represented a number of publishers who were filming and selling government publications in microform. They included the Congressional Information Service (congressional hearings, reports, and documents), READEX Microprint Corp. (all the publications listed in the *Monthly Catalog of United States Government Publications*), Greenwood Press (urban documents), and Information Handling Service (the *Congressional Record, Code of Federal Regulations,* and the *Federal Register*).

In 1973, the IIA decided to confront the threat of government micropublishing by bringing the two sides together with congressional, GPO, and Library of Congress (LC) staff at a Forum on the Legislative Needs of the U. S. Depository Library System. The meeting was held in the Caucus Room of the Cannon House Office Building. Paul Zurkowski, IIA president and organizer of the forum, explained that

even the selection of the meeting location and the proper placement
of chairs could affect the outcome of a meeting. Holding the meeting in a congressional building showed that someone in the IIA had
clout with a member of Congress since those meeting rooms have to
be sponsored by a member or committee. The meeting did not change
any minds about micropublishing, but it did identify areas where the
two groups could work together. Holding the forum was a smart
move on the part of the publishers because they had an opportunity
to assure the librarians that they supported the depository program,
to influence congressional staff, and to size up their opponents. The
publishers wanted to stay on good terms with the librarians because
they were customers for other products besides microforms.

Government agencies often have their own legislative goals.
Agencies that play a role in funding and supporting libraries and
access to information are the ones you need to concentrate on. On
the national level, the Institute of Museum and Library Services,
the National Commission on Libraries and Information Science
(NCLIS), and the Office of Management and Budget are good examples. On the state level, the governor's office, budget agencies,
departments of education, and state libraries play key roles in information and library policy and funding. Agencies work with
their authorizing/legislating and appropriating committees. You
need to get to know the staff of those agencies. Meet with agency
staff and ask them what their legislative requests are. Many times
those legislative requests are included in their budget submission.
See whether you share the same goals. If you agree with their goals,
offer to help them influence the budget and legislative staff. Try to
influence the agency's legislative proposals. Your opponents, if they
are wise, will also meet with agency staff.

Agencies may decide that their authorizing/legislative committee
is not supportive of the agency's version of legislation, so they may
go to their appropriating committee to get legislation enacted. This
will happen if the committees have opposing philosophies or goals
and the agency agrees with one of the committees. Although authorizing committees frown on legislation being included in appropriation laws, agencies often get their way. Since agencies are under
the control of an executive officer, such as the president, governor, or
mayor, they may have an ace up their sleeve because their chief executive can veto a bill that the agency does not like. This chief executive can influence legislation because he or she has the power to

provide patronage jobs, allocate money and projects to certain geographic areas dear to a legislator's heart, or even influence the political party that provides money for election or re-election.

Remember you are working with individuals who are being influenced by other individuals and groups. For example, the legislative leadership may pressure the legislator into following a set agenda so no matter how worthy your cause, it will go nowhere. The legislator's or policymaker's political party has a strong influence on its members, and the party may consider certain goals more important than your goals. Since there is limited time and power, your goal will take a back seat to theirs. There are two major political parties in the United States, Democrats and Republicans. There are other parties, but as of yet they have not been powerful enough to get their members elected to many offices. It is important which party wins because they control who gets to chair committees as well who gets on the committee. They also control whether a piece of legislation is considered and whether it is voted out of committee. Political parties are composed of people who organize to win elections so they can control government and its policies and actions. You need to know who the influential people are in the political party of the person you wish to influence.

It is helpful to read the party's platform. Platforms address the issues that are important to the members of the parties. They are developed and voted on by the members on the county and state levels and then are incorporated into a national platform. Party members expect their candidates to uphold the principles in these platforms, although once elected, some officials do not pay attention to them because their constituents or their financial supporters don't agree with parts of the platform.

Be realistic. You may not be the best person to lobby the policymaker. Another policymaker may be more effective in reaching colleagues. Work to get the policymaker with influence to convince others on your behalf. It may be another member of your group who is better suited to lobby a particular policymaker. That person may have campaigned for him or her, supported this person financially, or known him or her at school, church, or someplace else. It is a good idea to identify these people as you work on your cause so when you need their help, you already know who can and will help you.

An example of how even policymakers on the top rung have to lobby each other for their causes is the story of how the Peace Corps

legislation got through Congress. President John F. Kennedy set up
the Peace Corps on a temporary basis with Executive Order 10924,
made his brother-in-law Sargent Shriver the head, and told him to
convince Congress to pass the needed legislation. Shriver not only
had to convince Congress but had to fight the administration to make
sure that the Peace Corps was an independent agency. He turned to
Vice President Lyndon Johnson for help. It was Johnson who lobbied
Kennedy for Peace Corps independence and advised Shriver that he
needed to sell every member of Congress individually on the idea.
Shriver followed his advice and visited with every member of both
parties. Near the end of the process, he asked President Kennedy and
Vice President Johnson to lobby personally the key leaders of the
Senate and House. It was not a given that the Peace Corps would ex-
ist just because President Kennedy had promised the American people. He and his staff had to fight for it every step of the way.[1]

Once you have identified people who can help you promote your
cause, make a list of them and how you can contact them when you
need them. You may want to set up your traditional and e-mail address books in categories of people who have indicated a willingness to work on certain causes. You might also want to note in your
address files something unique about the person that will help you
visualize them when you communicate with them.

Work with a Group

Groups, such as associations, unions, and organizations, lobby all
the time. Those groups generally have units that are responsible for
most of the lobbying. Those units are charged with notifying the rest
of the members of the group when it is appropriate to lobby on behalf of the group's issues. For example, the American Library Association has close to sixty-three thousand members who work on
many issues. They depend on a special office in Washington, D.C.,
to track legislation and do the day-to-day work of lobbying. The
Washington office keeps track of the interests of the units of ALA
and contacts them when their concerns are being addressed by policymakers and legislators. Those units usually provide expert witnesses to testify. They also contact the members of their units to support the Washington office with lobbying.

Some groups forget the key element, which is keeping their members educated about and interested in the issues, so when it is time

to lobby, they are knowledgeable, motivated, and capable of effective lobbying. Large groups need to remember that it is not enough for only their specialized units to lobby. Every unit has access to different levels of the political spectrum, and to succeed, you must use all those access points. For example, if a group specializes in government information but the issue affects the entire library, it is not enough for only the government publications librarians to lobby, it must be the library directors, the boards of trustees, friends of the library, and the users of the libraries. Many a quilt has been left undone because not all the quilters were asked for help.

Sometimes it is best to lobby as a coalition. Such a coalition is formed when a group of organizations and/or individuals come together to pursue a common goal. Their aggregate numbers may impress the policymakers. Their diversity shows the policymakers that this is an important issue and they should pay attention.

Coalitions are good because they bring new perspectives to an issue, and the members may come up with ways to strengthen the arguments for supporting the goal. Cooperating in a coalition spreads the work over a number of groups and divides up the cost of phone calls, letters, printing, postage, and travel to meetings and hearings. The coalition can afford to publish a joint newsletter. Other newspapers and media outlets are more likely to cover coalition issues. If this particular effort is successful, it will make it easier to work together on future issues. Working together helps educate all the groups about the issues most important to other coalition members.

However, lobbying as a coalition creates unique challenges. For example, a strong position on an issue by an organization may be diluted by having to reach consensus with their coalition partners. Some coalition members may be constrained from lobbying because of their tax status, or they may not see themselves as lobbyists but as educators. These groups can work on background issues and conduct educational campaigns but cannot or will not actually lobby.

Some organizations and associations may not like coalitions because if the lobbying is successful, the credit must be shared. Of course, victory and therefore credit cannot be predicted until you try to win as a coalition. There may be differing styles of governance, and this may prevent some of the groups from being able to change position, if needed, without polling all their members. This problem can be alleviated if organizations adopt policies that cover a number of situations and provide some flexibility for compromise.

If you decide to form a coalition, use a few simple stitches. Start out with a specific issue, one that you are fairly sure that everyone can support without a lot of negotiating. Ask for a key contact person, who will be responsible for getting their group to agree and work on issues. Have regular meetings of the coalition. Recruit new members. Make sure that everyone is introduced at every meeting so newcomers feel welcome and know who the players are. Publish a list of coalition members and their key contact person. Have a standard procedure for groups to use in identifying issues and their proposed solution. Consult on strategy.

In a crisis, if all you have is names printed on the letterhead, with no one in the group committed to making the coalition work, you do not have a viable coalition. Each group must have a liaison doing things like testifying or identifying a good witness for hearings and making sure that person gets to the hearing with well-written testimony. The liaison must be able to (1) help in the writing of position papers, testimony, and news releases; (2) be responsible for contacting the members of their own group for help; (3) work to persuade their group to adopt policies and activities that will promote the work of the coalition; and (4) persuade their group to contribute money and expertise to make the coalition work.

Coalitions need to keep bringing in new members since new groups are constantly being formed and other groups are dropping out. Some coalitions need to work on multiple levels, including national, state, and local—with people on each level willing to contact policymakers, participate in meetings, and discuss issues. Other coalitions need participants on only one level, particularly if the cause is very focused and can be achieved in a short time frame.

Participate in Public Meetings

Public meetings are held by many legislative, executive, and regulatory bodies to gather public comments before making a decision on a regulation, new program, or bill. Check with your own state, county, and local bodies about the rules for participating in public meetings. Many state constitutions require open meetings of public bodies. These are often called sunshine or open meeting provisions. The Montana Supreme Court ruled in 1998 that the Montana constitution requires that even the Montana legislature's political party caucuses must be open to the press and the public. Some states require notice in local newspapers; others have online bulletin boards; others post meetings on traditional bulletin boards in the city and county courthouses or in the library. Many public bodies do not do a good job of letting the public know about meetings or how to acquire documents for those meetings. They may post the notice in such a way that the majority of citizens do not see it. If that is the case, you should insist that the public body that you are interested in provide notice in a variety of ways. For example, one library board of trustees meetings were consistently listed incorrectly in the local newspaper, and the board made little effort to change that until the chair of the friends of that library requested that they make a greater effort to notify the paper of the correct times and meeting places.

On the national level under the Administrative Procedures Act, agencies are required to hold public meetings. Their advisory committees must open meetings to the public except when it is determined that any portion of the meeting is to be closed to the public consistent with the provisions of section 552b of title 5 of the *United States Code*. Meetings may be closed or information resulting from meetings may be denied to the public if they come under the exceptions of 552b(c)(1) through (10). Reasons for nondisclosure range from information that must be kept secret in the interest of national defense, information exempted under statute, internal personnel rules and practices, trade secrets, information accusing a person of a crime, information restricted because of privacy laws, investigatory records that would interfere with enforcement proceedings, the right of a person to a fair trial, and the identity of a confidential source. For every meeting closed and information not made available pursuant to these exceptions, the general counsel or chief legal officer of the agency shall publicly certify that, in his or her opinion, the meeting may be closed to the public and shall state each relevant exemptive provision.

Meetings must be advertised in the *Federal Register* giving the time, place, and subject of the meetings. The public is entitled to an opportunity for public comment. Minutes of the meeting must include a record of attendees and a description of the discussion. The *Federal Register* is available online through GPO Access. Copies of documents distributed for the use of the committee must be made available to the public. Some of these documents are published in the *Federal Register*, some are available on agency websites, and others must be requested from the agency or viewed at the agency. Some agencies deposit these types of documents at public libraries, and many of them are distributed to the federal depository libraries. For example, there may be a draft environmental impact statement outlining the effects of a mine on a park, river, or community. Unless it is determined under U.S.C. title 5, section 552b, that a record or portion of a record is not to be made public, all records pertaining to the meeting must be made available to the public.

I was confronted with closed advisory committee meetings when I served on the Advisory Committee to the Public Printer on Depository Libraries. The first two meetings in February and June 1973 were closed to the public, including depository librarians. I knew about Public Law 92-463 passed in October 1972 requiring that federal advisory committees be open because we were observing the law at the Environmental Protection Agency. After the first closed meeting in February 1973, I wrote to Rowland Darling, acting superintendent of documents, raising questions about whether GPO's advisory committees were subject to Public Law 92-463, OMB directive circular A-63, and the president's executive order 11686.[2] GPO's response, on advice from counsel, was to change the name of the committee to the Advisory Council to the Public Printer for Depository Libraries, and our next meeting in Las Vegas in June 1973 was also closed.[3] I understood from talking to staff at GPO that GPO considered itself exempt from this law because it is part of the legislative branch. After the meeting in June 1973, I spoke privately with the new public printer, Thomas F. McCormick, about how unhappy the members of the Government Documents Round Table of ALA were about being excluded from observing the meeting. The meeting in January 1974, held in Chicago in conjunction with the ALA midwinter meeting, started out closed but was then opened at the direction of the public printer. A dozen GODORT members waiting outside the door happily accepted the invitation to be observers.

In later years, portions of some of the Depository Library Council (DLC) meetings were closed, and the library community was quick to complain. In March 1985 at its Albuquerque, New Mexico, meeting, the council closed the morning session of its opening day so council and GPO staff could have a private dialogue. I was admitted only after I insisted that as a representative from GPO's oversight committee, the Joint Committee on Printing, I should be there, and if they denied me access, they would have to write a letter of explanation to the chair of the JCP. Dr. James Veatch was the only council member to object to the closed meeting during the closed meeting and later introduced a resolution supporting open meetings at the next open session. The resolution was not opposed and ensured that citizens could attend the depository library council meetings. Veatch stood up for the rights of Americans to know what is going on in a tax-supported meeting. Veatch's resolution was supported by several past chairs of the DLC who had been denied access to the closed meeting. Jeanne Isacco, a past chair of DLC, presented a petition with forty-four signatures requesting that all meetings of council members be open to all attendees.[4] Members of library associations that had nominated several of the DLC members reminded them of their association's support of open meetings.

During the closed meeting, several council members said they were more comfortable and could express their opinions more easily without an audience. I was told by one of the council members attending her first meeting that she had expected an open meeting and was surprised when told that it was closed. Because she was new and confused, she did not object during the closed meeting. Later she voted for open meetings. If you are serving on a board or committee and the chair or other authority suddenly declares a closed meeting, be sure to raise questions as to what law or regulation allows such a closure. Often just raising the question will force the opening of the meeting.

Often the openness of meetings to the public depends on the philosophy of the head of a department, agency, or commission. Some, like Public Printer of the United States Michael DiMario, strongly believed in open meetings and his agency's accountability to the public. He believed in including all the attendees at Depository Library Council in meetings, receptions, and other functions. It was during his tenure that the DLC meetings and educational seminars were held at the same time in order to encourage attendance and to provide a venue for the interaction between GPO staff, agency publishers, and librarians. Public Printers Thomas McCormick and Jack Boyle also believed in open meetings. Several other public printers saw the DLC meetings as opportunities to promote their own political fortunes. They limited attendees at receptions, held off the record meetings with DLC, and did not allow many of their staff to attend the meetings.

It is important to attend public meetings, learn about the issues, and express your opinion. If you don't, public officials can legitimately say that they gave the public a chance to influence their decisions and the public did not choose to do so. If you cannot attend in person, find out whether you can submit a written statement.

Use the Legislative Process

Design a Bill

Developing a bill and getting it passed is similar to designing a quilt and completing it. No matter what kind of a bill is being created, several steps are the same. The legislative process, whether on the national, state, or local level, goes through similar steps: the idea; drafting of the bill; introduction by a member of the legislature; referral to a committee; committee hearings, discussion, and vote; report on the bill by committee to the House or Senate; debate by the House or Senate on the bill; vote on the bill; and referral to the other body where the same process is replicated. If there are differences in the bill as reported out by each of the houses, the bill goes to a conference committee composed of members of each body and is voted on a final time by the two bodies. The bill is then sent to president, governor, county executive, and mayor to be signed, amended, vetoed, partially vetoed, or ignored. If vetoed or amended, the bill returns to the legislature for another vote. The legislature can override the executive's veto or accept the amendment. The number of options available to the legislature and the chief executive varies from locality to locality, so you must carefully review the options available to the bodies you wish to influence. Most legislative bodies publish the rules by which they operate. For example, Montana publishes a booklet that includes the joint rules, Senate rules, House rules, and an index to those rules, the Montana constitution and its index, as well as a list of deadlines and time limitations for the session.

First, someone has an idea as to what legislation is needed. An elected official or an interested citizen develops the idea and then gathers facts and arguments to support the idea. Next that person must either write the bill or find someone else to do so. The writer could be an elected official, the official's staff, or an interested citizen. If written by a citizen, a sponsor for the bill is needed. Only an elected legislator can actually introduce the bill. The sponsor ideally should be on the committee that has jurisdiction over the subject area in the legislative body. It is even better if the sponsor is the chair of the committee (if the legislative body is partisan, the chair is from the majority party). The bill will be more likely to pass if it is cosponsored by the ranking member of the committee (the ranking member comes from the opposition party). If the chair and ranking members are not interested, the sponsor should be a member of the committee. If no member of the committee is willing to sponsor the bill, find as powerful a member of the legislative body as possible to sponsor the bill. If the legislative body is partisan, the bill is more likely to make it through the process if the sponsor of the bill is from the majority party, that is, a member of the party with the most members in that unit of the legislature.

If you as a citizen write a bill and want a sponsor, you can either talk with the legislator or with a member of the legislator's staff asking the staffer to present the bill to the member for consideration. Or if you do not believe that the member or the staff would welcome a bill from you, then find someone else in your group who has a good relationship with the member to ask for sponsorship. That person could be someone from the member's legislative district, someone who worked with the member on another bill, or someone who holds a position that inspires trust in the legislator. It could also be another legislator, perhaps the legislator who represents your district.

If the legislative body is divided into two houses, it might be a good idea to find a sponsor in both parts of the body. This works best if the bill is identical on both sides. Sometimes even when sponsors introduce identical bills, they may end up being different because in the process they get changed. Then the bills will have to go to a conference committee composed of members from each of the bodies. The conference bill may end up looking very different from the bill that was first introduced.

In the process of developing the idea into a bill, it is wise to discuss the bill with legislative staff from the committee of jurisdiction as well as the staff of the member who will introduce the bill. You can usually determine the committees of jurisdiction by looking at the document that establishes the committee structure, by checking with the library that serves the legislature, or by looking at similar bills and seeing which committees receive referrals.

Each member of a legislative body usually has personal staff designated as legislative staff. Committees usually have political legislative staff, as well as nonpartisan professional staff. It is wise to talk to as many of these staff as possible to determine the best way to write the bill and any pitfalls that may await the bill. All the elected members of a committee will eventually turn to staff for analysis of the bill before they determine their position.

Try to Have Your Bill Referred to the Right Committee

You want to work behind the scenes to make sure that your bill is referred to a committee that will act favorably on the bill. For example, when law librarians wanted a bill that would allow law school libraries to become federal depository libraries, they ran into a road block, Representative John Brademus (D-Ind.), chair of the Committee on House Administration Subcommittee on Printing, who was convinced there should be no more special categories of depositories. He believed that it would open the program up to other groups of libraries, such as medical schools. The chair of the full committee, Representative Wayne L. Hays (D-Ohio), referred the bill to another subcommittee, the Subcommittee on the Library, chaired by a supporter of the bill, Representative Lucien Nedzi (D-Mich.). Representative Nedzi had some Michigan constituents who wanted their libraries to be depositories. At the same time, Representative Hays also had constituents who wanted their library to be a depository library. The bill ended up becoming law because the subcommittee chair and the full committee chair wanted to make their constituents happy.

Work hard to keep your bill from being referred to multiple committees. This is a sure way to end up with a bill so complicated that it will never pass. It also delays the completion of the bill if it is sequentially referred. The National Publications Act of 1979 was referred to Committee on House Administration, the House Committee on Government Operations, and the House Rules Committee. After completion of work by the Committee on House Administration, the other two committees had up to sixty days to review and amend the bill. The bill did not make it for several reasons, but multiple referrals did not help.

Sometimes overlapping jurisdictions may be in your favor, if you can get your bill before the more favorable committee. If you oppose a bill, work to get it referred to a committee that will try to kill it. During the battle over the Paperwork Reduction Act, opponents of the bill encouraged the Committee on House Administration and the Senate Committee on Rules and Administration to ask for joint or sequential referral on the grounds that elements of the PRA were part of the jurisdictional authority of those committees.

Committees with overlapping jurisdiction often carry on long battles over the direction that government should go. For example, the Committee on House Administration and the House Committee on Government Operations, which had disagreed on the contents of H.R. 5424, the National Publications Act of 1979, continued to battle for years over government printing and publishing policies. In 1987, the Joint Committee on Printing and the Committee on House Administration asked the Office of Technology Assessment for a study of how the GPO could best use technology to prepare for the future. A number of other committees—including the House Committee on Government Operations Subcommittee on Government Information, Justice and Agriculture; the House Committee on Science, Space, and Technology; and the House Appropriations Committee Subcommittee on the Legislative Branch—asked to be included as corequestors. As a result, the study covered so many issues that it was of little help to the initiating committees in their work to modernize the GPO. The introduction of the report, *Informing the Nation: Federal Information Dissemination in an Electronic Age*, describes the broader purpose:

> This report addresses the opportunities to improve the dissemination of Federal information. It also highlights two major problems: maintaining equity in public access to Federal information in electronic formats, and defining the respective roles of Federal agencies and the private sector in the electronic dissemination process. The report focuses on current and future roles of the U.S. Government Printing Office (GPO) and Superintendent of Documents, the Depository Library Program (administered by GPO), and the National Technical Information Service (NTIS). In addition this report examines electronic dissemination of congressional information, the Freedom of Information Act in an electronic environment, and electronic dissemination of government information to the press.[5]

The Joint Committee on Printing and the Committee on House Administration did not appreciate their study being hijacked to question their vision of the GPO's role and to promote the role of the GPO's competitors, the private sector publishers, and the National Technical Information Service. Those opposing the GPO's role as an electronic publisher and disseminator wanted this report to justify changes in laws that would support their assuming a greater role in the publishing and dissemination of government information.

For example, the House Committee on Government Operations wanted the Office of Management and Budget and the executive branch to control the printing and dissemination of government information produced by the executive branch. They argued that requiring executive branch agencies to go through the GPO for their printing and dissemination services was unconstitutional and threatened the separation of powers. The House Committee on Science, Space, and Technology wanted to increase the authority of the NTIS by requiring that publishing agencies provide their publications to the NTIS for reproduction and dissemination. They wanted to authorize the NTIS to move into electronic publishing and to engage in joint publishing projects with private publishers. Private publishers worked to convince all of the committees that government should limit its role to collecting information and allow the private sector to disseminate it.

There is also the danger that a bill will fail on the floor if the deliberation and work on a bill is limited to a subcommittee and the full committee simply accepts the work of the subcommittee with no review or work of its own. The bill may fail because the chair of the full committee does not understand it well enough to defend it or because there are members of the full committee who feel left out of the process and choose to present amendments on the floor either to change the bill or kill it. You should lobby staff and members of the full committee and encourage them to work with the subcommittee on the bill.

Sometimes there is a lot more work done on the bill by full committee staff than one might imagine while it is still at the subcommittee level. The full committee chair may want to make sure that the bill as reported out of the subcommittee is acceptable to the full committee. This work is most likely done behind the scenes. This usually happens if the full committee chair thinks there is a possibility that the bill will make it out of the subcommittee. At other times there is public acknowledgment that the subcommittee and full committee staff are working together on the bill. This is a good sign that the bill has a chance of making it through the entire process. You should let the full committee chair know about your support for the subcommittee efforts. This may stimulate interest and result in the two staffs working together. At a minimum you should keep them informed about what you would like to see in the bill.

To track the progress of a bill, you can call the appropriate committee or use publications like the Library of Congress Congressional Research Service's *Bill Digest* and the *Legislative Hotline Directory*[6] (which lists telephone numbers to call for bill status in all fifty states). You can also go online and use GPO Access, LC's Thomas, or a committee, state, county, or city website. Political parties also provide information on bills via websites. For example, the Republican Party has a site at www.gop.gov/committeecentral. The site includes bill summaries, issue briefings and sample op-eds. Republican Congressman J. C. Watts, the House Republican Conference chair, promotes it as "One-stop shopping for Republican members and staff to get information in plain English on every aspect of a bill. Our only fear is that Members will catch on to the ease of this site, realize all they need is Committee Central and a scheduler, and the rest of the Washington staff will lose their jobs."[7]

Many federal depository libraries maintain websites that lead you to other resources, such as the University of Michigan Government Resources on the Web, Louisiana State University's online federal agency directory, and the GODORT Federal Documents Task Force's page on frequently used sites related to government information, hosted by Vanderbilt University.

There are many commercial websites such as the CIS Congressional Universe, CIS State Capital Universe, and Bernan's Government Information on the Internet Online. You can also refer to books that help you identify how to access a wide range of government information resources such as *Guide to Finding Legal & Regulatory Information on the Internet*,[8] *Government Online: One-Click Access to 3,400 Federal and State Websites*,[9] *Locating United States Government Information: A Guide to Sources*,[10] *Tapping the Government Grapevine*,[11] *Government Information on the Internet*,[12] and *Using Government Information Sources Print and Electronic*.[13]

Many state legislatures provide online access to bills and draft proposals. Montana created the Legislative Automated Workflow System (LAWS), which is available free to the public. Users can set up their own preference list of bills on the system and generate a report with the latest update or status of each bill, including the measures, short titles, and primary sponsors. Montana's preference service is free, but some states charge up to $1,000 to create such a list for their users.

Try to Influence the Hearings Process

Once the informal process of working with staff is finished and sponsors have agreed to work to get the bill passed, the bill will generally receive a hearing. Hearings are an important means to influence those who have the vote, members of Congress, state legislators, county and city commissioners, and members of advisory bodies of all kinds. Hearings are held by legislators as well as regulators. Do not wait to be invited to testify at a hearing. If you know or suspect that one will be held, find out how you or someone from your organization can testify. In some states, counties, and cities, any citizen can testify on any bill; you just have to get on the schedule. In some states, such as Montana, you just have to show up on the day of the hearing and sign a register indicating whether you are for or against the bill and wait until you are called to testify. If time runs out for statements, the chair of the committee may ask those for and against the bill to line up and give their name and hand their written testimony to a clerk. Even if you cannot testify in person, you can often submit written testimony.

Those who organize hearings usually have a result in mind and will often select witnesses to support the outcome they want. They may not be eager to hear your point of view. Keep in mind that if it is a hearing held by a legislative body, there will be both majority and minority members. The majority controls the selection of most of the witnesses, but the minority can also select witnesses.

Many committees hold field hearings so constituents in their state or district can testify about the issue. When Representative Charlie Rose chaired the Joint Committee on the Library, he held one in North Carolina to talk about the needs of users of libraries. It was an unusually moving hearing during which library users from poor and minority families testified how the library had helped lift them out of poverty and despair.

Usually the ranking member from the other party will participate in the hearing. The committee often asks the executive branch agency responsible for administering the laws under the jurisdiction of that committee to assist in organizing the hearing. Most executive branch agencies have field offices and know who on the local level is interested in the issue and should be invited to testify. The agency staff must suggest a balanced slate of witnesses, particularly if the president is of the opposite party of the chair of the committee. The chair of the committee is a member of the majority party.

If the legislative body is split down the middle, the body must decide whether the committee will have joint chairs or use some other device to determine the chair. For example, in the first six months of 2001, the U.S. Senate was split between Republicans and Democrats but because the vice president of the United States functioned as the tie breaker, the chairs were held by the Republicans. In June 2001, Senator James Jeffords (R-N.H.) left the Republican Party, became an independent, and aligned himself with the Democrats for determining the majority, thus shifting the majority control to the Democrats.

I helped staff a congressional field hearing on agricultural pollution when I was the Librarian for the Environmental Protection Agency (EPA), Kansas City Region. I worked with the office of public relations in selecting a hearing room, providing backup technical support, identifying possible witnesses, and providing guests at the hearing with name tags, agendas, witnesses' statements, and information on agricultural pollution. Each witness is encouraged to provide written statements. Our director of public relations, Randall Jesse, a Democratic political patronage appointee of President Lyndon Johnson, warned us to treat the Democratic and Republican senators with equal enthusiasm and respect. He said that the legislation depended on the support of both parties. The hearing seemed to go well with the chair, Senator Thomas Eagleton (D-Mo.), joking that he had Senator Robert Dole (R-Kans.) to the right of him and Senator James Buckley (R-N.Y.) to the far right of him. In spite of our efforts at being evenhanded, we were dismayed to learn that someone in the congressional delegation had complained to William Ruckelshaus, the EPA administrator, that the Democrats had been treated better than the Republicans. That complaint did not affect the outcome of the legislation since the real underlying problem was the tension between Republican President Nixon and the Democratic-controlled Congress.

It is important to pick up witness statements at hearings since hearings are not published until later. Sometimes the hearing record is not published at all, or only the statements submitted in writing are included. Some legislatures save money by not hiring court recorders to record the oral statements and the questions and answers. If you want your statement to be part of the permanent record, be sure to bring a copy for the committee's clerk. Those whose statements are part of the record shape the debate.

Communicate with the Policymaker
through Traditional and New Technologies

There are so many ways to contact an elected official or policy person that sometimes it is hard to decide on the best format. Use the approach that you are most comfortable using and that also meets the deadline that will get your message to the right person at the right time. If you get a frantic message saying that the vote is this afternoon, your medium will be phone, fax, e-mail, or personal delivery of a message. If you have more time, you may use the traditional letter; an e-mail letter developed on an association website; a faxed message; an ad on radio, TV, the Internet, or newspaper; or a protest march in front of the Capitol. The important thing is to communicate in some way with the person you want to influence. Don't worry if the message is not perfect, if the official gets enough messages supporting your position; he or she won't have time to do anything but quickly read your message anyway.

Keep Sending Those Letters and Postcards

Letters and postcards still work. Don't believe people who tell you that politicians don't pay attention to postcards. Politicians tally everything, even if it is obvious it is an organized mail campaign. After all, you cared enough to take the time to send a postcard, and that counts in the minds of elected officials. Many elected officials instruct their staff to keep two simple tallies, one for yes and one for no, so it hardly matters whether your vote comes in as a postcard, letter, fax, or Internet message.

In 1975, two other Joint Committee on Printing staffers and I shared an office in the former Carroll Arms Hotel, the location of the infamous Quorum Club run by Bobby Baker, secretary for the majority under Senator Lyndon Johnson (D-Tex.). The Quorum Club was a private meeting and drinking place for senators, members of the House, lobbyists, government officials, and others. In 1963, Drew Pearson, in his column "Washington Merry-Go-Round," wrote about the club and Baker's connection to it. Senator Williams (R-Del.) made an issue out of Baker's conflict of interest role in the club, others chimed in about other activities of the secretary, and it wasn't long before Baker was no longer secretary for the majority. Walking into this infamous hotel everyday reminded me of the importance of avoiding even the appearance of impropriety in order to preserve the power to influence policies and events.

We shared the sixth floor of the Carroll Arms with staff debriefing witnesses for the Watergate hearings and one of the busiest letter reviewers on the Hill, a case worker for Senator Hubert Humphrey. Every morning she pushed a shopping cart full of mail addressed to the senator across the street from his office in the Russell Senate Office Building to her office. I asked her how she handled that much mail. She said she sorted the mail by issue, then by those for or against the Senator's position, and then by unique cases. The majority of the mail got a pattern or standard letter crafted for that particular issue, and others were given to staff who had expertise in the subject for follow-up, investigation, and an answer.

If the subject is more complicated than "Vote for this bill" or "Fund my library," a well-thought-out personal letter is always a sound choice. That does not mean that you have to come up with the entire content of the letter by yourself. You can use a pattern letter, adapt a letter on an Internet website, compose a cover letter for a resolution or petition, or use the facts provided to you by someone else. If you use sources for your letter, be sure that you personalize your letter by using examples from your own life or that of your community, by referring to your relationship with the elected official, or by identifying yourself as a constituent from his or her district or state. Make sure that you sign the letter and include your address, phone number, and e-mail information so you will get an answer.

Use Electronic Mail, Websites, and Discussion Groups

The new electronic world is wonderful for getting the word to the people you want to influence. Many organizations, associations, unions, and individuals are using the Internet to lobby. Many of them conduct classes and workshops on how to lobby electronically. A good source for obtaining the URLs for the websites of those lobbying and being lobbied is *Cybercitizen: How to Use Your Computer to Fight for All the Issues You Care About*[14] by Christopher Kush. He is president of Soapbox, LLC, a Washington, D.C., grassroots consulting firm that educates individuals and groups on how to lobby public officials both online and offline.

Some elected officials and other policymakers love the Internet. Many candidates for public office campaign over the Internet. They host websites where they post policy statements, list their home town and state campaign appearances, run polls, and ask for feedback. They issue e-mail news releases, contact volunteers, and even compete over the Internet for supporters. In the 2000 Presidential election Democratic primary fight, according to *USA Today*:

> Vice President Gore and Senator Bradley gave new meaning to the idea of a virtual stalemate. Bradley's campaign had designated Tuesday as "Let Congress Know" day and, via E-mail, encouraged supporters to "reach out to your member of Congress and ask them to support Bill Bradley." Gore's campaign responded in kind, asking its supporters to place calls as well. Bradley's campaign then sent a follow-up message saying Gore was trying to "counter our efforts." Gore's camp then forwarded that message to its supporters, saying, "The Bradley folks are nervous and are now re-energizing their efforts as evidenced in their attached E-mail. So, keep up the good work!" Staffers at several Democratic House offices said they noticed little surge in contacts.[15]

Once officials get into office, many use the Internet to communicate with their staff, constituents, other elected officials, and the press. But for some office holders the Internet and fax machines are a nightmare because they generate so many e-mails and faxes that the official and staff cannot review all of them. According to a study by the Congress Online Project, the U.S. House of Representatives received forty-eight million e-mails in 2000, and the number was growing by some one million messages per month.[16] Members of Congress may simply delete or set their machine to reject any message that does not come from their home district or their state or from someone they know. Sometimes fax machines are so overloaded that the important documents needed by the official cannot get through, or the fax breaks down and no messages get through. Some offices get other people's faxes and get tired of delivering them to the right offices. Other offices fear that an e-mail response will allow someone to alter their message and use it against them. Some offices cannot handle the increased work load generated by groups that send e-mail messages to every member of Congress instead of just to their own member.

If you send an e-mail or fax to a policymaker, follow a few basic rules:

- Send it to a policymaker who has jurisdiction over the issue.
- Copy your message to your own senator, representative, councilor, or commissioner.

- Use the subject line to identify your issue.
- Use your own words, not those of a mass mailing.
- Make sure you have the right fax number and e-mail address of the policymaker.
- Include your full name, e-mail, and address including ZIP code and phone number. Adding the ZIP code is important because some policymakers' systems automatically ignore messages not from their home ZIP code.

Some elected officials underestimate the power of the Internet. The enemies of their policies can use that lack of knowledge to harm the candidate's efforts. Public officials and others should reserve their Internet domain name so no one else can use it. There are companies that will register your name so it cannot be used by others. For example, Marty Lord, a Helena, Montana, webmaster, set up a satirical website poking fun at the new governor and her policies. He uses her name as the name of the website. The site makes such claims as "A governor as crazy as the rest of us—she sleeps with two guns under her pillow." It pokes fun at her statement about being the industry's lap dog and at her economic policy with a mock interview: "I propose to have all Montana newspapers to stop just comparing states. Like it or not, Montana is part of NAFTA; so all we got to do is add all the Mexican States to our list, thereby propelling Montana a walloping 30 places from the bottom. We would no longer be in last place. Isn't that just dandy?"[17]

Electronic discussion groups and websites are good tools for lobbying. They are best used to educate those who are going to do the lobbying. They are great for (1) sharing information, testimony, agendas, and schedules for demonstrations; (2) developing position statements, resolutions, and petitions; and (3) for gathering signatures for petitions and letters. They are essential for (1) posting lobbying alerts, (2) letting people know when a bill will be up for a vote, and (3) giving them information on how and when to lobby. A number of websites also allow the lobbyist to access a letter online, personalize it, and send it from that site to the policymaker. This also allows the website owner to get a copy of the letter and keep track of how many people are lobbying and whom they are contacting.

The demonstrations held in Seattle in 2000 to protest the World Trade Organization (WTO) policies were primarily organized over the Internet. The organizers were so pleased with how they brought the meeting and the city to a standstill that they have held similar demonstrations and gatherings at other meetings of the WTO and other international organizations connected with globalization. Some governments have reacted harshly to the demonstrations and a protestor was killed at a demonstration in Genoa, Italy in 2001. Protesting in the streets with the danger of loss of life is an extreme form of lobbying. Sometimes people who have exhausted every other form of lobbying feel that street demonstrations, even violence, is their only means of making their voices heard by those in power. The use of violence undermines other means of lobbying and often turns a sympathetic policymaker against the lobbyists and their cause. On the other hand, those in power who meet peaceful street demonstrations with violence must examine their policies to determine whether those policies really are in the public's best interest.

Librarians in Canada used the Internet to educate other librarians and the public about the dangers of trade agreements that might lead to the privatization of libraries and information access. They sent resolutions adopted by the Canadian Library Association (CLA) and information generated by other groups to library discussion lists all over the world. The International Federation of Library Associations and Institutions (IFLA) soon joined CLA with a resolution of its own, which was sent out to its member institutions and associations all over the world. They in turn shared it with other librarians in their country. As a result of the actions by the CLA and IFLA, the American Library Association joined the fray. All three associations were invited to attend the WTO meeting in Seattle as nongovernmental organizations (NGOs) and were allowed to present their case to the delegates to the WTO. Unfortunately, not many of the delegates heard their arguments since the meeting hall was blocked by demonstrators, but they were heard by enough delegates to get the issue on the table.

The ALA and the American Association of Law Libraries use electronic services and websites with great success. The ALA Washington office maintains a website providing information on current issues, draft letters to be used to lobby members of Congress, and a simple mechanism where a letter can be composed and sent via the website to a member of Congress. ALA also publishes the *American Library Association Washington Office Newsline (ALAWON)* and e-mails it to members who have signed up for the service. This makes it easy for members to send urgent news and lobbying alerts on to other discussion groups and alerting services, particularly those maintained by ALA's state chapters, other units of ALA, and public interest and professional organizations.

The Washington, D.C., office of the American Association of Law Libraries (AALL) maintains an electronic page called *Washington Brief* where they post key information about legislative activities and urge their members to lobby on particular issues. For example, in the April 27, 2000, issue they advertised the upcoming advocacy workshops at their annual meeting with the following promotion: "We hope to turn our workshop participants into energized chapter leaders and advocacy experts on legislative issues of concern to the law library community." AALL also maintains an advocacy e-mail service where it sends out special alerts to key members who can be counted on to act and to get others involved by forwarding the information to electronic sites in their own institutions and to local chapters of AALL.

The Law Librarians Society of Washington, D.C., annually publishes the *Legislative Research SIS Membership Directory and Source Book*, which lists over one hundred telephone numbers and websites with legislative information. It also includes questions and answers concerning legislative and regulatory research, a table of congressional publication volumes and presidential issuances from 1873 to 1999, and a table describing Internet and online sources of legislative and regulatory information. Portions of the publication are available on the society's Internet home page (www.llsdc.org), *LLSDC's Legislative Source Book*.

Librarians can influence elected officials by urging them to link their sites to the library's website. This is a convenient way for a member of Congress, a state legislator, or a city or county commissioner to answer a constituent's request for information about pending bills and government programs. Many libraries are depositories for federal and/or state publications. Some libraries are depositories for county and city publications. Offering a website link is a way to remind elected officials indirectly of the value of the investment they are making in depositing government information in libraries when they vote on appropriations bills that support those depository or access programs.

Use Radio and Television to Shape Policy

Radio and television are powerful tools for shaping policy in the area of the public's access to information. Librarians, trustees, friends, and others need to think creatively about how to influence what is conveyed through these popular formats. Radio and TV are not simply places to insert public interest spots promoting the library's programs, get out the vote drives, and fund-raisers but also means to promote discussion about the value of access to information to our communities.

Radio discussion is dominated by radio personalities and their talk shows. Talk show hosts range from Dr. Laura Schlesinger, who denounced the American Library Association and librarians as pornographers and child molesters, to Jim Hightower, who praised librarians for being agitators, educators, and civilizers fighting the forces of ignorance and arrogance. Hightower at the January 2000 midwinter meeting of ALA described librarians as having ideals that support the essential founding values of this country—economic fairness, social justice, and equal opportunity. He said, "We need the spirit of agitation, the spirit of ALA and the spirit of the folks in this room."[18] On the other hand, Dr. Laura used her pulpit to promote the filtering of the Internet in libraries. She started out by protesting the ALA link to a website called Go Ask Alice and ended up calling for filtering of the Internet in all libraries. Go Ask Alice is run by Columbia University for teenagers who anonymously want to ask questions about physical, sexual, and emotional health.

Dr. Laura and other talk show hosts should not be taken lightly. Before Dr. Laura went off the air, she inspired some of her listeners to launch campaigns to force libraries to filter the Internet and in at least one case to eliminate Internet access altogether. I discuss just such a campaign in Michigan in the following section on petitions. Dr. Laura said her crusade was to save children from pornography, but the end result for some library patrons has been censorship for all.

Many radio stations have what they call coffee hour talk shows where the host invites local people to discuss the issues of the day and promote events such as fund-raisers. Try to get on one of these shows to discuss an upcoming library fund-raiser, program, or a vote on a levy. It is worth asking if you can simply talk about the values of public libraries and the public's need for information. It is best to go on a talk show as a member of a group supporting libraries, such as Friends, Library Board of Trustees, a library association, or a foundation.

Television stations assign a certain amount of time to public interest issues and events. Their news shows sometimes do a series of stories about a local institution like a library. Don't wait for the library to burn down or for a flood to approach your local TV stations to ask them to do a public interest story about the library. Ask them to cover a visit by the governor reading to the preschoolers, a special exhibit, an author's reading, or a library fund-raiser.

Promote Your Causes through Advertisements

If you want to promote a program at your library, a get-out-the-vote campaign, or a fund-raiser, advertise in all the media outlets such as newspapers, weekly shoppers, newsletters, magazines, radio, TV, the Internet, billboards, and bulletin boards. Print your message on flyers, buttons, bumper stickers, magnets, book marks, cups, T-shirts, calendars, and pencils. Hand them out at state, county, and street fairs, craft shows, parades, street dances, association meetings, exhibits, supermarkets, political gatherings, the Chamber of Commerce, doctors' and dentists' waiting rooms, local bookstores, and the library.

Start out by asking for free advertising space. If that does not work, ask for reduced advertising rates. The Fund Our Library's Future committee used all types of advertisements when promoting a get-out-the-vote for an increased mill levy for the Lewis & Clark Library in Helena, Montana. The advertisements that most delighted the readers were those in the shape of bookmarks that ran in the local newspaper for several weeks before the vote. The bookmarks included the logo of children reading, a box in which to vote yes, several points on how the money would be spent, and catchy literary sayings. The sayings, take-offs on what characters in popular books might have said in this context, were Scarlett O'Hara, stating, "Not tomorrow, fund our library today"; Captain Ahab, stating, "An open library; it's a whale of an idea"; Lewis and Clark, stating, "We found it, you fund it"; Aladdin, stating, "Open library"; and Dorothy, stating, "There's no place like the library."[19]

Influence Policy through Resolutions, Petitions, Initiatives, and Referendums

Many associations pass resolutions that state their concerns about a program, a bill, or an issue and urge a solution that reflects the beliefs of the association. These resolutions are usually composed and debated at conferences since they are intended to reflect the will of the membership. Associations use the debate over the resolutions as a means of alerting their membership to an issue. Once the resolution is adopted, the association's members are advised to send the resolution along with their letters to a policymaker. The resolutions, like road maps, help the association's lobbying unit keep track of the issues of importance to the association. The lobbyists can also include them in testimony and share them with policymakers. Passage of a resolution is a good reason to call a news conference to share the resolution and other information with the press.

One of the first actions that the Government Documents Round Table (GODORT) took after its birth was to examine the state of the Federal Depository Library Program. GODORT drafted a resolution for consideration by the ALA Governing Council. The resolution directed ALA to establish a committee to "prepare a report considering the possibility of proposing a revision to the Depository Act of 1962, incorporating such criteria as adequate financial support, provision of more non-GPO material, consulting services to the depository libraries," and to "report to the several appropriate units, the Legislation Committee, and to the Council at the 1973 Annual Conference in Las Vegas." As coordinator of GODORT, I was allowed to present the resolution on the floor of council, and then Jane Robbins, a councilor and member of GODORT, moved the resolution. The resolution passed.[20] The ALA Ad Hoc Committee on the Depository Library System was established, and it recommended that an independent National Depository Agency (separate from GPO) be established. The new agency would be responsible for obtaining, cataloging, and distributing federal documents (classified and unclassified) to depository libraries. It would also be responsible for maintaining a permanent archival set of federal documents to fill reference and photocopy needs of libraries.[21] Lois Mills and I served on that committee. Later when I went to work for the Joint Committee on Printing, knowing what the library community wanted, I was able to lobby other JCP staffers on the need for the law to be updated. They in turn convinced the representatives and senators on the JCP that all of the printing and distribution of government documents laws needed to be examined and updated to benefit from changes in technology.

Some associations also have a petition process to enable units to be established, candidates not nominated by nominating committees to run for office, and for other purposes. A number of petition candidates have been elected to office in the ALA.

The public can affect public policy through initiatives and referendums. The U.S. Constitution and the constitutions of states can be amended. The right of the people to use initiatives and referendums to amend state constitutions and enact laws varies from state to state. Almost half the states and the District of Columbia allow the people to petition for changes to the state's constitution or laws through initiatives or referendums. Initiatives are either direct or indirect. A *direct* initiative places a proposed measure on the ballot after the legally required number of citizen signatures on a petition are certified as valid. An *indirect* initiative is placed on the ballot after submission and authorization by the legislature. A referendum is the process where a state law or constitutional amendment is passed by the legislature and then placed on the ballot for citizen approval.

Citizens use initiatives when they believe that their elected officials will not address an issue or will pass a law that will harm them. For example, Montana voters passed an initiative that banned mining companies from using cyanide in the process of extracting gold from the ore because they were concerned about the damage done to their drinking water as a result of cyanide getting into wells, rivers, and lakes. The mining industry went to the courts to get the initiative overturned, but the courts sustained the people's vote.

A group of women are trying to resuscitate the Equal Rights Amendment (ERA) by getting it ratified by the state of Missouri. The ratification process was stopped at thirty-eight states in 1982 because Congress had put a ten-year voting deadline on the states. As Ellen Goodman describes it:

> The Missouri vote is the cutting edge of the "three state strategy." This is a long-shot plan to bring the amendment back to life by getting it passed by three more state legislatures. This strategy is an unexpected inheritance from James Madison. Back in 1789, the Founding Father proposed an amendment that would force Congress to take a roll-call vote whenever it approved a pay raise. The amendment languished in a state of suspended animation for 203 years. Finally, in 1992, it was ratified—after Congress agreed to accept the original 18th century state votes in the 20th century tally. Of course the Madison amendment didn't have a time limit. None of the amendments did until Prohibition. Indeed, suffrage never would have passed with a 10-year deadline. But the ERA did have one. Nevertheless, in 1995, three young

women law students saw the Madison amendment as a way to resurrect the ERA. If the pay-raise amendment could be resurrected after 203 years, why not the ERA after a mere 18? If Congress can do this for a Founding Father, why not do it for a Founding Mother?[22]

These three women—Allison Held, Sheryl Herndon, and Danielle Stager—and others set up a website promoting their three state strategy. Bills were introduced in the Missouri Legislature in 1998 and 1999, and finally in the spring of 2001, the bills (SCR 32 and HJR 42) were approved by Missouri House and Senate Committees and were waiting action by the full bodies. In 2001, the Missouri Women's Network and the Missouri ERA Ratification Fund formed a political action committee to wage an ongoing fight for ratification of the ERA. Representative Robert E. Andrews of the U.S. House sponsored H.R. 37 in the 106th Congress requiring that the House take any legislative action necessary to verify ratification of the ERA when three more states ratify the ERA.

Most cities and counties also allow their citizens to petition for changes in the local constitution and laws. A battle in Holland, Michigan, over whether the local library should be forced into filtering the Internet was settled by a public vote on a petition for an ordinance brought by the American Family Association. Another group, Families for Internet Access, organized voters to oppose the ordinance. The ordinance was defeated by a vote of 4,379 to 3,626.[23] A day after the Holland citizens defeated the proposed ordinance, the Hudsonville, Michigan City, commission voted to rescind a filtering ordinance and restore Internet activity at their city library. The commission had passed the ordinance because of another petition promoted by the American Family Association. The commission, rather than risk a lawsuit by citizens over limits to Internet usage, had simply ended all Internet services at the library. After the ordinance was rescinded, the Hudsonville Library installed "a software system that allows children different levels of Internet access according to their parents' wishes."[24]

NOTES

1. Elizabeth Cobbs Hoffman, *All You Need Is Love: The Peace Corps and the Spirit of the 1960s* (Cambridge, Mass.: Harvard University Press, 1998), 50–53.

2. Unpublished letter from Bernadine E. Hoduski, member of the Advisory Committee to the Public Printer on Depository Libraries, to Rowland Darling, acting superintendent of documents on February 13, 1973.

3. Memorandum for members of the Advisory Committee to the Public Printer on Depository Libraries on Renaming of Committee, U.S. Government Printing Office, May 4, 1973, signed by Rowland E. Darling, acting superintendent of documents.

4. *Depository Library Council to the Public Printer Summary of Meeting at Albuquerque, New Mexico, March 27–29, 1985,* 8.

5. U.S. Congress, Office of Technology Assessment, *Informing the Nation: Federal Information Dissemination in an Electronic Age,* OTA-CIT 396 (Washington, D.C.: U.S. Government Printing Office, October 1988).

6. "Legislative Hotline Directory" is part of *State Legislative Source Book,* 15th ed. (Topeka, Kans.: Government Research Service, 2000).

7. Juliet Elperin and John Lancaster, *Washington Post,* July 8, 2001, A15.

8. Yvonne J. Chandler, *Guide to Finding Legal & Regulatory Information on the Internet* (New York: Neal-Schuman, 1998).

9. John Maxymuk, *Government Online: One-Click Access to 3,400 Federal and State Websites* (New York: Neal-Schuman, 2001).

10. Edward Herman, *Locating United States Government Information: A Guide to Sources,* 2d ed. (Buffalo, N.Y.: Hein, 1999).

11. Judith Schiek Robinson, *Tapping the Government Grapevine: The User-Friendly Guide to U.S. Government Information Sources,* 3rd ed. (Phoenix: Oryx, 1998).

12. Greg Notess, *Government Information on the Internet,* 2d ed. (Washington, D.C.: Bernan, 1998).

13. Jean L. Sears and Marilyn K. Moody, *Using Government Information Sources Print and Electronic,* 3d ed. (Phoenix: Oryx, 2001).

14. Christopher Kush, *Cybercitizen: How to Use Your Computer to Fight for All the Issues You Care About* (New York: St. Martin's Griffin, 2000).

15. "E-Watch" in "Election Line," *USA Today,* January 13, 2000, 10A.

16. *E-mail Overload in Congress: Managing a Communication Crisis,* report from the Congress Online Project, George Washington University, and Congressional Management Foundation, February 19, 2001, 1.

17. Kathleen McLaughlin, "Website Takes Satirical Look at Governor-Elect," *Helena Independent Record,* December 28, 2000, 2A.

18. Brad Martin, "Hightower Calls for 'New Politics,'" *ALA Cognotes* (January 2000): 1, 10.

19. Gail Hewitt, a member of the Friends of Lewis & Clark Library and the Fund Our Library's Future Committee, created the sayings.

20. "Report on ALA Midwinter Meeting, Washington, D.C., January 28–February 3, 1973," *LC Information Bulletin,* February 23, 1973, A-43.

21. "Report by James Riley on the Federal Library Committee Meeting," *LC Information Bulletin,* August 23, 1974, A-199.

22. Ellen Goodman, "Show-Me State Is Showing Us How," *Great Falls* (Mont.) *Tribune*, February 17, 2000, 6A.

23. "Filters Rejected," *Holland Sentinel: Online Edition*, February 23, 2000; available: www.thehollandsentinel.net/stories/022400/new-hudsonville. html.

24. "Hudsonville Library Users Have Web Access Restored," *Holland Sentinel: Online Edition*, February 24, 2000.

4

Who Are the Quilters/Lobbyists?

Quilters/lobbyists range from the new quilter to the old-timers. New quilters will suffer pin pricks and may have to tear out stitches, but actually quilting/lobbying is the only way to learn. Old-timers can help new quilters by sharing their methods and including them in the designing of the quilt. They should encourage new quilters to learn from expert quilters while developing their own patterns of lobbying. Quilters/lobbyists quilt best when they are comfortable with the pattern and their fellow quilters.

The Congress and other levels of government have established rules to enable them to identify lobbyists and the source of their money. For example, Congress passed its first law regulating lobbyists in Title III of the Legislative Reorganization Act of 1946, which requires that

> (1) persons or organizations receiving money to be used principally to influence passage or defeat of legislation before Congress must register; (2) persons or groups registering must, under oath, give their name and address, employer, salary, amount and purpose of expenses, and duration of employment; (3) each registered lobbyist must report quarterly full information on his or her activities, which is then published in the *Congressional Record* and (4) failure to comply with any of these provisions will result in severe penalties prescribed, ranging up to a $10,000 fine and a five-year prison term and including a three-year ban against further lobbying.[1]

United States v. Harriss clarified the law by saying that the act only applies to those who directly try to influence legislation, not to those who lobby indirectly by influencing public opinion. This is an important distinction. Many organizations, in an effort to avoid registration and regulation as lobbyists, concentrate on influencing their members. Members in turn can directly influence elected officials because they are not paid lobbyists.[2]

The Lobbying Disclosure Act of 1995 was the first major revision of the 1946 law. It requires that lobbyists who receive at least $5,000 in a six-month period from one client and organizations that use their own staff and spend at least $20,000 in a six-month period must register with the clerk of the House and the secretary of the Senate. Lobbyists have to list the congressional chambers and federal agencies they contacted, the issues they lobbied on, and how much money was spent. The requirement to file lobbying reports was changed from quarterly to semiannual. Bernan published the *Directory of Federal Lobbyists* (2000), in an attempt to identify lobbyists who lobby members of Congress and their staff on a regular basis and to provide information on how to contact the lobbyists. The directory describes the top lobbyists based on their reported income, as well as the top organizations based on the amount of money spent lobbying and the number of people employed to lobby for them.

Keep in mind that elected officials usually respond more readily to their constituents. A constituent is someone who resides in the area from which the government official is elected. It is always more effective to have a constituent contact an official to present the case for your cause. As noted earlier, some elected officials block e-mail from nonconstituents.

EVERY CHANGE IN POLICY STARTS WITH AN INDIVIDUAL

Every change in policy starts with an individual. That individual identifies a problem, realizes that the solution is a policy change, and then lobbies to get the policy changed. The individual may act on his or her own or may persuade an association or institution to take up the cause. Following are some of the individuals who have impressed me with the courage and tenacity they have shown in pursuing their causes. They persuaded others to support their causes some times at the loss of their own jobs.

- Maryellen Trautman, a member of the Depository Library Council from 1973 through 1975, persuaded DLC and the Government Printing Office to hold federal depository libraries accountable for serving the public. She worked to improve the standards used by GPO to grade and inspect those libraries. She urged GPO to hire knowledgeable librarians to inspect the libraries in person, not by mail, and to require that libraries post signs indicating that they are depositories and open to the public. Some libraries at the time denied access to anyone but their own faculty and students or when they did provide access made it difficult for the public to find the documents and use them. Some did not open their boxes of documents for months, even years and others did not catalog, bind, or shelve the documents. Trautman changed policy by first convincing the superintendent of documents Robert E. Kling Jr. to resurrect the defunct depository library advisory committee in 1973 and then by being appointed to it and convincing Kling to appoint other working documents librarians like myself to the council. She met Kling at a Special Libraries Association conference and asked whether she could spend her vacation learning about the depository library operation. When he agreed, she sweetened their meeting at GPO by bringing his book, *The Government Printing Office*, for an autograph and a sample of her homemade wine. He was so charmed that he gave her a personal tour and called her later to ask her for suggestions about whom to appoint to the committee, insisting that she would be the first one appointed.
- Zoia Horn started the Right to Know Project at the Data Center in Oakland, California, and persuaded the American Library Association to establish the Coalition on Government Information. She served on the ALA committee that organized the coalition, using the list of organizations that she had prepared as part of her Right to Know Project.
- Roberta Scull of Louisiana State University, Karlo Mustonen of Utah State University, and Richard Leacy of Georgia Tech, while members of the Depository Library Council lobbied for the inclusion of scientific, technical, and agricultural government documents and contractor reports in the federal depository library program. They also argued that these documents should be cataloged using AACR2 and included in the *Monthly Catalog of United States Government Publications*. In response to

their efforts the Department of Energy (DOE) was an active participant in the electronic pilot projects for depository libraries. DOE and GPO have launched several cooperative electronic services that provide libraries and the public with free online access to thousands of scientific and technical reports as well as information about ongoing projects and scientific journal articles.

- Richard Leacy, documents librarian at the Georgia Institute of Technology, spearheaded the effort to keep the economic census in the depository library program in the early 1970s. A census official had decided not to publish the census through the government and instead allow a private publisher to have sole rights to publication. Leacy launched a very effective campaign to alert other depository librarians about the potential loss to the public and persuaded them to lobby members of the congressional appropriations committees to keep the Commerce Department from privatizing public information.

- Elizabeth Morrissette, while director of the library at the University of Montana School of Technology, persuaded the International Federation of Library Associations and Institutions (IFLA) to establish a working group on peace. She did this during the Cold War and at IFLA meetings behind the iron curtain in Czechoslovakia and East Germany. She enlisted the aid of E. J. Josey, longtime American Library Association councilor, and me in persuading IFLA powers to allow the working group, but she was the driving force that made it happen. Morrissette also coordinated and energized a peace task force within the Social Responsibilities Round Table of ALA.

- Joan Marshall and Sandy Berman waged life-long struggles to eliminate biases, prejudices, and cultural insensitivity in subject headings used by libraries. Marshall spent several months at the Library of Congress analyzing subject headings assigned to books about women and wrote *On Equal Terms: A Thesaurus for Nonsexist Indexing and Cataloging*. She lived at my house during that time and gave me a daily education on how to change an institution for the better. Berman issued a cataloging bulletin that provided alternative terms to those used by the Library of Congress. When Marshall, Berman, and I represented Round Tables on the ALA committee that rewrote the cataloging rules in the late 1970s, we learned that asking for and getting changes in something as sacred as cataloging rules and subject headings takes patience and diplomacy. It also requires lobbying every member of the committee since rational arguments alone will not sway those who consider cataloging an art and not a science.

- E. J. Josey forced the American Library Association to fight segregation in libraries by expelling chapters whose states allowed racially segregated libraries. He served as ALA president and spent twenty-nine years on the ALA Council persuading ALA to adopt policies that encouraged the recruitment of minority librarians, the provision of library services to minorities, and the diversification of library collections to reflect the communities that use them.

- Stephen Hayes, documents librarian at Notre Dame, courageously confronted Donald Fossedal, superintendent of documents, about depository libraries being unable to serve the public because of the lack of government documents due to the microfiche disaster of the late 1980s. The GPO contractor was years behind in producing the fiche, and the fiche produced was of such poor quality that it was unreadable. Libraries that had chosen microfiche rather than paper did not receive any publications. Hayes confronted GPO officials at ALA and DLC meetings. At the DLC meeting in Charleston, South Carolina, he explained that faculty were complaining about not having access to publications that were available for sale but not sent to depository libraries. He demanded that GPO live up to its slogan of "demand-driven, service-oriented." Fossedal responded that he was not going to allow the tail to wag the dog and that the libraries should buy the publication while waiting for the depository copy. Hayes did not agree, urging librarians to stop asking GPO to solve the problem and lobby Congress instead. The Joint Committee on Printing was listening and after an initial investigation determined that the problem was that GPO had only one contractor and that contractor was not providing quality fiche on a timely basis. GPO then terminated its contract with the sole contractor and broke the work out into nine separate contracts. The terminated contractor won one of the nine bids and protested several others that it failed to win. The ongoing dispute further disrupted distribution of the fiche to libraries. JCP then asked the General Accounting Office (GAO) in July 1988 to investigate the problem and report back to JCP. As a result of the GAO report, additional steps were

taken by GPO to institute quality control procedures to assure
that only qualified contractors were awarded contracts. Hayes's
campaign was a public one, but unknown to the library community, the GPO staffer responsible for the day-to-day operation of the microfiche program resigned in protest over the refusal of other GPO officials to disqualify the contractor for poor
performance.[3]

- Carl LaBarre, superintendent of documents, chose to fight to
keep twenty-seven out of the thirty GPO bookstores open
rather than close them down as directed by Dan Sawyer, public
printer, in 1981. LaBarre, with the help of the bookstore managers, marshaled statistics showing that the stores paid their
own way and were needed by the public. When this data failed
to convince the public printer, he gave the information to the
Joint Committee on Printing and resigned rather than implement a decision he believed to be detrimental to the public's
right to know. JCP was convinced by the statistics and an outcry from the public and librarians and voted to keep the bookstores open.

- John Gordon Burke, editor of the *Missouri Library Association
Newsletter* and *American Libraries*, insisted on editorial independence so the journals could objectively report about library and
policy issues. He believed so strongly in that principle that he
resigned as editor of *American Libraries* after he was forced to
fire a reporter for investigating the financial reimbursement of
commissioners on the National Commission on Libraries.

- LeRoy Schwarzkopf, regional depository librarian at the University of Maryland and longtime editor of *Documents to the People*,
helped bring down a superintendent of documents by taping his
speeches at public meetings and courageously taking those tapes
to the deputy public printer. As a depository librarian whose library was inspected by that superintendent, he could have suf-
fered for complaining to the superintendent's boss.

- Arne Richards, documents librarian at Kansas State University,
lobbied Congress in the 1960s and 1970s to provide congressional committee prints to depository libraries. Committee
prints are special reports and studies issued by committees.
When I was hired by the Joint Committee on Printing in 1974,
that became my first project, and now the majority of the prints
are in libraries.

CAMPAIGN TO REFORM LC'S AND GPO'S
CATALOGING POLICIES FOR GOVERNMENT DOCUMENTS

I launched my campaign to persuade the Library of Congress to reform its government documents cataloging policies as an individual but used my position within several institutions to support that lobbying campaign. I became concerned with the completeness and quality of the cataloging provided by the LC in 1965 when I started a project at Central Missouri State University to catalog the school's entire government documents collection. I found very little government documents cataloging performed by LC and that cataloging often left out key elements needed to identify the item as a government document. Looking for other sources of cataloging, I turned to the cataloging performed by GPO. Unfortunately, I could not use the cataloging by GPO because it did not conform to the Anglo American Cataloging Rules, use the LC subject headings, nor was it available in LC's MARC data format, which would allow the cataloging records to be easily incorporated into library catalogs.

Only after I established a library for the EPA Kansas City Region in 1970 did I get the financial support of my institution in my campaign to persuade LC to improve the cataloging of government documents and GPO to adopt the library world's computer format and cataloging rules.

Sooner or later, an individual needs the support of his or her institution, whether it is financial, administrative, or moral. It is important that you educate your institution or association about why it is important for you to spend time, energy, and money pursuing your cause. Your cause must in some way help your organization in furthering its own goals. EPA wanted publicity and worldwide recognition for its fight against pollution. Having its publications included in the national catalog was one way to get attention. EPA sent me to Washington, D.C., to meet with staff at LC and to national library meetings to work with others to persuade the policymakers to change their approach to cataloging government documents. I got the opportunity to lobby people on the national level by first lobbying my boss. But relying on the initial support of your boss is not enough. Update her or him about your progress to ensure that you continue to receive the support that you need to pursue your cause.

As the only professional librarian at an EPA Library with a very small staff, I depended on catalog cards purchased from LC. After several years, there was a box full of order slips that had never been filled. I knew that LC had most of the publications because at LC's request I had sent them the publications issued by our Kansas City, Missouri, office, and those publications had been given preassigned catalog card order numbers. On a visit to LC, I found that many of those publications had been rejected by LC's Exchange & Gift Division and were being offered to other libraries. I was upset not only because I had no catalog cards but because rare copies of my agency's publications were being given away to other libraries. LC could have at least returned them to me. I had persuaded reluctant scientists to give me copies of their precious documents with the promise of a permanent home at the Library of Congress. If they had known that LC did not value their sacrifice, I would have had a hard time persuading them to share any more documents.

As it turned out, there were several problems. The Library of Congress asked for and accepted government documents that either received preassigned order card numbers but were later discarded and never cataloged or that were given a low cataloging priority. I did not persuade LC to change their selection or cataloging priorities, but LC did agree not to assign an LC catalog card order number until after the Exchange & Gift Division decided to add the publication to LC's collection.[4] Knowing what will be cataloged by LC and what won't means that books will not sit on shelves for days, weeks, and even years waiting for LC cataloging. Libraries will catalog the publications themselves or use another library's cataloging so publications will be available to the users of the library.

LC's policy of demanding government publications under the law but rejecting many of them for retention and cataloging persuaded me that a more likely candidate for providing cataloging and preservation services was the United States Government Printing Office. GPO also demanded government publications under the law. When I visited with Mae Collins, head of the Library Division at GPO in 1970, she pointed to an empty table and said, "As you can see, we have no backlog and would welcome EPA's publications." Because I wanted to be able to use GPO's cataloging in my agency's catalog, I had to figure out a way to convince GPO to automate their cataloging and use LC and ALA's cataloging rules, subject headings, and computer format.

I decided to work through five groups—the ALA Government Documents Round Table, the Special Libraries Association Government Information Services Committee, the Depository Library Council to the Public Printer, the Committee on Information Hangups, and the Federal Library Committee—to convince GPO to adopt the Anglo American Cataloging Rules and LC MARC format and subject headings. Each of those groups stitched a square of what became the library community's consensus quilt that GPO adoption of those standards would be good public policy.

After I was hired in 1974 as a staffer for the Congressional Joint Committee on Printing, adopting those standards became a priority at GPO. I was assigned to work with James Livsey and Milton McGee at GPO to implement those standards. We needed help in deciding how to design a system that would best serve the needs of the users of the cataloging records. We turned to two groups for assistance, the Committee on Information Hangups (an informal group of D.C. area librarians) chaired by Ruth Smith and the Special Library Association's Government Information Services Committee chaired by Mary Lou Knobbe. They agreed to act as a sounding board as we struggled through the transition.

The two groups decided to conduct an "intensive study of the Government Printing Office" because of the "concern of heavy users of government information in the metropolitan D.C. area about the quality of service given by the Government Printing Office" and "the desire of Government Printing Office officials to have an unprejudiced, independent assessment of its services."[5] While one group designed a survey instrument and selected a sampling of academic, public, special, school, and government libraries to answer the survey, another worked with us on identifying the most important elements of an automated cataloging record, including which numbers associated with government contracts and reports should be included in the record.

We knew that we needed technical support. I turned to William Welch, deputy librarian of Congress, and James Riley, executive director of the Federal Library Committee, for help. I had lobbied Welch in 1970 for the inclusion of government documents in LC's program, Cataloging in Publication. I met him because I got to the ALA meeting on CIP early so I could sit in the front row and be the first person at the microphone to ask why government documents were not in LC's plans for CIP. I knew he noticed me because I was wearing a white dress, holding a red rose, and sitting next to my friend George Caldwell, LC federal documents librarian. After the meeting, Caldwell introduced me to Welch, who expressed surprise at my attending the CIP session instead of the SRRT program with fireworks being held at the same time. Welch and I were so absorbed in discussing my plans to ask SRRT to establish a task force on CIP and documents that I followed him into an elevator on his way to another meeting. He encouraged me to start the task force and to lobby government agency publishers and my colleagues in federal libraries to support CIP.

James Riley had taken over the Federal Library Committee just about the time that I started at the Joint Committee on Printing. I had been attending FLICC meetings for several years as a field librarian and had lobbied Riley's predecessor, Kurt Cylke, to urge federal librarians to encourage their agencies to work with LC on the CIP program.

Welch assigned David Remington, assistant chief of the LC Subject Cataloging Division, to work with the Joint Committee on Printing and the Government Printing Office on the transition. Remington had been LC's liaison to the Government Documents Round Table and was familiar with GODORT's desire to have GPO adopt the library community's standards. LC agreed to provide training and technical support for the catalogers at GPO. LC, at the urging of John Kountz, library automation guru for the California State University System, even paid for Philip Long, an automation consultant to LC, to advise the GPO automation staff on how the LC MARC format worked. Long persuaded the automation staff and the Superintendent of Documents, Carl LaBarre, that it would be cheaper and easier for GPO to catalog into an already-existing cataloging utility rather than establish its own.

Once GPO agreed to input government documents records into a cataloging utility, David and I tried to convince the Library of Congress to allow GPO to catalog directly into LC's computers. LC librarians were not ready to accept GPO's cataloging so I turned to Riley for help. The Federal Library Committee had established the Federal Libraries Information Network (FEDLINK), a system where federal librarians cataloged directly into OCLC, a utility using the MARC format and AACR2. Riley welcomed GPO as a member of FEDLINK, therefore allowing GPO to catalog into OCLC. By July 1976, the first issue of the newly designed *Monthly Catalog of United States Government Publications* was published. GPO produced both a tape and a paper version of the cataloging records. We had convinced LC to (1) sell the GPO cataloging tapes as part of its regular tape service, (2) incorporate some of GPO's records into its own cataloging database, (3) work on a cooperative cataloging program with GPO, and (4) accept authority records established by GPO librarians as a part of the national authority file.

It took a lot of patience, persistence, and belief in our cause, but the library community succeeded in persuading (1) GPO to automate using library standards, (2) LC and federal libraries to accept that cataloging, and (3) OCLC to welcome GPO as master cataloger. A master cataloging agency can upgrade other libraries' records by adding or changing information.

Real-Life Quilters/Lobbyists

James Bennett Childs

One of my mentors, James Bennett Childs, was tireless in his efforts to lobby both his institution, the Library of Congress, and other librarians about the importance of collecting, cataloging, and preserving government documents. Childs worked at the Library of Congress until his death in May 1977, twice as chief of the Division of Documents and once as chief of the Catalog Division. After his retirement in 1965, he was an honorary consultant in government documents bibliography. But his most important work is what he did to inspire librarians all over the world to fight for what they loved: government documents. He understood that lobbying the librarian to lobby the policymakers was the best use of his time.

As a representative of the Library of Congress, Childs established agreements for the exchange of government documents with other national libraries. He served on the IFLA Official Publications Committee and lobbied librarians worldwide about the importance of collecting and cataloging government publications in a way that would make it easy for the public to find them.

Childs met resistance from librarians who preferred to spend cataloging dollars on other kinds of publications and from catalogers who wanted to catalog government documents as if they were ordinary publications. He insisted on using the corporate body as the main entry, arguing that any other type of cataloging would mean that the cataloging records would never be discovered since many documents' titles are nondescript and only mean something connected to the issuing government body. When he failed to convince the catalogers of the world, he turned to the growing community of documents librarians for help. He wrote hundreds of letters to documents librarians encouraging them to fight for fair treatment for government documents. Since he was writing as an individual, he asked recipients not to share his letter but to use his advice and evidence in the fight to provide better collecting and cataloging of government documents.

At Childs's urging, I became deeply involved in the struggle to reform the cataloging rules to provide for better treatment of government publications. When ALA, The Library Association (of Great Britain), the Canadian Library Association, and LC decided to rewrite the cataloging rules, resulting in the Anglo American Cataloging Rules 2 (AACR 2), ALA established the Resources and Technical Services Division, Catalog Code Revision Committee. I was a representative to that committee for the Government Documents Round Table.

Childs sent me hundreds of examples of the cataloging of government publications annotated with comments indicating what was wrong with the cataloging and why the rules needed to be changed. He would call me on Sunday mornings to give me a pep talk and to find out what progress had been made. I remember telling him a week before his death that I was persistently arguing our position but that the voting members of the committee considered me a troublemaker. He replied, "Keep making trouble because change only happens when someone is willing to make trouble."

Childs also convinced me to carry on his work on the international level as a member of the IFLA Official Publications Committee. He wrote so many letters urging me to get involved that I finally accepted an invitation from the committee to speak about the work of the ALA Government Documents Round Table at their meeting in Brussels in 1978. In honor of Childs and his loving support of my lobbying efforts, I served on the Official Publications Committee from 1979 until 1994. He must have been doing his usual behind-the-scenes lobbying because at the Brussels meeting, the outgoing chair, Suzanne Honore, announced that she was putting me on the committee, much to the surprise of the incoming chair. I insisted on being elected and was subsequently nominated for the spot by LC, ALA, the American Association of Law Libraries, and the Association of Research Libraries.

Morris B. Schnapper

Morris B. Schnapper of Public Affairs Press was, as the *Washington Post* put it, "a tenacious challenger of high-level government officials' practice of copyrighting their public speeches."[6] His crusade started in the 1950s when Admiral Rickover denied him permission to publish two of his speeches issued in official Defense Department news releases, saying that the speeches were copyrighted. Schnapper took him to court, arguing that "the speeches were an official act and therefore public property."[7] He argued his case against the copyright of government publications in his book *Constraint by Copyright*.[8] In 1984, he sent me a copy of this book with a letter in which he said, "When I wrote this book 25 years ago I naively thought it would inhibit privatizing of government produced works. I couldn't have been more mistaken. Here's hoping that the Joint Committee won't let itself be taken in by privatizing proponents."[9]

Schnapper continued to fight against the copyright of government publications up until his death at eighty-six in 1999 by writing articles, persuading newspapers to cover the issue, and lobbying the Joint Committee on Printing and the judicial committees of the Congress. He was concerned about government agencies allowing contractors, paid by the government, to research and write publications, to copyright and publish them. He initiated the writing of the statement signed by dozens of editors of newspapers, scholars, and librarians that said, "We the undersigned view with apprehension the rapidly growing tendency to place copyright restrictions on the contents of Government publications and documents. The situation seems alarming in that such restrictions now apply to literally hundreds of official works despite the fact that Section 8 of the Copyright Law expressly stipulates that 'No copyright shall subsist in any publication of the United States Government, or any reprint, in whole or in part thereof.'" Signers included William F. Buckley, editor of the *National Review*; Daniel A. Poling, editor of *Christian Herald*; Roger Baldwin, founder of the American Civil Liberties Union; and R. C. Swank, director, Stanford University Libraries.

I first met Schnapper when he came to JCP offices to research the committee's minutes. I learned that he had been active in convincing the Joint Committee on Printing to add paragraph 38 to JCP's *Government Printing & Binding Regulations*, which said:

> When a department uses appropriated funds to create information for publication, the printing and binding of that information is subject to the provisions of Sections 103 and 501 of title 44, *United States Code*, and it shall not be made available to a private publisher for initial publication without the prior approval of the Joint Committee on Printing.

Schnapper continued to provide JCP staff with information that proved agencies were still allowing contractors to copyright reports that they had been paid by the agency to produce. He was particularly concerned about the Department of Education because it was working with a firm to actively promote the publishing and copyrighting of information produced by contractors.

JCP approved some agency publishing agreements with private publishers but always insisted that the agency provide copies of the publications free to depository libraries and that the underlying government information not be copyrighted. In 1985, JCP required that each department and agency submit a comprehensive printing program plan to JCP. The plan required reporting about

> the number and titles of all Government publications, e.g. monographs and journals, for which the department intends to seek a private sector publisher; the number of articles which the department intends to publish in privately published journals or compilations including the names of the journals and compilations; the number of articles to be published in each, and the total dollar amount of page charges to be paid; and the procedures used to notify the Superintendent of Documents of intent to publish and the procedures used to provide all required copies of Government publications to the Superintendent of Documents.[10]

The reports showed that thousands of articles written by government employees were being published in private publications and that the government was paying hundreds of thousands of dollars in page charges to have those articles published. The government was also subsidizing the publishers by buying reprints of the articles. It is not surprising that commercial and academic (university and college) publishers objected to any controls over their agreements with agencies. Publish or perish is just as important to researchers and others in the federal government as to those in academic institutions. An academic institution having both a depository library and a publishing operation may take opposing positions—the library opposing copyright and insisting on the publications being made available free in the depository program and the academic publisher supporting special publishing arrangements with government agencies.

PERSUADE AN ASSOCIATION TO SUPPORT YOUR CAUSE

An *association* is a group of persons or entities sharing a common interest or purpose. They range from associations composed mainly of professionals in a certain area of expertise, such as library, history, archives, or publishing, to those composed of corporate entities ranging from nonprofit educational institutions to companies that print, publish, or create and sell technology. Other associations cover a subject area, such as genealogy, the environment, and retirement. They invite anyone interested in the subject to join. Associations are funded primarily by membership dues, but some are good at generating revenue from the sale of publications, insurance policies, credit cards, and from convention revenues. Some associations receive grants and donations from various sources.

Many associations work to affect policy in the areas of libraries and access to information. There are some like library, archival, and history associations that spend considerable time lobbying in these areas, whereas other associations only get involved when it is an issue of particular concern to them. Most of these associations have legislation or public affairs committees. All groups have formal leaders, either elected or appointed, and informal leaders. You need to identify and work with both kinds of leaders.

According to George Bobinski in an article in *American Libraries*, there are some 152 library associations in the United States with about 228,000 members. These include fifty-six national associations; seven regional associations; fifty state associations; associations in the District of Columbia, Guam, Puerto Rico, and the U.S. Virgin Islands; and thirty-five state associations limited to school librarians.[11] Bobinski asks whether the profession is overorganized. I would ask instead, Are they using the power of being organized to promote their causes? Are they forming coalitions among the associations? Or are they wasting a lot of energy on internal organizing and procedures?

On the national level, the major library associations include the American Library Association (ALA), the American Association of Law Libraries (AALL), the Special Libraries Association (SLA), the Medical Library Association (MLA), the Music Library Association (MLA), Art Libraries Society of North America (ARLIS/NA), the American Society for Information Science (ASIS), and the Catholic Library Association (CLA). ALA has chapters in all states, the District of Columbia, Guam, and the Virgin Islands that elect a representative to the ALA Council, ALA's governing body. AALL, SLA, CLA, and the Medical Library Association also have chapters in states or regions.

Other associations represent smaller groups of libraries or librarians, such as the Chief Officers of State Library Agencies (COSLA), the Urban Libraries Council, the Association of Research Libraries (ARL), the Theater Library Association, the American Indian Library Association (AILA), the Chinese-American Librarians Association, REFORMA (National Association to Promote Library Services to the Spanish Speaking), the Asian/Pacific American Librarians Association, and the Ukrainian Library Association of America.

Other organizations represent special concerns such as the Freedom to Read Foundation, the American Booksellers Association, the American Association of Publishers, the Software and Information Industry Association, the Society for American Archivists, and Reading Is Fundamental.

There are many national and local groups that represent writers rather than publishers. They include groups such as PEN American Center (PEN) and the National Writers Union. PEN "stands for the principle of unhampered transmission of thought within each nation and between nations and members pledge themselves to oppose any form of suppression of freedom of expression in the country and community to which they belong."

Within these organizations are units that specialize in specific subject areas. For example, ALA has units with particular interest and expertise in the areas of government information, intellectual freedom, technology, and standards. Most of these groups have committees that work on legislation and public policy issues. In the larger organizations, joint committees may be formed when a particular issue crosses unit lines and the issue is at a crucial stage. In ALA these joint committees cover issues like copyright and changes to the federal depository library laws.

The American Association of Retired Persons (AARP) is an association that anyone interested in promoting libraries and the public's access to information should cultivate. According to an article in *Roll Call*, the director of AARP's Advocacy Office "envisions the group becoming 'the No. 1 organization in the country working for social change.'" One of its goals in 2001 is better education.[12] Older and retired people are big users of libraries and are active in many volunteer groups that need information. They are also more likely to vote than younger citizens. AARP has some thirty-four million members, a budget of over $450 million, offices in every state, a think tank, and a large lobbying staff located in Washington, D.C. This group is active in issues that cut across age lines. According to Dychtwald in *Age Power*:

> Like a thousand-armed octopus, AARP reaches out to wield its power in countless ways: lobbying on Capitol Hill, hosting or co-hosting hundreds of conferences and meetings, sponsoring thousands of workshops and programs, conducting research into dozens of aging-related subjects, advising employers, serving as an ongoing "source" for the media, and mobilizing grassroots activism that can put an instant stranglehold on its opponents' efforts.[13]

Many library associations encourage membership by offering free memberships to students in library schools, lower cost memberships for recent graduates and first-time members, grants for first-time attendees at conferences, special units in their organization for new members, and mentoring programs for new attendees. I joined ALA in library school and have been a member ever since. I was encouraged to join by a library school dean who believed that library organizations can make a difference in such areas as fighting for faculty status for academic librarians and good pay for librarians. Dr. C. B. Ford, the dean of libraries at Central Missouri State University and the person who hired me out of library school, taught me the value of library associations for the working librarian. He insisted that every librarian who worked for him attend the state association annual conference and participate in every breakfast, luncheon, dinner, and association-wide meeting. He also persuaded the university to provide funding for our attendance. He encouraged us to attend the meetings of school and public librarians and to work with all the members of the association on common issues. Ford also encouraged us to attend the ALA conference when it was held in a nearby city. He believed that membership in library associations would make us better librarians and provide lifetime education.

PERSUADE A NONPROFIT INSTITUTION, THINK TANK, OR ADVOCACY ORGANIZATION TO SUPPORT YOUR CAUSE

Since many lobbyists for libraries and the public's access to information are either working for a nonprofit or lobbying one, it is important to understand the role they play in our society. Nonprofits help shape the philosophical and political underpinnings of our communities by their activities. Understanding the size and composition of the nonprofit sector helps you decide who to lobby and why. It also helps you determine who is on what side and whether you can enlist them to aid you in your cause.

There are more than six hundred thousand tax-exempt nonprofit institutions, associations, and groups in the United States. They include libraries, museums, hospitals, mental health and educational institutions, professional and social action groups, foundations, think tanks, and research centers. According to Reynold Levy in *Give and Take: A Candid Account of Corporate Philanthropy*, "Nonprofits are the fastest growing part of the nation's economy. If donations of money and time are to the Third Sector organizations what voting is to democracy, it is worth observing that more than twice as many Americans participate in nonprofit life as cast a ballot in the 1996 presidential elections."[14] Nonprofits receive their support from membership dues, payment for services, publishing, grants, and donations. Levy explains why for-profit corporations give money to nonprofits:

> Philanthropy can help minimize potential damage to a firm's performance and to its reputation. Philanthropy can please customers, strengthen brand recognition, bolster morale, express the values of a business, and provide employees with leadership development opportunities. Philanthropy can also enhance the quality of life in communities where employees live and work and encourage key executive relationships with opinion leaders, customers and government officials. Not the least, philanthropy can help expose leading executives to new ideas, important social movements, and points of view they might not otherwise encounter. . . . Philanthropy can be no less than a source of sustainable competitive advantage difficult to attain by other means.[15]

Nonprofit institutions, such as universities, colleges, libraries, schools, museums, and archives have staff who lobby for them. These staff are probably not called lobbyists, but they are there to influence policymakers. Nonprofit institutions also belong to associations that attempt to represent institutional interests. Staff working for the institution are called upon to identify witnesses to testify to legislative and regulatory bodies when the institution's budget or programs are being reviewed by the legislature or when regulations are being promulgated or changed. Some nonprofits are very active in lobbying Congress and state legislatures for research money. Some have spent hundreds of thousands of dollars in their efforts. This often pays off in millions of dollars earmarked for specific universities, colleges, or research centers. The ability to persuade a legislative body to appropriate big money for institutions in their states is one reason why legislators lobby to be put on appropriations committees.

Think tank is an informal term used to describe an institution, foundation, or research center established to study issues or to give money and support to others, thereby influencing the policies regarding those issues. Some of these organizations could be better described as advocacy organizations. Think tanks are established by individuals and groups. Their methods of influence range from the scholarly research and analysis approach of institutions like the Brookings Institution and the American Enterprise Institute, to the investigative and confrontational methods used by the groups established by Ralph Nader. Some groups operate like investigative reporters and attempt to change policies by exposing wrong doing. In some cases, their work may lead to the investigation of government officials by law enforcement agencies. Groups like OMB Watch attempt to influence policy by closely monitoring the work of government and recommending changes that will improve the government's track record in providing information to the public. Wealthy individuals like Andrew Carnegie, George Soros, and Bill Gates and families like the Bentons establish foundations and use them as a means of distributing wealth in order to influence policies and lives.

These organizations raise money through membership dues, sale of newsletters and publications, speeches, contracts, grants, and donations from individuals, corporations, governments, and others. It is as much where they get their money as what they do with it that causes concern. Some think that the source of the money has too much influence on what the group does.

The National Committee for Responsive Philanthropy (NCRP) argues in its report *$1 Billion for Ideas: Conservative Think Tanks in the 1990s* that conservative think tanks like the American Enterprise Institute "are likely to increase their strength and impact in the new millennium with their unflagging commitment to marketing their policies, sophisticated political communication, seemingly unlimited resources, and strong grassroots networks."[16]

NCRP president Robert Bothwell commented, "When it comes to winning political battles, ultimate success results less from who's doing the right thing and more from whose view of reality dominates the battlefield. It doesn't take a rocket scientist to figure out that the millions effectively spent by conservative think tanks have enabled them virtually to dictate the issues and terms of national political debates."[17]

$1 Billion for Ideas asserts that the top twenty conservative think tanks probably spent over $1 billion between 1990 and 2000, more than doubling their budgets since 1992. The five largest and most well known—the Heritage Foundation, Hoover Institution, Center for Strategic and International Studies, American Enterprise Institute, and Free Congress Research and Education Foundation—expended half of the $158 million total in 1996, but the remaining $80 million was spent by fifteen smaller policy organizations. The report argues that these conservative think tanks argue for privatization of the public sphere and dependence on the market as the prime mechanisms for dealing with society's problems. They receive much of their money from corporations that want to influence the political process. They work closely with lobbyists for corporations, political groups, and activists at the grassroots level.

NCRP thinks corporations give too much money to right-leaning organizations, while the Capital Research Center (CRC) of Washington, D.C., thinks that they give too much money to left-leaning organizations. CRC publishes *Patterns of Corporate Philanthropy* annually with subtitles like *The Suicidal Impulse, Funding False Compassion, The Progressive Deception*, and *Executive Hypocrisy*. CRC staff use an in-house formula to place the recipients of corporate funds on a scale from radical left to radical right and then grade the donating corporations based on the amount of money they give each recipient. Large donations to numerous groups on the right earn them a high grade, whereas the same on the left earns them a low grade.

The following is a sampling of nonprofit entities with a brief description of how they influence public policy in the area of public access to information.

Brookings Institution

The Brookings Institution caught the attention of the library and information world when Daniel Ellsberg, who was associated with

Brookings, gave the *Pentagon Papers*, a classified history of the United States military and diplomatic actions concerning Vietnam, to the *New York Times* for publication. The subsequent debate about whether the papers should have been published led to the 1974 amendments to the Freedom of Information Act (FOIA). Those amendments make it possible for documents classified by the government to be released to the public through an appeal process that includes going to court.

The Government Documents Round Table supported the FOIA bill by sponsoring a panel discussion on the bill in 1973 and persuading ALA to work for the bill. The panel speakers, Ronald Plesser and William G. Phillips, went on to play important roles in the revision of laws affecting access to government information. Plesser, a lawyer and director of the Press Information Center supported by Ralph Nader and later a private law firm, advised NCLIS in 2000 on its study about public information dissemination. Phillips, staff director of the Subcommittee on Foreign Operations and Government Information of the Committee on Government Operations, played an important role in the adoption of amendments to FOIA. He later became the staff director of the Committee on House Administration. I worked with both Phillips and Plesser in an attempt in the late 1970s to revise the printing and dissemination laws of the federal government. Phillips acknowledged the library community's support for FOIA by including language in the National Publication Act of 1980, which added government information in electronic and audiovisual format to the depository library program.

Center for Democracy and Technology

The Center for Democracy and Technology (CDT), founded in 1994, operates out of Washington, D.C., and is directed by Jerry Berman. According to its website, "CDT works for practical, real-world solutions that enhance free expression, open access and democracy in the rapidly evolving global communications technologies."

Berman served as the American Civil Liberties Union's chief legislative counsel and director of the ACLU Project on Privacy and Information Technology from 1978 to 1988. He was director at the Electronic Frontier Foundation prior to founding CDT. Berman's dream was to expand the Freedom of Information Act to include

access to electronic government records. Berman and others convinced the Congress to pass the Electronic Freedom of Information
Act Amendments to the Freedom of Information Act (Public Law
104-231) in October 1996. As a result, the federal government must
treat electronic information such as e-mail messages as official government records subject to access by the public. The act requires that
agencies establish online reading rooms and make information
available electronically to those making FOIA requests.

Berman and I met when we were speakers at the joint spring
workshop of library associations in the metropolitan Washington,
D.C., area discussing the issue "High Technology & Politics in
1984: A Look at the Impact of Information Technology on Society
and the Political Issues Facing Our Profession This Election Year."
He was at the ACLU and just launching his Information Technology Project. Because some of the members of the Joint Committee
on Printing and their staff were leery of ACLU and Nader activities, I did not dwell on my work with those groups. We attended
the same public meetings and forums on government information
policies so we had ongoing contact. On the other hand, JCP members and staff approved of my close working relationship with library associations. When I needed some behind-the-scenes inter-
vention to reverse the Joint Committee on Printing's short-lived
policy to make citizens pay for legislative bills and other material,
I needed help from someone who could get to the chair without it
being traced to me. I turned to Berman for assistance. JCP was re-
sponding to the cost cutting provisions of the 1986 Gramm-
Rudman-Hollings balanced budget law. Anthony Zagami, JCP'S
general counsel, and I advised the staff director that making citizens pay for bills would be against Senator Mathias's philosophy
of the public's right to information. The staff director insisted that
the senator had read the letter announcing the decision and supported the change in policy. Zagami said that when he took letters
over to be signed, the chair sometimes read only one side of the
letter, trusting staff to look out for his interests. Once the senator
heard from the influential constituent contacted by Berman, the
policy was rescinded and never suggested again. Understanding
the underlying philosophy of the person or organization that you
work for can help you influence policies.

Congressional Accountability Project

The Congressional Accountability Project, run by Gary Ruskin, is a Ralph Nader–supported investigative and advocacy organization. Ruskin argues that citizens cannot play an active and effective role in the crafting and passing of legislation unless they have access to that legislation at every stage from draft to final bill, including the votes of members at each stage of the bill. He advocates online access to the draft, marked-up version, and final bills; hearings; votes of members; and Library of Congress Congressional Research Service (CRS) reports.

Ruskin persuaded U.S. senators John McCain (R-Ariz.) and Patrick Leahy (D-Vt.) to introduce Senate Resolution 21 on February 14, 2001, to put CRS Reports and Issue Briefs, CRS Authorization and Appropriations products, lobbyist disclosure reports, and Senate gift disclosure reports on the Internet. The resolution was cosponsored by Senate Majority Leader Trent Lott (R-Miss.) and Senator Joseph Lieberman (D-Conn.). This would provide public access to some 2,700 CRS reports, available only to members of Congress and their staff on an internal congressional intranet. Making lobbyists' disclosure reports available over the Internet would allow citizens to track patterns of influence in Congress and find out who is paying whom how much to lobby about what.

Ruskin put together an impressive coalition of supporters, including the Alliance for Democracy, American Association of Law Libraries, American Conservative Union, ALA, American Federation of Government Employees, American Society of Newspaper Editors, AOL Time-Warner, Better Government Association, Center for Democracy and Technology, Center for Media Education, Center for Responsive Politics, Common Cause, Computer Professionals for Social Responsibility, Congressional Accountability Project, Consumer Federation of America, Electronic Frontier Foundation, Electronic Privacy Information Center, Federation of American Scientists, Friends of the Earth, Government Accountability Project, Intel Co., National Federation of Press Women, National Newspaper Association, National Security Archive, National Taxpayers Union, OMB Watch, Progressive Asset Management Inc., Project on Government Oversight, Public Citizen, RealNetworks Inc., Reform Party of the USA, Regional Reporters Association, Reporters Committee for Freedom of the Press, Society of Professional Journalists, Taxpayers for Common Sense, and U.S. Public Interest Research Group (USPIRG).

Ruskin's effort in 2001 was not his first attempt to persuade Congress to share Congressional Research Service publications with the public. He persuaded Senators McCain and Leahy, Representative Christopher Shays (R-Conn.), and Representative David Price (D-N.C.) to introduce similar bills in 1999 (S. 393 and H.R. 654) requiring online access to LC CRS reports. According to a story in *Federal Computer Week* on February 15, 2001:

> Efforts in 1998 and 1999 failed in part over concern that publishing the reports online might make CRS vulnerable to legal liability. Researchers who recommended canceling a military program, for example, might be sued by a weapons manufacturer. McCain said he has redesigned his legislation to avoid the legal problem by having the Senate Sergeant-At-Arms post the reports, which will be available via the websites of Senators and Senate committees. The arrangement will ensure that CRS is protected by the immunity to legal action that members of Congress enjoy, a McCain aide explained.

The American Library Association had urged access to CRS reports since the late 1970s. ALA supported Ruskin's efforts in 1998, 1999, and 2001. The association issued a 2001 press release saying, "The CRS reports are well researched and balanced products addressing a wide variety of current public policy issues. It will be a great public benefit to have access to these materials." ALA encouraged Congress to take immediate action to ensure that publicly released CRS reports and information products are distributed in a timely manner to the general public through the federal depository libraries and on the Internet.

The congressional members who introduced these bills did not chair the authorizing committees of the Congressional Research Service, Senate Rules, and House Administration. Those chairs opposed making all CRS reports available from the CRS site and instead supported making selected reports available on committee websites. Librarians started lobbying the Joint Committee on Printing and the Joint Committee on the Library in the 1970s for dissemination of CRS reports to depository libraries. In the 1980s, the Joint Committee on Printing persuaded the Joint Committee on the Library and the Congressional Research Service to provide the CRS *Bill Digest* and several other publications to depository libraries. JCP was unable to persuade JCL to direct CRS to provide the bulk of the reports to depositories even though JCP suggested that the reports be sent a year after publication in order to give Congress time to determine whether it wanted them released. Many of the reports are prepared at the request of a member or a committee, and the requester may not want them released until after a hearing is held or a bill is passed. The Congressional Research Service argued that many of the reports are publicly available because they are published as congressional committee prints and as part of congressional hearings records. The Joint Committee on the Library argued that the members of Congress preferred sending out copies of the reports in response to constituent requests for information. Much to the frustration of the advocates for free public access, Pennyhill Press manages to obtain many of the CRS reports and sells them to the public.

OMB Watch

OMB Watch was founded by Gary Bass in 1983 to keep tabs on the Office of Management and Budget (OMB), part of the Executive Office of the President. Bass is the executive director. OMB Watch issues *Government Information Insider*, a quarterly publication with reviews about how agencies implement the law; files comments on draft OMB circulars and directives; testifies at regulatory and legislative hearings; and organizes meetings with other interested parties to discuss information policy issues. OMB also maintains a website.

The director of OMB reports directly to the president, making OMB one of the most powerful agencies in the executive branch since it reviews agency budgets and testimony for congressional hearings. OMB's Office of Information and Regulatory Affairs also issues official binding advice to agencies about how to interpret and implement a number of information laws such as the FOIA and the Paperwork Reduction Act (PRA). OMB Watch monitors how well agencies are complying with laws passed by Congress and the directives based on those laws issued by OMB. For example, in 1997, OMB Watch's *Potholes on the Information Bridge to the 21st Century* criticized OMB for not pressing government agencies to build their part of the Government Information Locator Service (GILS), an online catalog of government information services and products. OMB Watch's report charged that fewer than half of the seventy-seven federal departments, agencies, boards, and commissions had listed their holdings online since the project was started in 1995.

OMB Watch plays an active role in trying to influence the contents of each revision of the Paperwork Reduction Act and the Freedom of Information Act since those laws are the basis for most of the powers of OMB's Office of Information and Regulatory Affairs in the area of government information policies.

Taxpayers Assets Project

James Love of the Taxpayers Assets Project, another Ralph Nader–supported endeavor, was instrumental in the formulation and passage of the GPO Access Act of 1993. Love worked closely with the ALA Washington office on efforts to get the bill introduced and passed. He lobbied for free public access to the Securities and Exchange Commission filings and to the legal information generated by the U.S. Court system. Love was a leader in the fight against West Publishing's attempts to copyright and claim sole ownership of legal information generated by our nation's courts. West republishes and organizes court decisions using a unique citation system that has become the standard used by the legal profession. West tried to keep other publishers from publishing the same information by claiming copyright. When the other publishers challenged West in court, West resorted to persuading a member of Congress to insert language in a bill that would have allowed them to copyright the information. Love organized the opposition, and the language was deleted.

Freedom Forum

The Freedom Forum was established in 1991 under the leadership of its founder, Allen H. Neuharth, as successor to the Gannett Foundation. It receives income from an endowment worth more than $700 million. It funds only its own programs such as the Newseum at the Freedom Forum World Center in Arlington, Virginia.

The Freedom Forum is a nonpartisan, international foundation dedicated to free press and free speech for all people. It supports these causes through conferences, educational activities, publishing, broadcasting, online services, fellowships, partnerships, training, and research. Starting in 1998, the Freedom Forum joined with the Coalition on Government Information to present a program on Freedom of Information Day. The coalition presents its Madison Award to recipients at that event. By 2001, the American Library Association had taken over sponsorship of the Madison Award.

Benton Foundation

The Benton Foundation, a private grant-making foundation, is a legacy of Senator William Benton (D-Conn.). "Through projects that staff initiate and direct, Benton bridges the worlds of philanthropy, public policy, and community action—to shape the emerging communications environment and to demonstrate the value of communications for solving social problems."[18]

The Benton Foundation has attempted to influence the shape of policy in the area of communications and information through the funding of a number of activities. In early 1988, the foundation commissioned a series of eight papers to explore options for public policymakers. Those papers included *A Federal Right to Information Privacy: A Need for Reform* by Jerry Berman and Janlori Goldman of the American Civil Liberties Union, *Strengthening Federal Information Policy: Opportunities and Realities at OMB* by Gary Bass and David Plocher of OMB Watch, *A Presidential Initiative on Information Policy* by John Shattuck and Mauriel Morisey Spence of Harvard University, and *The Federal Structure for Telecommunications Policy* by Henry Geller of the Washington Center for Public Policy Research at Duke University.

The Benton Foundation and the Bauman Family Foundation moved the debate along by funding a two-day conference in October 1989 called "Electronic Public Information and the Public's Right to Know." The conference brought together representatives of public interest; library and information industry associations; policy experts; litigators; and congressional and federal agency staff to "explore key legal, policy, and technical issues involved in establishing public access rights to federal electronic government information."

The conferees concluded, "Electronic technologies blur the boundary between FOIA access, in which an agency is essentially passive until a FOIA request is received, and electronic dissemination, involving agency initiative to distribute information to potential consumers wherever they are." They added that "it now is technologically feasible to provide the public with a computer window into the databases actually used by agencies."[19]

The Benton Foundation encouraged librarians to examine their role in an electronic world by conducting a study of the public's opinion of library leaders' visions of the future and publishing their findings in *Buildings, Books and Bytes: Libraries and Communities in the Digital Age*. The study concluded:

> Americans continue to have a love affair with their libraries, but they have difficulty figuring out where libraries fit in the new digital world. And many Americans would just as soon turn their local libraries into museums and recruit retirees to staff them. Libraries are thus at a crossroads, for they must adjust their traditional values and services to the digital age. But there is good reason for optimism as libraries and their communities take up this challenge. Libraries have enormous opportunities nationwide to influence and direct public opinion because strong public sentiment already supports key visions for the future of libraries. . . . So libraries and their leaders now must chart a role for themselves, giving meaning and message to their future institutions and their central role in community life.[20]

Carnegie Corporation of New York

Andrew Carnegie made his money through steel and gave away 90 percent of his fortune to support "the improvement of mankind." He was particularly generous in funding the building of about 2,500 libraries. He supported library associations, library schools, library conferences, studies, and publications. The Carnegie Corporation of New York is still carrying out his directive to support libraries and librarians. The latest attempt to influence the development of library services worldwide is an award of $249,400 to the Library and Information Association of South Africa (LIASA). LIASA, established in July 1997, means "the new dawn or dawning" in the Pedi, Sesotho, and Zulu languages. In a July 21, 2000, LIASA news release, the purpose of the award was explained as follows:

> The Carnegie Corporation feels strongly that LIASA, as the national representative body of librarians and information workers in South Africa, has the potential to become a leading force in the transformation and development of South Africa in this post-apartheid era. The grant will enable LIASA to conduct an extensive recruitment drive, to support continuing education programmes and capacity-building among librarians and information workers, to lobby government and politicians to support the development of library services and to promote the image of the library profession.

LIASA will use the money to support an executive director, staff, and an office to carry out the wishes of Carnegie. This grant comes at a crucial time in the development of libraries and librarians in South Africa. I spent almost a month in South Africa in 1997 advising the library, government, and public interest communities on how to strengthen the public's access to government information through libraries. I met with the directors of most of the major libraries in South Africa. I gave the keynote address in Durban at the historic last conference of the South African Institute of Library and Information Science (SAILIS), the white-segregated library association, where SAILIS members voted their association out of existence and transferred their members and money to the integrated Library and Information Association of South Africa.

Carnegie has supported libraries in South Africa since 1928 and in 2001 awarded financial grants worth more than $3 million to six public library systems following a competitive selection process. Libraries receiving grants are the City of Johannesburg Library and Information Services, the Nelson Mandela Metropolitan Library Services, the Durban Metropolitan Library, the Free State Provincial Library and Information Services, the Northern Cape Provincial Library and Information Services, and Mpumalanga Provincial Library and Information Services. The goal of Carnegie is "the revitalization of public libraries in South Africa with the intention to strengthen the infrastructure of a selected number of public library systems to help them move to the next level of service delivery and to assist them to develop centers of learning and communications within each system."[21]

Soros Foundation

Financier George Soros is spending his money through foundations with the intent of influencing the development of an open and democratic society in countries that emerged from behind the iron curtain or from repressive societies. These countries include parts of the former Soviet Union, the former Communist bloc in Central and Eastern Europe, South Africa, and Haiti. Programs supported by his money include the education of librarians and others; expansion of a free press, Internet, and e-mail communication; publishing; human rights; arts and culture; and social, legal, and economic reform.

Soros received the James Madison Award from the Coalition on Government Information in 1997 and Barbara Ford, president elect of ALA, praised him with these words:

> What Andrew Carnegie did for libraries and public dissemination of information in the United States, George Soros is doing around the world. It has been said that he is the only modern philanthropist who ranks with Andrew Carnegie. George Soros' personal commitment to open societies, open and accountable government, cultural tolerance, mutual respect, diversity of views and voices make him an outstanding choice to receive the James Madison Award.[22]

One way that Soros seeks to influence the future of the newly democratized Eastern Europe and the former Soviet Union is to fund the Library of Congress–Soros Foundation Visiting Fellows Program for librarians. He believes that educating librarians about how to improve their libraries and assist the policymakers of their countries will provide a strong foundation for democracy. To have a say in which fellows will be selected, he insists that staff in local Soros Foundation offices throughout Eastern Europe conduct the initial interviews of applicants and then lets LC make the final selections from that group. The first group of fourteen selected in 1992 included librarians, library professors, and a recent library school graduate, each from a different nation. They spent one month learning about the activities of LC and two months working in their areas of specialty.[23]

After their work at LC, the visiting fellows spend up to a year at the University of Illinois at Urbana-Champaign, Mortenson Center for International Library Programs, studying and collecting books in their area of interest. My friend Tatiana Ershova, then chief of the Department of Foreign Acquisitions and International Book Exchange at the Russian State Library (formerly the Lenin State Library), was selected as a fellow because she spoke excellent English and was a leader at the national library and a supporter of democracy in Russia.

Ershova and I became friends during the August 1991 coup attempt against President Mikhail Gorbachev in Moscow. In a speech entitled "The Lenin State Library of the U.S.S.R. as a National Library and Official Publications" at the IFLA Official Publications Committee program, she explained that since perestroika, interest in foreign documents had increased greatly as a valuable source of information about the experience of highly developed countries in forming democratic institutions. Government documents received by the Lenin State Library from the Library of Congress were studied by those working toward democracy. Ershova and other Russian librarians used their talents as information disseminators to assist those who were with President Boris Yeltsin at the "White House" barricades during the coup. She told me that we librarians, who stayed in Moscow and held our IFLA meetings in spite of the coup, provided cover for Russian librarians as they disseminated information to the populace about who was behind the coup and who was behind the barricades. The librarians posted flyers in the subway stations and on the walls of buildings. In thanks for my help in "saving his wife's life," Tatiana's husband gave me an intricately carved plaque of a horse and rider and a photo of the rocket ship that he had helped design.

After the coup attempt failed and we were celebrating with vodka and dancing at a party in the Kremlin, Ershova asked me to thank the U.S. Congress for supporting the international exchange program. Her thank-you vindicated the Joint Committee on Printing's defense of the exchange of information between the Library of Congress and libraries behind the iron curtain like the Lenin State Library. Several senators wanted to eliminate these libraries from the program. Senator Mathias directed JCP staffers to prepare a memo supporting the program. We argued that without the international exchange program the United States would suffer because it would be very difficult for Americans to obtain information from behind the iron curtain. The State Department and the Central Intelligence Agency (CIA), for example, are regular users of LC's foreign documents collection. I argued that libraries in Communist countries would still be able to access U.S. government information through the LC Exchange partner libraries in other Western countries. I based this argument on a conversation I had had with Eve Johannson, documents librarian at the British Library, and a librarian from the Lenin State Library in 1980. Over ice cream sodas in the back streets of Leipzig, East Germany, he told us how pleased he was that he could borrow American documents from the British Library. We had to meet in the back streets because the Russians had been told not to visit with the Americans except during official events. JCP staffers also argued that having information about our government available to the citizens behind the iron curtain would educate them about democracy and the Moscow coup proved us right.

Bill and Melinda Gates Foundation

Bill Gates, one of the founders of Microsoft, made millions of dollars providing software to the public, libraries, and businesses to help organize information and provide access to that information over the Internet. He and his wife established the Bill and Melinda Gates Foundation, which among other projects established the $250 million U.S. Library Program. Its goal is to assist libraries in low-income communities provide their users with access to electronic information. The Gates Foundation plans on providing equipment, software, and access to the Internet to some ten thousand libraries in all fifty states by 2003. It provides equipment, software, and assistance in the installation of the equipment and software as well as training for the librarians. For example, the Lewis & Clark Library in Helena, Montana, received a grant of $25,000 for expanding public access to computers and the Internet.

The Gates Foundation realized that for the initial investment in libraries to be successful in the long term, ongoing training needed to be provided to both librarians and patrons of libraries. Therefore, it provides grants for setting up regional training labs. The Lewis & Clark Library received a second grant of $36,000 to establish a training lab that is used to train librarians at Montana libraries receiving grants and for long-term training of library staff and patrons. The lab is also used by the Montana State Library to provide ongoing training for librarians throughout the state.

National Security Archive

The National Security Archive (NSA) was founded in 1985 by Scott Armstrong, a reporter for the *Washington Post* and coauthor with Bob Woodward of *The Brethren: Inside the Supreme Court*. It is "a not-for-profit District of Columbia-based corporation established to promote research and public education on U.S. governmental and national security decision making and to promote openness in government and government accountability through making government information more widely available to the public."[24] It is located in the Gelman Library at George Washington University. NSA concentrates on research on international affairs, runs a library and archive of declassified U.S. documents acquired through requests made under the Freedom of Information Act, and publishes books based on research in those declassified documents. Through its efforts, NSA has forced the federal government to release information such as letters written by President John F. Kennedy and Soviet president Nikita Kruschev during the 1962 Cuban missile crisis and the diaries of Oliver North kept during the Iran-contra affair. NSA staff hosts a steady stream of delegations from other countries who want to learn how to get information from their own governments. NSA works with scholars in other countries by helping them to expand open government laws and practices.

The National Security Archive celebrated the twenty-fifth anniversary of passage of the Freedom of Information Act on July 4, 2001, by issuing its first annual *State of Freedom of Information* report on its website. It reported that documents released under federal, state, and local freedom of information acts sparked more than three thousand news stories in 2000 and 2001. The site includes a user's guide to FOIA, a sample FOIA request and appeal letters, the addresses of every major federal agency FOIA contact, and guidance on how to use FOIA.

When Armstrong left the NSA, Thomas Blanton became its executive director. Blanton is a longtime member of the American Library Association and was a member of its Committee on Legislation Subcommittee on Government Information for several years.

INFLUENCE CORPORATIONS AND FOR-PROFIT INSTITUTIONS THAT BENEFIT FROM INFORMATION PROGRAMS

It is amazing how many corporations and for-profit institutions have a commercial/profit interest in libraries and the public's access to information. They include companies that

- publish books, journals, magazines, newsletters, documents and articles in traditional, electronic, and audiovisual formats;
- supply products that assist in publishing such as printing, paper, ink, microforms, floppy disks, CD-ROMs, computer tapes, printing and computer equipment;
- produce and provide the software and support services for electronic acquisition, cataloging, reference, circulation and documents management, and retrieval systems;

- provide communication services such as telephone, cable, satellite, and Internet servers;
- offer services such as book and journal jobbing, binding, training, indexing, cataloging, and preservation;
- provide bookmobiles, kiosks, signs, furniture, shelving, security, lawn care, maintenance of equipment, and cleaning services; and
- act as consultants, lawyers, accountants, auditors, architects, and building contractors.

Look around your own community and identify those for-profit corporations that benefit from libraries and their efforts to provide the public with information. Walk up and down the aisles of vendors at exhibits at library conventions, and you will meet many who are lobbying for policies that will assure them a profit in the library and information marketplace. Find out who is helping to pay for the receptions, luncheons, banquets, music, bus service, and speakers at library conventions. Find out who is funding the library scholarships, awards, grants for travel, and attendance at library conferences. Check out who is supporting the purchase of electronic equipment and software being used by the staff of your library association. Then ask yourself what do they expect in return for their generosity?

Librarians and the producers of information products and support services need each other. We need their products and they need our money to produce those products. But we do need to exercise caution when we are developing policies that affect the public's interest in libraries and not allow our gratitude to vendors to cloud our vision of what is best for libraries' users.

In the early days of the Government Documents Round Table, GODORT was hard-pressed to come up with enough money to publish its newsletter, directory of documents librarians, and other publications, hold receptions, and provide awards to deserving promoters of public access to government information. GODORT members turned to publishers of tools that helped them serve the public and asked for money. Publishers who shared GODORT's zeal in providing the public with access to government information responded enthusiastically.

William Buchanan, president of several presses including Carrollton Press and publisher of the *Declassified Documents Reference Sys-*

tem and the *Cumulative Subject Index to the Monthly Catalog of U.S. Government Publications 1900–1971*, supported GODORT workshops and receptions. He warned me when I was chair of GODORT, "I'll support your receptions as long as it helps me promote the sale of my publications, but when it no longer helps, I'll drop you like a hot potato." (And he did.) I responded, "If your support of our receptions ever interferes with our support of a policy that we consider good for libraries, we will drop *you* like a hot potato."

Buchanan was as much of a crusader for access to the public's access to government information as any documents librarian. After a career in government, part of it spent as a Central Intelligence Agency officer, he launched Carrollton Press to provide access to government documents declassified under the Freedom of Information Act. Among those documents were the diaries of Lee Harvey Oswald written during his time in the Soviet Union and the records of CIA experiments with the drug LSD. Buchanan told *Parade Magazine* in 1978, "Responsible American officials have already evaluated every document in our collection and have made a legal determination that its disclosure is no longer a threat to national security. Our service gets the truth out. It clears up misconceptions. Having this material accessible to the scholarly community does far more good than harm."[25]

I lobbied Buchanan on behalf of Mary Elizabeth Poole when she was looking for a publisher to publish the fourth edition of her *Documents Office Classification*. Poole was legendary among documents librarians as the compiler of an authoritative list of superintendent of documents classification numbers—a heroic task. Her tool was invaluable in classifying older obscure documents. Buchanan was delighted to work with her, and she used his United States Historical Documents Institute microfilm collection of the GPO Library's shelf list as another source for her compilation.

Many publishers turn to librarians for advice when they are developing new publications and services. In 2001, CQ Press, a division of Congressional Quarterly Inc., advertised on GOVDOC-L, a documents electronic discussion group, for academic librarians to participate in the evaluation and development of electronic reference sources. The librarians could help by answering a questionnaire, being interviewed by telephone or in person, and participating in a focus group.

Some publishing companies start as Mom-and-Pop operations in the homes of their founders. Some have the goal of supporting libraries and their users as their major purpose rather than making a big profit. Once publishers are successful, larger companies often buy them out. The founders may be tired or ready to move on to other endeavors; they may decide that the value of their company is diminishing and want to get out while they can still sell their company; or they may believe that being part of a larger corporation will help them market their publications or attract talented staff and authors. Whatever the reason, more and more independent presses have become part of large corporations. Sometimes that has meant that the presses have taken fewer chances in publishing unknown authors and scholarly or limited market publications. In 1994, Patricia Glass Schuman, president of Neal-Schuman Publications and former president of ALA, summed it up in her article "Librarians and Publishers: An Uneasy Dance":

> For many librarians, it is not the government that raises the spectre of monopoly control; it is the private sector. Since 1986, three of the six commercial online systems now used by libraries have changed hands. Once an industry made up of independent, often family run companies, trade-book publishing is now dominated by a handful of corporations; six publishers now control from 40 to 50 percent of school book sales in the U.S. According to some reports, fifteen companies may represent as much as 50 percent of the total revenue in the publishing industry, and 2 percent of the publishers now publish 75 percent of the titles. Foreign publishers control an estimated 25 percent of total U.S. book revenues.[26]

She adds:

> Many of the private sector companies lobbying for privatization of government information are multinational conglomerates. The serials pricing crisis university libraries are facing is largely caused by these same companies. Elsevier N.V. raised its serial prices 52 percent in a single year. In 1992, Elsevier and Reed International P.L.C. merged to create one giant publishing empire, with sales of nearly $5 billion a year. The group now controls a large portion of the world's scholarly, scientific, and technical journals, as well as *Library Journal*, *School Library Journal*, and *Publishers Weekly*.[27]

The Association of Research Libraries was so alarmed at the merging of publishing houses and the increase in the cost of journals that they launched the Scholarly Publishing and Academic Resources

Coalition (SPARC) in 1997. SPARC is a coalition of major libraries and affiliates with the goals of (1) creating a more competitive marketplace where the cost of journals acquisition, archiving, and use are reduced and where publishers who are responsive to customer needs are rewarded; (2) ensuring fair use of electronic resources while strengthening the rights of authorship; and (3) using technologies to improve scholarly communications. SPARC partners with publishers that agree with SPARC's principles to help assure them a viable market for their publications at a reasonable price to libraries.

The cost of scientific and medical journals has made it almost impossible for libraries in developing countries to provide such information to their users. Journal subscriptions, both electronic and print, have been priced uniformly for medical schools and research centers irrespective of geographical location. Annual subscription prices cost on average several hundred dollars per title. Many key titles cost more than $1,500 per year. The World Health Organization (WHO) as a part of the United Nations established the Health Inter-Network, which hopes to strengthen public health services by providing public health workers, researchers, and policymakers access to health information through an Internet portal. In 2001, working with the *British Medical Journal* and the Open Society Institute of the Soros foundation network, WHO lobbied the six largest medical journal publishers (i.e., Blackwell, Elsevier Science, the Harcourt Worldwide STM Group, Wolters Kluwer International Health & Science, Springer Verlag, and John Wiley) to develop a more affordable pricing structure for online access to their international biomedical journals. The result was a tiered-pricing model that will make nearly 1,000 of the 1,240 top international biomedical journals available to institutions in the hundred poorest countries free of charge or at significantly reduced rates.

Recognizing the growing distrust between the library and publishing communities, the International Federation of Library Associations and Institutions and the International Publishers Association established a joint steering group to improve library and publisher relations throughout the world through cooperative initiatives in August 2001. The group of eight members is cochaired by Ingrid Parent, member of IFLA's executive board, and Herman P. Spruijt, member of IPA's executive committee.

The group plans to share information on activities in favor of freedom of expression; promote zero or reduced VAT rates for books and electronic publications, exchange statistical information, discuss deposit and archiving of electronic publications, clarify the price components of electronic publications; participate in metadata and Digital Object Identifier (DOI) activities, discuss electronic interlibrary document delivery, and work on a draft joint statement on copyright aimed at promoting agreed principles within and beyond the IFLA and IPA memberships.

On the other hand, Chemical Abstracts, Cambridge Scientific Abstracts, Elsevier, and Thomson successfully lobbied the House of Representatives in 2001 to defund PubScience, an online citation service run by the Department of Energy (DOE). PubScience provides free access to articles in 1,250 journals from thirty-five publishers in which DOE researchers report their scientific discoveries. Much of the research reported in the journals is funded with federal dollars. The publishers contribute their information free of charge. The private companies argued that DOE is competing with their citations services. The supporters of PubScience persuaded the Senate not to agree with the House, and PubScience was not eliminated by the Congressional Conference Committee.[28] The secretary of the Department of Energy then directed that PubScience be eliminated in September 2002. Its proposed closure was announced on the PubScience website, and users were asked to comment. Out of 240 comments, 230 favored retention of the service. Seven comments submitted by industry favored elimination. DOE discontinued PubScience in November 2002.

Congressional Information Service

James and Estee Adler started the Congressional Information Service (CIS) out of their home. They sold CIS to Elsevier, who sold it to LexisNexis. In 2001, CIS's name was changed to LexisNexis Academic and Library Solutions. The Adlers saw the need to provide indexing of congressional publications to improve access for the users of libraries. They recognized that even though the paper version was being provided to libraries and the public, a complete microfiche version with multiple indexes might be of interest to libraries. While James organized the business, Estee spent a lot of her time convincing congressional committee staff to give her copies of their hearings, prints, and reports, many of which were printed in limited numbers or not printed through GPO at all. In return, the committees got free copies of the indexes.

CIS turned to librarians in the late 1960s to get advice on the best way to index congressional hearings and to determine whether they would be willing to buy the hearings on microfiche. They surveyed librarians, met with them at conferences, visited them in their libraries, and hired them as consultants. CIS also hired librarians to index and help develop and market their publications. It was successful because they took their customers' advice and developed good products.

CIS promotes its products by doing a number of things to please its primary market, documents librarians. For example, CIS has held an annual breakfast for documents librarians since 1971 where they provide a well-known, sometimes controversial speaker and give a cash award to the recipient of the CIS/GODORT/ALA Documents to the People Award. The GODORT main program has traditionally been held right after the breakfast in the same hotel. CIS publishes GODORT's *Directory of Government Documents Collections and Librarians,* advertises in *Documents to the People,* and supports GODORT's receptions.

As the chair of GODORT, I negotiated the contract with CIS to publish the first edition of the directory because GODORT did not have the funds to publish and market it. CIS is still publishing the directory some twenty-five years later. CIS shares the profits with GODORT. The goodwill that CIS garnered by publishing a tool needed by the user community helps them in marketing their other products to librarians.

CIS treats librarians as valued customers, and their customers value their products. But not all is as it appears. There is an underlying conflict between the two communities revolving around who is going to produce and disseminate the publications produced by the government. Librarians value CIS indexes to government publications but oppose the CIS position that commercial publishers and not the government should be the major disseminator of government publications. Librarians support commercial publishers' republication of government publications in different formats, especially in silver microfiche. Librarians also support the government's right to use new technologies to produce and disseminate their own publications. Librarians oppose copyright of government publications so that all citizens, including private publishers, can republish them. Librarians do not support turning government publications over to private publishers so they can own them through copyright.

At times during the almost thirty years of struggle over who is going to control production and dissemination in the new formats, the two communities have had to balance their own interests and still work together to provide needed services for their users. Over the years, CIS worked to influence government policies through directly lobbying Congress and its customers and indirectly through the lobbying efforts of the Information Industry Association. A number of the letters that were sent to the Joint Committee on Printing asking JCP not to allow GPO to produce publications in microfiche were from CIS library customers who were afraid that CIS would go out of business if the government competed with them in producing microforms. CIS expressed support for the depository library program but preferred that the government give the libraries money so they could buy from the source of their choice, and, of course, CIS hoped to be that source.

Corporations as Lobbyists

Like the publishers of CIS, the people who own and work for many corporations and for-profit institutions lobby. It may be the president of the corporation putting in a good word at an inaugural ball, a dinner at the White House or Governor's mansion or on the golf course. Many corporations also have staff, often called *public affairs officers*, who lobby for them on a formal basis. Those who lobby for corporations usually have more money than lobbyists for other entities. They can afford to take policymakers to lunch and dinner, hold receptions for them, offer them trips to exotic places, and contribute to their election campaigns. These lobbyists usually work full-time and are able to attend most of the legislative and regulatory hearings, briefings, and news conferences in the area of their interests. Rather than stand in line for limited seating in hearings, some will pay others to wait in line for them. They have the time and resources to serve on advisory committees, commissions, and task forces. They also have the time to visit the offices of the policymakers on a regular basis. They can attend meetings of associations to promote support for their causes. They even attend the conferences and briefings of rival associations and organizations. They have the help of their corporation's lawyers, librarians, subject experts, and clerical and technical support staff. I vividly recall when a fellow congressional staffer took a job as a lobbyist with a big oil company and said, "Now I will get a decent salary and an expense account."

Milton J. Esman in *Government Works: Why Americans Need the Feds* warns those who value the public's access to information:

> Perhaps the greatest threat to freedom of expression comes not from government harassment or censorship but from the creeping monopolization of the major media-newspapers, radio, TV, cable, films, and even publishing houses—in the hands of a few large corporate conglomerates. The willingness of the federal government, beginning in the Reagan era, to tolerate such concentration of the information media in so few hands by failing to enforce the anti-monopoly laws (a tendency not reversed sadly, by the Clinton Administration) should be troublesome to progressives, for it handicaps the efforts of original, dissenting, and heterodox thinkers and writers to find public outlets for their views. The unlimited web space available on the Internet represents a countervailing force, but by no stretch of the imagination can the web compensate for the emergent concentration of ownership and control of the mass media.[29]

During 2000, a number of Montanans sued the W. R. Grace Company, claiming that exposure to the mine's hazardous substances (primarily asbestos) led to the illness and death of many workers and their families. Some federal government officials were criticized because they knew in the 1980s that the by-products of W. R. Grace were harmful and yet the information was not shared with the workers or local officials. One of the reasons for their silence might be connected to J. Peter Grace (chairman of W. R. Grace from 1948 to 1995), chairmanship of President Reagan's Private Sector Survey on Cost Control Commission in 1983. The Grace Commission argued that private publishers should determine "whether the material gathered by or prepared for the agency is worthy of publication at all by or under the sponsorship of the Government."[30] The report advocated the imposition of user's fees on government information, saying it could generate some $80 million per year. User fees would have limited even further the access to information needed by all.

Because more and more publishers of information are being bought by large corporations, they have more money to spend and may be tempted to use some of the tactics described by Reed E. Hundt, former chair of the Federal Communications Commission, in his book *You Say You Want a Revolution: A Story of Information Age Politics:*

> An innovation of the Gingrich Congress was to permit business lobbyists to draft legislation in committee rooms, as if they were staff to the

member. Indeed, many of the new Republican members acted like staff to the business lobbies. Some new Republican Congressmen demanded, from me, rulings "on behalf of" a particular business—a locution that appeared to dispense with the traditional assumption in our Republic that elected officials represent voters, not corporations.

No one outside Washington seemed to know about the new deal for moneyed interests. The reason for the national ignorance of this stealthy scandal was that the degradation of the legislative process by money was not on television. It did not meet the requirements of television news. Nothing is broadcast unless it sparks at least one of four basic emotional reactions—regret, bathos, horror, prurient interest.[31]

In 1991, Herbert I. Schiller warned of a possible society where only data with a commercial value would be collected and disseminated in his article "Public Information Goes Corporate."[32] He argued that there are two contrasting approaches to the information function. "One is to regard information as a central element in the development and creation of a democratic society. Under this premise, information serves to facilitate democratic-decision making, assists citizen participation in government, and contributes to the search for roughly egalitarian measures in the economy at large." And the other "is to view information collection, organization, and dissemination as a neutral activity, absent of social direction." He further argued that "expanded corporate wealth and power, deregulation, and the preemption of social space with commercial messages and perspectives—culminate in still another far-reaching change in the economy. What once were social and public spheres of activity have been steadily privatized." He added that the

> [n]ational informational system especially has borne the brunt of the privatization pressure. The national government has been, and remains, the largest generator, collector, and disseminator of information. The drive to privatization has cut deeply into these functions. . . . As the idea of information as a good for sale, a commodity, advances, the idea of information as a social good, the cornerstone of democratic life recedes.

Sometimes the Goals of For-Profit and Nonprofit Entities Are the Same

Sometimes the goals of corporations and the associations that represent them are also the goals of nonprofit organizations and associations. A good example is the joint effort by the Association of American Publishers (AAP), Bowker Company, and the American Library Association Government Documents Round Table to persuade the Government Printing Office to use the International Standard Book Numbering System (ISBN). Bowker publishes *Books in Print* (*BIP*), which lists all books with ISBN numbers and is used by bookstores and libraries for identification and ordering of publications. Being listed in *BIP* is a useful marketing tool. An ISBN number uniquely identifies one title from one publishing area or language group and one specific publisher within that area or group.

The struggle started in 1972 when Carol Nemeyer of the AAP wrote to me as chair of the ALA Social Responsibilities Round Table Task Force on Government Publications.

> I hope you have been successful in getting signatures sufficient to establish your Government Documents Round Table. If this SRRT Task Force takes hold, perhaps your group will be concerned with helping the Superintendent of Documents to understand the need to adopt the ISBN numbers for government documents. You know my interest in standardization, and here, I think, is a golden opportunity to mesh government documents into an international mainstream.[33]

Many people worked to convince GPO and the Joint Committee on Printing to use ISBN for government publications. In 1975, Robert Frase, consulting economist and former vice president of AAP, wanted to include statistics on government publications for publication by UNESCO. He believed that GPO adopting the use of ISBN would further that goal. Several JCP staff lunched with him in 1975 when he offered his help in assisting GPO in adapting the ISBN for their sales publications by incorporating some of the information in their GPO stock numbering system.[34]

After Frase moved on to other issues, Emery Koltay, director of serials bibliography and standards at Bowker, took up the cause. Koltay and I joined forces in 1980 to convince GPO and government publishers to adopt ISBN. James Young, director of the GPO Library and Statutory Distribution Service, arranged for Koltay to speak to the GPO's Interagency Council on Printing and Public Services about the ISBN in May 1981. As a result of that meeting and a meeting with JCP staff in August 1981, we wrote a paper arguing that the government should assign the ISBNs and offered four alternatives as to which agency or agencies should assign them. We debated whether each agency should have a block of numbers and assign their own numbers (some agencies already had blocks of numbers) or whether GPO and NTIS should control the numbers and assign them to the publications that they sold.[35]

Toni Carbo Bearman, executive director of the National Commission on Libraries and Information Science (NCLIS), devoted her December 1981 brown bag lunch to a discussion about ISBN. She invited agency publishers, as well as staff from the Joint Committee on Printing, the Library of Congress, the General Accounting Office, the Federal Library Committee, the National Archives, the Government Printing Office, and the National Technical Information Service. Patricia Berger, chief of the Library and Information Services Division at the National Bureau of Standards, argued that if ISBNs were adopted, it should be limited to selected publications and administered by the depository library program, not by the government. She added that there were four times more government publications than commercial ones and that would make it too expensive to implement.[36]

In March 1982, Ruth Smith, chief of the Office of Customer Services at the National Technical Information Service, argued, "There already is a government-wide Standard Technical Report Number (STRN) system" that is administered by NTIS; since it was not being fully implemented, to add another system would be "economically insupportable." She opposed depository libraries running the program.[37]

In spite of GPO sales staff's reluctance to implement ISBN because GPO had its own stock numbering system for tracking inventory, GPO began receiving ISBNs for monographs in 1985. Koltay and I lobbied for the ISBN in all sales publications, and, in 1987, we got the support of Don Fossedal, the superintendent of documents, who wrote to Koltay inquiring "about the possibility of re-opening discussion of the assignment of ISBN to publications distributed by GPO." He argued, "I believe the issue is sufficiently important to warrant another attempt at resolution. Our interest in ISBN is to provide better service to our commercial customers, some of whom are quite inconvenienced by the absence of numbers. We also believe that the presence of ISBN would signify a greater willingness to participate in the international book selling community."[38]

In 1987, GPO issued *Circular Letter No. 285 International Standard Book Numbers (ISBN)* to all the printing and publishing officials of the federal government announcing that GPO planned to assign

ISBNs to publications selected for sale by GPO and asked which agencies were already assigning ISBNs to their publications. In 1988, Bowker gave GPO a string of ISBNs with a unique stem, but because agencies also assigned ISBNs, it was not possible to pre-assign and print the ISBNs on the publications until it was determined whether one had been assigned by the agencies. When GPO assigned a second ISBN to a publication that already had one, the result was confusion.

In July 1990, Dr. James Veatch, head of Technical Services at Nashville Tech Library, testified on behalf of ALA at a hearing held by the House Committee on Administration Subcommittee on Procurement and Printing. He urged, "Plans to implement ISBN at GPO should be highly encouraged, with ISBN assigned to at least all sales items and printed on the items." After the hearing James Young, director of the GPO Sales Service, called Bowker to discuss how all GPO sales publications with ISBNs could appear in *Books in Print*. Koltay replied in a letter that *BIP* carried 1,212 active GPO titles, but adding another 5,000 titles with ISBN would require a copy of the GPO sales catalog tape. He argued, "If the GPO wants to develop any effective sales plan, it should be a priority to list your titles in all the important information providing services. As a publisher, you should not be charging DIALOG or anyone else and you should be using all the free promotional channels available to you." He also urged GPO to print the ISBN in bar code format on the publications.

In 1990, Public Printer Robert Houk accepted the recommendation of a GPO Sales Publications Pricing Panel to "accelerate the process, which had already been started, to convert the sales program to the ISBN and ISSN identification systems." In August 1991, a circular was sent to printing and publishing officials outlining GPO's plan for printing ISBNs on monographs handled by the central office. Some agency officials objected to the use of GPO generated ISBNs on their publications. GPO decided to wait until the implementation of a new automated sales system to replace the GPO stock number with the ISBN.

By 2001, most of the GPO sales titles were assigned an ISBN and were listed in *Books in Print*, Amazon.com, and other sales outlets.[39] Some agencies just print the ISBN in the book while others also include the number in a barcode. GPO still uses a unique number called SKU (stock keeping unit) for organizing their warehouse stock.

GOVERNMENTS

Governments are all around us on the town, city, county, state, regional, national, and international levels. Think of the hierarchy of governments as an inverted pyramid with the smallest governments, towns, and cities on the bottom and the others progressively covering more geography and people until you reach the national government. National governments interact with other national governments directly through treaties and other agreements. National governments also belong to international organizations such as the United Nations where they work together on common issues.

Governments are not permitted to lobby in the usual sense. But most of them have someone on staff who is available to talk to and educate staff and policymakers in other governments, other branches of their own government, nongovernmental organizations and associations, and the public. Staff titles vary: Some are called public affairs officer, press director, or congressional or public liaison. Some states such as Montana require that government employees supplying information and testifying before the legislature on a regular basis register as lobbyists. Some states, counties, and large cities have lobbyists at the national level. If you are lobbying for library and public access interests in Washington, D.C., or your state's capital, don't forget to check in with your state, county, and city lobbyists. They can give you good advice about whom to lobby and how to approach them. Educate the lobbyists so if your issues come up in their daily activities, they will remember to lobby for them.

One way you can learn about the structure and purposes of organizations such as governments is to read their organizational manuals, annual reports, budget requests, and the appropriations records. For example, the federal government issues the *United States Government Manual* and the *Congressional Directory*. Many states publish organization manuals called blue books, although in Missouri the Irish American secretary of state changed the traditional color of the book, and it became the green book. On the county and city levels, telephone directories usually have government sections that list the elected officials and government offices. Many government bodies, corporations, associations, and think tanks have websites with information about their organization, including names of key officials. Some include information so you can go from the website directly to the key people working for the organization. Many libraries, including the Library of Congress, have electronic websites that lead the user to international, federal, state, and local sites that give information about government and those who work for government.

A number of private publishers also publish guides to government organizations and officials. For example, Staff Directories of Mount Vernon, Virginia, publishes *Congressional Staff Directory* and *Federal Staff Directory*. Bernan publishes the *Almanac of the Executive Branch* and *Almanac of the Unelected*, a detailed glimpse of those who work for members of Congress. Oryx Press publishes the *American Political Landscape Series* about the people who drive the political process, including elected and other government officials and those outside government. The series includes *Encyclopedia of Women in American Politics*, *Encyclopedia of Religion in American Politics*, *Encyclopedia of Minorities in American Politics*, and the *Political Market Place USA*. Oryx also has a series of books on distinguished African, Asian, and Native American political and government leaders. Carroll Publishing of Washington, D.C., publishes a series of directories covering federal, state, county and municipal government bodies and government officials.

The *U.S. Government Printing Office's Ben's Guide to U.S. Government for Kids* (bensguide.gpo.gov) is a good place to start for an introduction as to how the federal government works. With Benjamin Franklin as a guide, the kids' pages cover topics such as the U.S. Constitution, how laws are made, the branches of the federal government, and what it means to be a U.S. Citizen. *Ben's Guide* offers resources tailored to four specific age groups, plus special information for parents and educators. It also provides instruction on the use of the primary source materials on GPO Access, a free web service that provides electronic access to government information produced by the federal government. GPO Access is run by the U.S. Government Printing Office.

COALITIONS

Coalitions come into existence when associations, institutions, or corporations realize that they cannot accomplish their goals alone. The Coalition on Government Information (COGI), Coalition Networked Information (CNI), the Inter-Association Working Group on

Government Information Policy (IAWG), and the Cartographic Users Advisory Council (CUAC) are examples of coalitions. Some coalitions are formed to lobby for one cause and dissolve when that purpose is accomplished. Some coalitions start out with a cause and gradually include other causes. Some become practically permanent and develop an independent life of their own. Coalitions are usually funded either by members paying an agreed-on amount of money each year or by member organizations providing services, office space, and staff. Some coalitions receive grant money.

In 1985, E. J. Josey chose the theme "Forging Coalitions for the Public Good" as his president's program at the American Library Association's annual conference. Librarians spent a day discussing the value of coalitions and how to form them. During Josey's term, the Coalition on Government Information was established. ALA has since formed or joined many coalitions, and I have worked with a number of coalitions over the years. Following are descriptions of some of them and their accomplishments.

Coalition for Networked Information

A good example of a coalition that became permanent and has its own staff is the Coalition for Networked Information, founded in 1990 "to help realize the promise of high performance networks and computers for the advancement of scholarship and the enrichment of intellectual productivity."[40] CNI is a partnership among the Association of Research Libraries (ARL), CAUSE, and EDUCOM. ARL membership comprises over one hundred of the largest university and other libraries in the United States and Canada. CAUSE is the association for managing and using information resources and technology in higher education, with members from 1,400 colleges and universities and more than eighty corporations. EDUCOM is a nonprofit consortium of colleges, universities, and other organizations. CAUSE and EDUCOM merged in 1998 and became EDUCAUSE. The letter of merger intent gave several reasons for the merger, but the one that is important to us is "the ability to speak with a single and more forceful voice on issues of policy at the intersection of higher education and information technology."[41]

CNI works with what it calls a task force of almost two hundred other institutions and organizations. Members of the task force include higher education institutions, publishers, network service providers, computer hardware, software, and systems companies, library networks and organizations, and public and state libraries. CNI promotes its causes through cooperative projects, meetings of its task forces, regional briefings, publications, meetings, conferences, and public policy activities. In other words, CNI attempts to influence the policies affecting current and future use of technologies to benefit its members.

CNI does not directly lobby Congress or other legislative bodies; instead, it depends on its partner bodies to talk to legislators and their staff, to testify at hearings, and to rally its members to support or oppose legislation. However, CNI testified in support of the GPO WINDOW/Gateway/Access bills at a hearing in 1992.

Coalition on Government Information

The Coalition on Government Information (COGI), organized in 1986 by the American Library Association at the urging of ALA Councilor Zoia Horn and the then president of ALA, E. J. Josey, has been effective in getting congressional support for legislation. Josey asked Francis Buckley to organize the coalition. Buckley at that time was serving as the chair of the Committee on Legislation Subcommittee on Government Information. Nancy Kranich, associate dean of New York University Libraries, and Daniel O'Mahony, government documents coordinator of Brown University's library, served as chairs of COGI and the subcommittee after Buckley. The *ALA Handbook of Organization* describes COGI as being

> composed of public interest and library organizations united in their concern about the public's right to be well informed about the activities of the federal government. COGI's objectives include: (1) developing support for improved access to government information, (2) focusing national attention on efforts that limit access to government information, (3) identifying organizations and individuals who are concerned with limitations on access, and encouraging them to advocate appropriate actions to improve access to government information, and (4) alerting the public to the importance of government information through public awareness campaigns.[42]

COGI, at the suggestion of Scott Armstrong, founder of the National Security Archive, instituted the James Madison Award given to recipients for championing freedom of information and the public's right to know. The award, named after President James Madison, often called the "Father of the Constitution," has been given to members of Congress, journalists, government agencies, government officials, and philanthropists like George Soros.

In 1993, this award was given to several key members of the Senate Committee on Rules and Administration and the Committee on House Administration for their efforts in supporting the GPO Access Act of 1993, which directed that government information in electronic format be made available free to the public through depository libraries. Although these members were already committed to passing such legislation, recognizing their good work was an added push to make sure that the legislation got passed since other groups were asking them not to support this legislation.[42]

Vice President Al Gore was one of the recipients of the Madison Award, but he was unable to attend the awards ceremony. His parents, however, had an apartment in the Methodist building where the ALA Washington Office was located. Anne Heanue and I were in the parking lot of the building when we spotted Gore's mother. Heanue mentioned that she still had Gore's award, so I suggested that she give the award to his mother and ask her to give it to the vice president. She did, and Mrs. Gore wound up inviting us to her apartment for a cup of coffee. Mrs. Gore showed us the dining room where Vice President Gore had written his book on the environment, including where he had pinned notecards on the wall and organized them on the table. She also showed us the Russian boxes that she had collected over the years. She was reluctant for us to leave because she was worried about her husband and asked us to stay until he returned. He had gone to the White House to visit his son. Fortunately, Al Gore showed up and explained that he had stopped off at the Senate gym so he could keep in shape for the next presidential campaign. As a former senator, Gore still had special access to Senate facilities. This story illustrates how ALA Washington office staff wisely took advantage of having an office in a building where many members of Congress had apartments, including the Gores and the Gingriches, to lobby for libraries.

COGI also published a newsletter from the mid-1980s to the early 1990s, provided along with other support services by Anne Heanue of the ALA Washington office. Without financial support from other members, it was difficult to provide all the services needed for a viable coalition, but the coalition was instrumental in securing the passage of the GPO Access Act of 1993.

Cartographic Users Advisory Council

The Cartographic Users Advisory Council (CUAC) is a coalition made up of representatives from six national and regional library organizations. CUAC "functions in an advocacy capacity as liaison between U.S. agencies producing cartographic products and CUAC's constituency." It has been very successful in persuading government bodies to provide libraries with maps and other cartographic materials. CUAC has representatives from the American Library Association Map and Geography Round Table and the Government Documents Round Table, the Special Libraries Association Geography and Map Division, the Geoscience Information Society, the North American Cartographic Information Society, and the Western Association of Map Libraries.

Once a year CUAC organizes a meeting in D.C. and invites staff from federal map publishing agencies, the Library of Congress, the superintendent of documents, and congressional committees to meet with them to discuss their concerns. CUAC has worked with agencies to identify material not in the federal depository library program; has advised agencies on alternative publishing programs such as microfiche, CD-ROMs, and online publishing; has worked to increase and improve bibliographic control of maps; and has advised agencies on the content of maps and other cartographic publications. CUAC has also lobbied the Congress for increased funding for mapping agencies.

CUAC was very effective in lobbying the Joint Committee on Printing to direct mapping agencies to provide their maps to depository libraries. Their lobbying included dinner with JCP staff at La Brasserie, a Capitol Hill French restaurant with everyone paying for his or her own meal. Sharing a meal at a charming Hill landmark encouraged JCP staff to think of the librarians as interesting constituents worthy of the considerable effort involved in persuading dozens of agencies to change their policies and find the money needed to make the librarians happy.

The small number of maps sent to libraries stemmed from the authority of some mapping agencies like the U.S. Geological Survey and the Defense Mapping Agency to print their own maps. Since GPO did not print or procure the agency maps, it argued that it did not have the authority to ride the agency contracts and pay for copies of those maps for the libraries. Riding a contract means that

GPO can print extra copies of the material printed or procured through GPO and pay for them out of appropriations for the depository library program. Under *U.S. Code*, title 44, section 19, agencies must pay for depository copies if they produce the maps in an agency printing plant. The mapping agencies, claiming limited resources, said they could not afford to pay for all the maps needed by the libraries. With the help of JCP, a cooperative map-printing and distribution program was worked out so that map-producing agencies paid for the printing of maps and GPO paid for their distribution. I was happy with the results because my former employer, the Central Missouri State University Library, started receiving USGS and Army Corps of Engineers maps. I had asked those agencies to put CMSU on their agency depository waiting lists in 1965 when I was head of the documents department. Thanks to CUAC and JCP, hundreds of libraries on USGS and Corps of Engineers waiting lists started receiving maps.

Inter-Association Working Group on Government Information Policy

An example of a coalition set up for a brief time to influence public policy is the Inter-Association Working Group on Government Information Policy (IAWG) established in 1996 by the American Library Association.[43] Administrative support and meeting space for the coalition was provided by the ALA Washington Office.

> IAWG is a cooperative team of representatives from seven major library associations working to enhance public access to government information through the revision of Title 44 of the U.S. Code. Together these associations represent more than 80,000 librarians, information specialists, library trustees, libraries and others interested in library issues.[44]

The representatives of the library associations were chosen by their own associations from their legislative committees and their lobbying staffs. Many of them had worked on title 44 issues as members of association committees. Some had served on advisory committees to the Congress and the Government Printing Office.

IAWG, tired of rejecting bills written by congressional staff, decided to write its own draft bill expanding and protecting public access to government information through the depository library program and to present it to members of Congress in hopes that it would be incorporated into a congressional bill. In early 1998, IAWG transmitted a proposed bill called Federal Information Access Act of 1998 to Senators John Warner (R-Va.), chair, and Wendell Ford (D-Ky.), ranking member, of the Senate Committee on Rules and Administration.

IAWG promoted its bill by setting up a website where constituencies of the seven groups and others could read and support their goals and the proposed bill. They issued press releases and position papers. Representatives of member organizations wrote articles for their organizations' newsletters and gave briefings at meetings of their organizations. IAWG met with other parties affected by the legislation such as Government Printing Office officials and union representatives, representatives of the executive and judicial branches, and members of the private sector in an effort to understand their concerns and to persuade them to support the librarians' goal for legislation that would support expanded free public access to government information. IAWG spent countless hours working with key congressional staff to review IAWG's proposed bill and versions of bills drafted by the staff. IAWG held a series of discussions in person, through conference phone calls, e-mail messages, and faxes resulting in a bill acceptable to IAWG and congressional staff. The agreed-on proposal was part of a much larger bill that would affect GPO, the unions, and the rest of the government. No matter how good the library section of the bill, if the larger bill to be introduced by the senators did not meet the satisfaction of other lobbying groups, it had little chance of passage.

The IAWG bill had three goals: (1) enhance public access to government information in all formats from all three branches of government, (2) strengthen the Federal Depository Library Program to improve public access to government information, and (3) ensure the public has continuous and permanent access to electronic government information.

Library associations realized that by working together through IAWG, they could set the agenda and become initiators of policy instead of reactors to Congress and others. This would give them an activist role in influencing the contents of legislation. They knew that even if the current Congress did not pass legislation, the groundwork was being laid for influencing the next Congress.

Senators Warner and Ford introduced The Wendell H. Ford Government Publications Reform Act of 1998 (S. 2288), a bill that included much of IAWG's language. The bill stated, "It is altogether fitting and proper that this Act, the most comprehensive and far reaching proposal to ensure permanent public access to the Government's publications, regardless of form or format, to come before the Congress of the United States during the tenure of Senator Ford, be named in his honor." The Senate Committee on Rules and Administration held a hearing on the bill on July 29, 1998. S. 2288 (Report No. 105-413) was reported out of the Committee on Rules and Administration on October 16, 1998, with an amendment. The bill did not make it to the floor of the Senate, however, and died at the close of Congress.

It is unusual for a bill to be named after a current member of Congress. Senator Warner and his staff believed that naming the bill after a respected and retiring senator would assure its passage on the floor of the Senate. What Senators Warner and Ford and the librarians underestimated was the strength of the opposition from for-profit firms who opposed the bill because it continued a centralized procurement and production system for government publications. Firms such as Xerox prefer a decentralized system where government departments and agencies buy equipment from them and produce their own printing. Current law requires that agencies procure their printing through GPO. GPO processes agency printing orders and decides which will be produced in house and which ones will be advertised to thousands of printing companies, which bid on the work. It would seem that companies that produce printing for the government and unions who represent workers at GPO would support the bill, but both groups had concerns about it. Near the end, unions supported the bill, but the printing companies still had problems. Once the unions were satisfied that the bill would not harm their collective bargaining rights, some members of Congress decided to oppose the bill because reconfirmation of bargaining rights might mean that other workers within the legislative branch would insist on the same rights. Lack of consensus among the bills constituencies and agreement between the Senate and House caused the bill to die in the 105th Congress.

IAWG regrouped in the 106th Congress and drafted a proposed bill entitled the Next Generation Electronic Government Information Access Act of 1999. The coalition hoped to build on the support expressed by a number of members of Congress for two issues that they included as the purposes for the bill: to "(1) broaden, strengthen, and enhance public access to electronic Government information and (2) provide permanent public access to and ensure authenticity of electronic Government information."

IAWG then started to work on building support for the bill by presenting it to staff of the members of the Senate Committee on Rules and Administration and the Committee on House Administration in the hopes that members of those committees would introduce the bill. They also took the bill to the members of the Coalition on Government Information, asking them to support the bill and help them get it passed.

The library community was not successful in getting the bill introduced or passed in the 106th Congress, but early in the 107th Congress, ALA decided to try again. This attempt to draft and seek support for a bill was prompted by the wish to promote the library community's version of a solution to the need to get more electronic information into the depository library program and to obligate the federal government to preserve and protect that information. ALA also did not believe that the proposed bill floated by the National Commission on Libraries and Information Science late in December 2000 would meet the needs of the public and wanted to be ready with their own bill.

Instead of having their bill introduced the librarians were faced with S. 803, the E-Government Act of 2001 introduced by Senator Lieberman, which is basically the Paperwork Reduction Act with a new name. It gives the Office of Management and Budget great control over the generation, collection, cataloging, and dissemination of government information. The bill is intended "[t]o enhance the management and promotion of electronic Government services and processes by establishing a Federal Chief Information Officer with the Office of Management and Budget, and by establishing a broad framework of measures that require using Internet-based information technology to enhance citizen access to Government information and services."

The bill even proposed giving OMB control over cataloging standards. Cataloging rules and electronic formats for structuring cataloging records have traditionally been set by the American Library Association in conjunction with the Library of Congress. Sharon Hogan, ALA's witness at the July 11, 2001, Senate Committee on Governmental Affairs hearing, disagreed with the statement:

> Librarians and information scientists—not information technologists—
> are the specialists in establishing cataloging, classification, indexing

and metadata standards for government information products. Cooperative international bodies set current cataloging and classification
standards using the combined knowledge of information professionals
as a resource. The Library of Congress, the Government Printing Office, the national libraries, and other governmental agencies already
cooperate with professional library organizations to create internation-
ally recognized cataloging standards such as MARC cataloging
records, AACR II, GILS, and Dublin Core.

Representative Jim Turner (D-Tex.) introduced a companion bill
H.R. 2458 on July 12, 2001, with the public statement "The goal is simple. Decrease the amount of time citizens spend in line and increase
the resources they can turn to online. The E-Government Act of 2001
takes an important step toward this goal." The Senate Governmental
Affairs Committee reported out the bill early in 2002. The expressed
goal of the drafters of the E-Government Act is to enlarge the public's
access to government information. The Senate passed the bill in June
2002. S. 803 was then referred to the House Committee on Government
Reform and its Subcommittee on Technology and Procurement Policy,
and a hearing was held on September 18. The subcommittee reported
H.R. 2458 (instead of S. 803) out to the full committee on October 1,
which reported the bill out on October 9, 2002. The E-Government Act
passed the Senate and House as amended in November 2002.

The Uniting and Strengthening America (USA) Patriot Act (S.
1510) was passed by the Senate on October 11, 2001, and signed into
law on October 26, 2001. In spite of intensive lobbying by library,
public interest, and civil liberties organizations the law contains a
number of provisions that threaten the public's access to government and other information. Section 215 of the act allows the FBI
with a warrant or subpoena from the Foreign Intelligence Surveil-
lance Act Court to obtain from libraries and bookstores the names of
books bought or borrowed by anyone suspected of "international
terrorism" or "clandestine activities." Bookstore owners and librarians cannot reveal the request for information. They can contact a
lawyer after the fact, but since they do not have prior notice, their
lawyer cannot object to the seizure of information before it happens.
Because the actions by law enforcement cannot be made public, the
public has no idea how many libraries and bookstores have been ordered to provide information about their readers.

The Patriot Act and the establishment of the Homeland Security
Office have led to government agencies taking down government

information in electronic format from their websites. It also resulted in the withdrawal of a U.S. Geological Survey CD-ROM containing source water assessment data from the Federal Depository Library Program in October 2001. A number of agencies are reviewing publications that have long been in the public domain for their possible withdrawal from public use. The National Technical Information Service and the Defense Technical Information Service have both been directed to withdraw documents from public access.

An unforeseen side affect of IAWG's work was the appointment in December 1997 of its chair, Francis Buckley, as superintendent of documents by Michael DiMario, public printer of the United States. Some may argue that his appointment would have happened anyway, but his visibility as chair of IAWG working on issues of importance to the public printer and his interaction with key congressional staff certainly helped him. He had impressed all of them with his ability to get seven library associations to agree on policies. The superintendent of documents position is political, and certain members of Congress and their staff, as well as the White House, have a voice in approving the public printer's choice. DiMario had known Buckley since the late 1970s when Buckley represented ALA on the Joint Committee on Printing's Ad Hoc Advisory Committee on Revision of Title 44 and chaired its subcommittee on the depository library program. Buckley also served on the Depository Library Council to the public printer. In both those roles, he lobbied for the public's access to government information and for depository libraries. Buckley worked closely with DiMario when he was the superintendent of documents. Buckley ended up in a key position because he treated all players with respect and lobbied for his association's causes in a positive and persuasive manner.

The *Congressional Serial Set* Advisory Committee

The *Congressional Serial Set* Advisory Committee to the Joint Committee on Printing established in February 1979 was called a committee but really functioned as a coalition. The *Serial Set* Committee included representatives from the Joint Committee on Printing (the legal publisher of the set), the Government Printing Office (the producer and disseminator of the set), the Library of Congress, Senate and House Libraries, the National Archives, and Federal Depository

Libraries (recipients of the set). The Library of Congress also represented the interest of the international exchange libraries.

The *Serial Set* is intended to be the permanent historical record of
the work of the Congress and is composed of the Senate and House
documents, reports, and other publications. It does not include hearings. The law specifically requires that the set be distributed to state
libraries and other depository libraries, thus recognizing the relationship between the United States and the states. The *Serial Set* has
been bound and numbered consecutively from the first Congress
until the latest. The quality of the paper and whether it is acid-free
has varied over the years, but the binding has always been very
durable.

When I went to work for the Joint Committee on Printing in 1974,
I was delighted to learn JCP was responsible for the *Serial Set*, one of
my favorite publications. After visiting staff at GPO, I was alarmed
to learn that only Virginia Saunders, editor of the set, knew the in-
tricacies of how the set was put together. There was no documentation and no plans to educate anyone else to take her place when she
retired. As of 2002, she was still guarding the set.

In 1979, I persuaded JCP to establish the *Serial Set* Committee. It
was a wonderful group to work with, almost a sacred, secret society,
since even JCP staff were unaware of the treasure JCP was responsible for publishing. The members of the *Serial Set* Committee not only
provided technical advice on how to improve the contents and production of the set but also lobbied GPO, JCP, and the appropriations
committees for sufficient funding and support to produce an archival
and a microfiche edition of the set.

The committee persuaded the units at GPO responsible for producing the set to document, improve, and streamline the process.
The members of the committee educated themselves by tracking the
production of the set from the initial printing and setting aside of
unbound copies of House and Senate reports and documents to the
collating, binding, and stamping of the set. Copies of the books were
stored in the bowels of GPO, sometimes in very dank and remote areas. At the end of a Congress, some two years later, these copies
were retrieved for binding. Many of the copies were damaged or
had been misplaced, and some beautiful and rare publications were
stolen. To produce complete volumes for all libraries, GPO had to go
back to press at a much greater expense than the original printing.
Once enough copies for a volume were available, the sets had to be

hand collated, sewn, hand bound, and marbleized, and a legend identifying the volume was stamped on it by hand.

As a result of producers and recipients working together, the procedures were changed to provide for safe, dry storage on shrink-wrapped pallets in locked facilities. Two editions of the sets were being produced, one for the posterity libraries and one for the depository libraries. *Posterity libraries* was the term used for the Library of Congress, Senate and House Libraries, and the National Archives. It was assumed that these copies would be kept as part of the nation's treasury of important publications. The committee persuaded the producers to merge the two editions, thus saving lots of money and yet using the best characteristics of each edition to assure durability, beauty, and use of archival materials such as acid-free paper and end sheets. The committee also convinced GPO to preserve the digital version of the Senate and House reports and documents included in the set. GPO had been reusing the tapes containing the original material over and over again in order to save money.

The committee lobbied the Joint Committee on Printing and the Senate and House Appropriations Committees for the very survival of the set. The members of the *Serial Set* Committee, at some professional risk to themselves wrote a letter in December 1992 to the chair of the Joint Committee on Printing, arguing:

> In our considered opinion, 44 U.S.C. 738 clearly requires that the Senate and House reports and documents be produced in paper format so that they can "be bound and distributed to state libraries and other designated libraries for their permanent files." It is our judgement that paper is the only currently available publishing medium that offers genuine permanence for documents of this importance. Consequently, GPO's recent directive, limiting distribution of the bound Serial Set merely to the 50 regional depository libraries—and not to the other 350, which have selected the Serial Set, fails to meet the permanence requirements of 44 U.S.C. 738.[45]

The letter went on to urge JCP to direct GPO not to dispose of the $300,000 worth of reports and documents waiting to be bound into the *Serial Set* so they would be available for distribution to the selective libraries that had requested them. GPO had taken these drastic actions as a result of a cut in appropriations for the depository program. The House Appropriations Committee believed that the provision of the

Serial Set in microfiche would be sufficient and would be an easy way to cut the cost of the depository library program. JCP directed GPO not to dispose of the copies and to produce the *Serial Set* for all the selecting libraries for the years in which the publications had already been printed. The Appropriations Committees went along with JCP directive.

Later Representative Bill Thomas (D-Calif.), chair of the Committee on House Administration and member of the Joint Committee on Printing, agreed with the House Appropriations Committee and introduced H.R. 4280, Government Printing Reform Act of 1996, which would have eliminated the permanent, bound, paper *Serial Set* starting with the 105th Congress. His bill was introduced after the House had already decreed in House Report 104-657 accompanying H.R. 3754 that "a reduction of $1.2 million would be possible by converting most *Serial Sets* to CD-ROM. Regional depositories, plus one depository in each state without a regional, and the international exchange program would continue to receive paper copies of the *Serial Set*." This action denied some three hundred libraries the bound, paper *Serial Set* for 1995 and 1996. The proposed bill by Thomas also would have denied the regional depositories and the international exchange libraries the paper *Serial Set*.

Fortunately, the library community helped defeat Thomas's bill to eliminate the paper *Serial Set*. The community cited the expert advice of the Joint Committee on Printing's *Serial Set* Committee that only paper met the permanence requirements of the law.

As of 2003, the bound *Serial Set* is still being produced and sent only to regional depository libraries. However, it is still in danger of being eliminated for the regionals by a Congress that does not understand the importance of preserving its own history for the use of future members of Congress and the public.[46]

NOTES

1. Jack C. Plano and Milton Greenberg, *The American Political Dictionary*, 10th ed. (Fort Worth, Tex.: Harcourt Brace, 1997), 181.

2. *United States v. Harriss*, 347 U.S. 612 (1954).

3. *Procurement: Government Printing Office Supply of Microfiche to Libraries Disrupted*, GAO/GGD-89-44, United States General Accounting Office Re-

port to the Chairman and Vice Chairman of the Joint Committee on Printing of the U.S. Congress, February 1989.

4. Letters between William Welsh, director, Processing Department, Library of Congress, and Bernadine E. Hoduski, librarian, U.S. Environmental Protection Agency, Library, Kansas City, Missouri, November 8, 1971, December 8, 1971, and January 5, 1972.

5. Special Library Association Government Information Services Committee and the Committee on Information Hangups, *An Evaluation with Recommendations for Action of the Government Printing Office's Services from the User's Point of View* (New York: Special Library Association, 1978), 1.

6. Louie Estrada, "Book Publisher Morris Schnapper Dies at Age 86," *Washington Post,* February 7, 1999.

7. Estrada, "Book Publisher."

8. M. B. Schnapper, *Constraint by Copyright* (Washington, D.C.: Public Affairs Press, 1960).

9. Letter from M. B. Schnapper, Public Affairs Press, to Bernadine E. Abbott Hoduski, staff member of the Joint Committee on Printing of the United States Congress, September 9, 1984.

10. Letter from Charles McC. Mathias Jr., chair of the United States Congress Joint Committee on Printing, to the heads of all federal departments and agencies, September 23, 1985.

11. George S. Bobinski, "Is the Library Profession Over-Organized?" *American Libraries* 31, no. 9 (October 2000): 58.

12. Morton Kondrake, "AARP's Agenda and Bush's," *Roll Call,* February 19, 2001.

13. Ken Dychtwald, *Age Power: How the 21st Century Will Be Ruled by the Old* (New York: Tarcher/Putnam, 1999), 27.

14. Reynold Levy, *Give and Take: A Candid Account of Corporate Philanthropy* (Boston: Harvard Business School Press, 1999), xviii.

15. Levy, *Give and Take,* xxi.

16. News release from National Committee for Responsive Philanthropy, Washington, D.C., March 12, 1999.

17. News release from National Committee for Responsive Philanthropy, Washington, D.C., March 12, 1999.

18. *Buildings, Books, and Bytes: Libraries and Communities in the Digital Age,* a report on the public's opinion of library leaders' visions for the future, prepared by the Benton Foundation and funded by the W. K. Kellogg Foundation, Washington, D.C., November 1996, inside cover.

19. Henry H. Perritt Jr., *Electronic Public Information and the Public's Right to Know,* (Washington, D.C.: Benton Foundation, 1990), 47.

20. Perritt, *Electronic Public Information,* 7.

21. News release from the Library and Information Association of South Africa in 2001.

108 *Chapter 4*

22. Barbara Ford, American Library Association president-elect, remarks on March 31, 1997, at James Madison Award ceremony in Washington, D.C.

23. Library of Congress, Public Affairs Office, *The Library of Congress News*, July 17, 1992.

24. Taken from National Security Archives website dated February 2001.

25. Joseph E. Persico, "The Man Who Sells Broken Secrets," *Parade*, October 8, 1978, p. 5.

26. Patricia Glass Schuman, "Librarians and Publishers: An Uneasy Dance" in *Wilson Library Bulletin* (December 1994): 42.

27. Schuman, "Librarians and Publishers," 42.

28. The 2002 Energy and Water Development Appropriations bills, H.R. 2311 and S. 1171, passed in 2001.

29. Milton J. Esman, *Government Works: Why Americans Need the Feds* (Ithaca, N.Y.: Cornell University Press, 2000), 144–45.

30. *President's Private Sector Survey on Cost Control: Report on Management Office Selected Issues*. Volume I: Publishing, Printing, Reproduction, and Audiovisual Activities (Washington, D.C.: U.S. Government Printing Office, September 15, 1983), 88.

31. Reed E. Hundt, *You Say You Want a Revolution: A Story of Information Age Politics* (New Haven, Conn.: Yale University Press, 2000), 84.

32. Herbert I. Schiller, "Public Information Goes Corporate," *Library Journal*, October 1, 1991.

33. Letter from Carol Nemeyer, senior associate, Education and Library Services, Association of American Publishers, to Bernadine E. Abbott Hoduski, chair of ALA SRRT Task Force on Government Publications, January 11, 1972.

34. Letter from Robert W. Frase, consulting economist, Washington, D.C., to Bernadine E. Abbott Hoduski, Joint Committee on Printing, U.S. Capitol, Washington, D.C., April 22, 1975.

35. *GPO Use of ISBN and ISSN*, Discussion Paper, December 10, 1981.

36. Memorandum for Federal Information Programs Consortium Members, International Standard Book Numbers (ISBN)—Some Pros and Cons for Government Managers from Patricia W. Berger, chief, Library and Information Services Division, United States Department of Commerce, National Bureau of Standards, Washington, D.C., December 7, 1981.

37. Memorandum to Patricia W. Berger, National Bureau of Standards, on the International Standard Book Numbers (ISBN) from Ruth Smith, chief, Office of Customer Services, National Technical Information Service, March 3, 1982.

38. Letter to Emery Koltay, RR Bowker Company, New York, from Donald Fossedal, superintendent of documents, May 4, 1987.

39. *Documents Sales Service ISBN Barcode Utilization: Issues and Recommendations*, paper prepared for Francis Buckley, superintendent of documents, in 1999.

40. Coalition for Networked Information, *Program Overview, July 1, 1993 through June 30, 1994*, September 27, 1993.

41. *EDUCOM*UPDATE**, July 23, 1997 (letter of intent signed by Susan Foster, chair of the CAUSE Board of Trustees, and Don Riley, chair of the EDUCOM Board of Trustees).

42. American Library Association, *ALA Handbook of Organization 1997–98*, supplement to *American Libraries* (Chicago: Author, 1997), 141.

43. Members of Congress receiving the Madison Award were Senators Wendell Ford and Ted Stevens and Representatives Charlie Rose and William Thomas. Vice President Gore also received the award for the work he had done on the GPO Access Act when he was a senator.

44. The IAWG is composed of the American Association of Law Libraries, the American Library Association, the Association of Research Libraries, Chief Officers of State Library Agencies, the Medical Library Association, Special Libraries Association, and the Urban Libraries Council.

45. Inter-Association Working Group on Government Information Policy, press release, "The IAWG Submits to Congress a Legislative Proposal to Improve Public Access to Government Information," March 1988.

46. Letter from the Congressional *Serial Set* Committee to Chair Charlie Rose of the Joint Committee on Printing, December 11, 1992; and a letter from the superintendent of documents, Wayne Kelley, to the Depository Library community, November 18, 1992. Signers of the letter to Chairman Rose were Roger Haley, Senate librarian; Gregg Harness, reference librarian, Senate Library; Richard A. Baker, Senate historian; Raymond Smock, House historian; Karen Reminger, chief of serials and government publications, LC; George Caldwell, senior specialist in U.S. government documents, LC; William W. Ellis, associate librarian for scientific and technical information, LC; Michael L. Gillette, director, Center for Legislative Archives, National Archives; Maryellen Trautman, U.S. government publications librarian, National Archives; Susan Tulis, documents librarian, University of Virginia; Page Putnam Miller, director, National Coordinating Committee for the Promotion of History; and Bernadine E. Abbott-Hoduski, professional staff member, Joint Committee on Printing.

5

Who Is to Be Lobbied?

Lobby everyone who has anything to do with the issue that you are interested in shaping, including people in and out of the government. As you identify key people to be lobbied, keep a list of their names and how they can be contacted. Those to be lobbied include

- legislative and executive branches of any level of government,
- those who influence the officials in the legislative and executive branches,
- members of the nonprofit and for-profit sectors,
- members of your own group,
- the media, and
- the public.

LEGISLATIVE BRANCHES OF GOVERNMENTS

Members of Congress and State, County, City, and Town Legislative Bodies

Legislative bodies enact laws and ordinances based on the rights and responsibilities given to them by the United States Constitution and the constitutions of the states. The state constitutions must be in harmony with the U.S. Constitution because states exercise all those powers not delegated to the national government. Counties and cities derive their power from their state constitutions and state legislatures. Therefore, their laws are actually ordinances enacted according to the authority of the state's constitution, laws, and charters.

The forms of city and county government vary. Most state legislatures have divided their states into counties as a means of carrying out state policies. Counties in Louisiana are called parishes and in Alaska boroughs. Cities are usually established by state charters. In some cases where the county and the city cover the same geographic area, they have decided to merge into one entity.

The responsibilities and rights of counties and cities vary from state to state. Some are divided into legislative and executive branches and others combine their functions. The governing boards are usually called councils or boards and those elected to them are called commissioners, supervisors, or aldermen. They are elected by the residents of the county or city on a partisan or nonpartisan basis. Both cities and counties are usually divided into smaller units called *districts* or *wards*. The *American Political Dictionary* and *State and Local Politics: Government by the People* are good beginning sources for understanding the structure of governments on all levels. But to understand the unit you wish to lobby, you need to read the constitution, law, and/or charter that authorizes that unit.

Members of legislative bodies are always willing to talk to their constituents, those voters from their district, city, county, and state who put them where they are. Never tell the legislator that you did not vote for them. As long as the vote is secret, they do not know. They may know you are of the opposite party, but they know that many voters vote for the person, not the party. Once they are elected, they are your senator, representative, or commissioner no matter what your party. In many cities and counties, the legislators are elected on a nonpartisan basis. If you are not from the legislator's district or state, you may not get as good a hearing as if you were, but if the legislator has indicated an ongoing interest in your subject area, he or she will probably listen.

The most effective way to lobby legislators is in person, in their office, at a public meeting, on the street, at the airport, wherever you can talk to them. If you do talk to legislators in person, follow up with a letter, postcard, phone call, fax, or e-mail, reminding them of when and where you talked to them. When you correspond in any media, make sure that you use his or her correct title and full name, since there may be more than one person with the same last name. If you are writing about a particular bill, try to identify that bill by title and bill number. Let the legislator know how that bill will affect you and the people in his or her district. Try to keep your message short. Keep to one issue or bill per letter. Staff try to summarize all the messages about an issue or bill for the legislator. Write a letter of thanks even if the legislator does not do what you want. But if the legislator does not do what you want, make sure that your follow-up letter reminds him or her of that. Make sure you include your own name, address, phone number, and e-mail address so the legislator or staff can follow up if necessary. This is particularly important if you are asking for special assistance, a copy of a bill, or a response concerning how the legislator is going to act on your issue or bill.

Many legislators on all levels of government are setting up their own websites where they have news releases and information about bills being worked on by the legislator. Some websites also offer the capability of accepting messages about issues from their constituents. When you send an electronic message to a legislator, if you are not in that legislator's district or state, you may get a message back saying that they have noted your concern but only respond to constituents. Other legislators' websites will indicate that they will not answer electronically but will send an answer by regular mail.

Some legislative bodies have e-mail addresses for the house and the senate, instead of for individual legislators, so you can send a message to that site and the message will be delivered to the legislator.

Senator Paul Wellstone (D-Minn.) in the *Conscience of a Liberal* reveals how he gradually realized that talking on the floor of the Senate about a bill or an issue was not enough. A senator, like others, has to personally lobby other senators to vote for his or her bill or amendment. When you witness discussions on the floor of the Senate, what you are seeing is last-minute lobbying. Senator Wellstone adds, "To have power in the Senate, you need to know only two words: I object. Much of the Senate work—procedural agreements, the passing of bills and amendments, the confirmation of presidential appointments—is done by unanimous consent. If you object—you have power—positive or negative depending on the situation."[1]

Committees of U.S. Congress, State, County, and City Legislative Bodies

Legislatures are called by different names depending on the jurisdiction in which they operate. On the national level, it is the Congress; on the state level, it is the legislature, general assembly, or general court; on the local level, it is usually called a county commission, city commission, or council.

Legislative bodies have a number of committees that perform different functions. There are legislative, oversight, and appropriations committees. Depending on the legislative body, these committees may be standing, select, or joint committees. A *standing* committee is one that has a long-term life, either because of a specific law or because when the legislature organizes itself, it determines that this will be a permanent, long-standing committee. Select committees, also called *ad hoc committees*, usually have a brief life, as they are organized for a specific amount of time to address a single issue. *Joint* committees can be either standing or select. State legislatures that meet every other year also have interim committees that work on legislative proposals between legislative sessions. The U.S. Congress and legislatures that meet all year do not have interim committees. I prefer to think of the committees by their areas of jurisdiction rather than by their type.

A committee's members' goals for the agencies and programs they oversee may be different from another type of committee because they are looking at the issue from their unique perspective. For example, the appropriations committees may be more interested in eliminating agencies and programs to cut the deficit or reach a balanced budget than they are in helping the agency reach the goals established by the authorizing committees. Additionally, appropriations committees may attempt to legislate in an effort to achieve their goals. Sometimes the name of the committee may not truly reflect the work of the committee. For example, the Committee on House Administration of the U.S. Congress has oversight over the Library of Congress and the Government Printing Office. LC and GPO are within that committee's jurisdiction because Congress considers them support agencies for the internal needs of Congress and the executive and judicial branches. Those agencies also support the needs of the public, but sometimes their responsibilities to the public are overshadowed by the daily needs of Congress and the rest of the government.

There are also joint committees that may perform one or more functions, depending on the will of the body. Joint committees have members from both houses of a legislative body and serve the whole legislature. The majority party has more members than the minority party. Even if a joint committee is described as only an oversight committee, it may have influence in the areas of legislation and appropriations. Keep in mind that you may have to lobby a joint committee along with the other committees.

Committees often have shared jurisdictions and may have opposing goals. Committees will fight each other to uphold their goals and jurisdiction. For example, the Senate Committee on Rules and Administration, the Senate Committee on Governmental Affairs, the Committee on House Administration, and the House Committee on Government Operations have overlapping jurisdiction over government publishing and dissemination that sometimes conflict.

It is to your benefit to get to know all the committees that share jurisdiction over policies, programs, and agencies of concern to you. On the federal level, you can find out about the jurisdiction of a congressional committee by looking at the *Congressional Directory*. Each committee and its members and staff are listed. If the committee was established by statute, the citation will be there. For example, the Joint Committee on Printing was created in 1846, the citation is *U.S. Statutes* 9 Statute 114, and that law is codified into the *United States Code*, title 44, section 101. You can also look at the names of subcommittees of the committee, which often clarify the areas of responsibility. Another method is to look at the calendars, hearings, and committee prints issued by the committee. The committee's calendar will alert you to the bills assigned to the committee, the hearings schedule, and when the bill will be voted on by the committee.

Legislative Committees

Legislative committees are established to develop legislation and get it passed. They are called *authorizing committees*. The membership is allotted between the majority and the minority parties. The majority will have more members on the committee than the minority, therefore controlling most of the votes. Each party determines its own members.

Before appropriations committees can appropriate, the entity or program must be authorized. Usually an agency or program is authorized in one legislative session and receives appropriations in the next session. It is difficult to get authorization and appropriation in the same session. Often in the course of reviewing the effectiveness of existing legislation, legislative committees will act as oversight committees. In the course of their oversight, they may develop new legislation. Legislative committees are jealous of their power and do not like appropriations committees passing legislation in the name of appropriating. On the other hand, some legislative committees may approach an appropriations committee and ask its members to include legislative actions in appropriation bills. Some committees do this because they may not have time to go through the authorizing process or prefer to have their bill hidden in a large appropriations bill where it is less likely to be spotted and potentially opposed. It is also a way to avoid a veto because appropriations bills are often passed at the last minute and are not usually subject to veto. Sometimes one member of a legislative committee will convince a member of an appropriations committee to put language in an appropriations bill that the member cannot persuade the legislative committee to include in a legislative bill.

Passing a controversial law in the late 1990s, Congress gave the president line item veto authority, the same authority most governors have. A number of entities, denied funding by use of this veto authority by the president, sued, and the Supreme Court declared the law unconstitutional.

Some members and staff of a committee are considered experts on specialized subjects by other congressional members and staff. Often members and staff will not have a discussion with outsiders without the expert staffer being there. If those expert staff are not at the meeting, it is likely that they will get a full report of the meeting and will be asked to clarify issues raised by lobbyists and others. They may be asked to explain what the outsider really wants. They may even be asked to formulate an answer for the other staffer or the member. Once a key staffer of Chairman Frank Thompson Jr., having been lobbied by commercial micropublishers, asked me to prepare a paper explaining the issue and the position of all interested parties. He did not want to get all his information from only one source. As a staffer with responsibility for providing professional nonpartisan advice on policies to members of the Joint Committee on Printing, I would often ask professional staff on other committees, such as Anthony Harvey, for their expert advice on an issue. Serving a joint committee, I was sensitive to the possibility that advice I gave might affect both the Senate and the House, and I wanted to make sure that JCP Committee members were aware of that.

According to the author of *Inside Congress*, one key staffer, Robert Gellman, was one of those experts who came close to controlling certain kinds of legislation. Gellman retired in the mid-1990s and became a consultant.

> For seventeen years, Robert Gellman was counsel and staff director on a House subcommittee that had jurisdiction over the Freedom of Information Act and the Privacy Act. Because these issues have little impact on business or labor, the chairman of the subcommittee left Gellman alone to develop laws he thought were in the public interest. "The acts apply to federal agencies," Gellman said. "We weren't regulating the private sector, so interest was limited." Gellman fended off Reagan administration efforts to gut the Freedom of Information Act. He also helped draft measures that reduced the fees charged for FOIA responses from government agencies.[2]

I agree that Gellman had a lot of influence in developing policies in the area of government information. He often represented the congressional members of the committee at meetings with constituents and lobbyists. They had a hard time getting past him to the chair of the committee, but I doubt that he ever did anything that went against the wishes of the chairman. In my experience, staff who go against the chair's wishes do not survive. Gellman was also key in several attempts to revise and reauthorize the Paperwork Reduction Act. His knowledge of the details of the issues and the players made him invaluable to the chair, and this know-how convinced a series of chairs of the House Committee on Government Operations Subcommittee on Government Information and Individual Rights to keep him on the staff.

Another powerful staffer, Edward Lombard, served as staff assistant for the House Appropriations Committee Subcommittee on the Legislative Branch during the 1980s and 1990s. He worked for a series of chairs, both Democratic and Republican, and survived because he mastered the complicated appropriations process, understood the numbers, and was able to figure out how to meet the goals of members of the Appropriations Committee. Staff who worked for the many units of the legislative branch feared him and his ability to control public policy decisions through encouraging budget officials to fashion their budget proposals in a way that met his approval before the members ever saw their requests. He was good at identifying weak links who would agree to cut their budget request rather than fight him.

Only two other staffers, in my estimation, were Lombard's equal and able to take him on directly and win. Both of them were staff directors of the Joint Committee on Printing. They could beat him because they had the support of their own chair. These two staff directors insisted that GPO's budget be reviewed by the Joint Committee on Printing before it was submitted to the House appropriations committees. In this way they were able to alert the chair of the JCP about budget requests that would undermine the intent of U.S.C. Title 44 as envisioned by the members of the JCP. Examples included attempts by the Appropriations Committee to pressure GPO to drop paper versions of important publications provided to depository libraries.

Staff often control what legislators see, and when legislators do see information, it is often annotated by staff. That is why it is important to get staff to trust you so your information gets to the elected members of the committee. Staff are also the gatekeepers of information produced by the committee. If they like and trust you, they will think about you when there is information to share. If you and the staffer share the same values and goals, she or he may help you behind the scenes by promoting your position on an issue. The staffer may also alert you when an issue becomes hot, when hearings are scheduled, when your rival has visited the committee, or even what a legislator says off the record about an issue.

Good relations with staff can help you get copies of statements submitted at hearings. Now that fewer hearings are published, or are published so late that they are of no help, the copies of statements provided by witnesses at the hearing may be the only record of the hearing. Since copies are limited, you may not get them even if you get to the hearing on time, so good relations with a staffer may result in her or him holding copies aside for you or agreeing to copy statements for you after the hearing.

Get to know legislative committee staff. Some staff will accept you as pseudostaff. If you think alike on issues, you may become part of the committee's team, particularly if a member wants a particular bill passed. If you convince the staff that you are an expert on a particular issue, they may call on you for help or information.

Oversight Committees

Oversight committees are established to provide ongoing monitoring of government departments and agencies to determine whether they are implementing the laws properly and effectively.

These committees may be given responsibility for subject areas rather than specific agencies, and those subject areas may be the purview of several agencies. They include such broad areas as education, environment, and health. This may mean that agencies are subject to the authority of several committees. Oversight committees may also be legislative committees or part of a joint committee. Oversight committees are in both houses of a legislature. In the library and information arena, the Joint Committee on the Library and the Joint Committee on Printing are oversight committees.

Appropriations Committees

Appropriations committees are very powerful because they are established to review the funding requests of the units of government and to decide whether a unit will receive money and how much. Legislators usually fight to get on an appropriations committee. In the U.S. Congress, members of the appropriations committees are called the *cardinals*. Appropriations are usually only good for one year. As long as the authorizing legislation is still there, the money can be restored.

In the 104th Congress, the appropriations committees convinced their colleagues to zero out the Office of Technology Assessment (OTA) in order to save money. OTA was defunded but not deauthorized by its authorizing committee. OTA could be restored to the quilt of government. In June 2001, Representative Rush Holt (D-N.J.) and other members of Congress introduced H.R. 2148, to Reestablish the Office of Technology Assessment, and to provide appropriations for its rebirth.

Another example of appropriations committees trying to undermine the intent of the law by eliminating program funding is the struggle over whether basic, substantial, historical publications like the *Congressional Record*, the *United States Code*, and the *United States Congressional Serial Set* will continue to be produced and bound as permanent paper copies or will only be produced in electronic formats. For a number of years, the appropriations committees cut back the number of permanent copies and, in the 104th Congress, eliminated offering the bound *Congressional Record* to selective depository libraries.

The House Appropriations Committee was not about to give up on its effort to eliminate the *Serial Set* and other historic documents of Congress and in 2000 voted to eliminate all paper copies for depository and bylaw libraries. The library community argued that this 62 percent cut in funding for fiscal year 2001 would seriously damage the ability of our national and depository libraries to preserve government information for the use of future citizens. The Appropriations Committee argued that the program should be totally electronic, ignoring the fact that in 2000, some twenty-five thousand publications were not available in electronic format, and other publications were totally unsuitable for electronic format. The Senate Appropriations Committee did not agree and voted to fund the program. After an intense lobbying campaign by librarians and others, the House voted in June 2000 to restore part of the funding but still required that some fifteen thousand publications issued in several formats (e.g., paper, microform, and CD-ROM) be distributed only in online electronic format. That would have eliminated paper permanent copies of such publications as the *United States Congressional Serial Set, United States Code, Supreme Court Decisions,* and the *Congressional Record.* The Senate and the House appointed a conference committee in July 2000 to arrive at a compromise.

The conference committee agreed to cut the Federal Depository Library Program appropriations from $29.9 million to $27 million, forcing the Government Printing Office to accelerate the change from a dual-format publications program to an electronic program. GPO had asked for $34.5 million. On August 25, 2000, Francis Buckley, superintendent of documents, wrote to the directors of Federal Depository Libraries explaining the actions needed to comply with the cut in depository appropriations. Here are a few paragraphs of his letter to illustrate the seriousness of the cuts:

> I am writing to you in my capacity as administrator of the Federal Depository Library Program (FDLP) and because your library is one of the Nation's 1,330 depository libraries. Over the past few years, there have been important changes in the way in which the FDLP makes Government information available to libraries and to the American public. The most profound of these changes is the FDLP electronic transition, which follows the general trend in the Federal Government to publish and disseminate information in electronic formats. Often this means that information previously provided for your collection in a tangible, printed format is now available via the Internet. During the most recent 12 months, more than 50% of the content provided through the FDLP has been online. However, due to the proposed congres-

sional appropriation for the FDLP, the shift to a primarily electronic program will accelerate.

Therefore, we are implementing a policy on distribution to Federal depository libraries that will accelerate the transition to a primarily electronic program. As an operational guideline, U.S. Government publications will be furnished to Federal depository libraries solely in online electronic format unless:

- There is no online electronic version available from the publishing agency.
- The online version is incomplete.
- The online version is not recognized as official by the publishing agency.
- The online version is unreliable; e.g., the content is replaced or over-written without notice.
- The tangible product is of significant reference value to most types of FDLP libraries. The online version poses a significant barrier to access; e.g., the product is very difficult to use, thus impeding access to data or content.
- The tangible product is intended to serve a special needs population; e.g., publications in Braille or large print.
- There is a legal requirement to distribute the product in tangible format.
- The costs associated with disseminating electronically exceed those for the tangible product, a situation that may arise with certain CD-ROM software licensing or fee-based online services.

This fiscal year, we estimate there will be about 27,000 tangible titles in the Program, down from about 40,000 last year, due to reductions in agency publishing and transition to online access. . . . Our analysis indicates that up to 40% of the products distributed in tangible format may also have an online version available. If that is the case, and they do not fall into one of these exceptions, GPO is changing the depository dissemination to electronic only.

These changes will impact the budget and operation of the depository program in your institution. Shipments of tangible FDLP products to your library will decline sharply over coming years, reducing your long-term requirements for shelving and space. However, I am concerned that we use the electronic transition as an opportunity to expand public access to electronic Government information products. In order to deliver this information effectively, libraries must take steps to ensure that the technological infrastructure is in place. Together we must address accelerating training and continuing education needs of depository library personnel, so that they may keep abreast of this rapidly changing technological environment.

In the new, primarily electronic environment, GPO will continue to provide Federal depository libraries administrative support, collection development, and access services (identification, evaluation, selection, authentication, organization, and cataloging), as well as systems for permanent accessibility.

In spite of efforts in 2000 and previous years to change the law through the appropriations process, the Appropriations Committee has not managed to eliminate the law that authorizes those publications. As long as the authorizing legislation stays on the books, those who understand that the historical record of the legislative, executive, and judicial branches will survive only if it is produced in a permanent format can continue to fight for the money for those publications.

Joint Committees

Joint committees are like community-made quilts with each group stitching pieces that are eventually sewn together. They bring together the community of a legislature, county commission, or city council into a committee that resolves differences between houses of the legislature or committees of a legislative body. Their membership comes from both houses of a legislative body. These joint committees can be permanent or ad hoc.

On the federal level, the U.S. Congress offers a good example of how joint committees work. They are established to provide a means for the Senate and the House to agree on a regular basis in areas of mutual concern. Most joint committees continue to have power during recess periods. During the struggle in 1995 over the House's attempt to abolish the Joint Committee on Printing, Senator Ted Stevens (R-Alaska) argued that the JCP was a dispute panel, and if it were abolished, there would still be joint committees established to resolve disputes between the two houses about congressional publishing and dissemination policies and issues. These joint committees usually do not generate legislation. In most cases they are oversight committees, although they do influence the committees of their parent body in the development of legislation. As of the 107th Congress, there were four U.S. congressional joint committees: the Joint Economic Committee, Joint

Committee on Taxation, Joint Committee on Printing (JCP), and the Joint Committee on the Library (JCL).

The Joint Committee on Printing and the Joint Committee on the Library are of particular interest in the areas of access to information. These committees are interesting structurally because they have the same parent committees: the Senate Committee on Rules and Administration and the Committee on House Administration. Five members of Senate Rules and five members of House Administration are elected by their respective bodies to the Joint Committee on Printing and the Joint Committee on the Library. By law, the chair of the parent committees serve on both joint committees. The chairmanships usually rotate between the Senate and the House every other Congress. The chair of the parent committee does not have to be the chair of a joint committee but can step aside so another member can be elected. The joint committees traditionally elect their chairs.

Caucuses, Commissions, Bicameral Organizations, and Coalitions

Members of legislative bodies form groups within one or more of the units called caucuses, commissions, bicameral organizations, and coalitions. These groups play different roles. Commissions and bicameral organizations are usually officially set up by the bodies to devote time to developing a solution to a problem that all the members believe is important. Caucuses and coalitions are formed by members who believe that their issue or cause will be ignored by the parent body if they do not bring attention to the issue. Sometimes caucuses can grow quite powerful and may pose a perceived threat to one political party, particularly if most of the members are from the other political party.

On the national level, several congressional caucuses, especially the Black, Hispanic, and Progressive ones, became so powerful in the eyes of the House Republicans that they voted unanimously on December 6, 1994, to stop funding all caucuses out of money set aside by the Congress for caucuses. Instead, members of Congress have to pay for them out of the money they receive for staff salaries and expenses. The Republicans argued that they were special interest groups. The caucuses continue to exist but with less staff. The

Black Caucus went outside Congress and started an independent organization called the Congressional Black Caucus Foundation with an
executive director and staff. Much of the work formerly done by the
Black Caucus is now conducted by this foundation. The Hispanic Caucus, according to Representative Robert Menendez (D-N.J.), has been
forced to become more cohesive and productive. Since it no longer automatically receives funds, it has to work harder to convince members
to join it and contribute money. The caucus convinced Congress to increase the funds for processing citizenship applications in 1999.[3]

Staff of Members, Committees, and Support Offices

Never assume that a person who works for a legislator, committee,
or support agency is unimportant. In politics and other similar institutions, you never know for sure who will end up being a key person or influencing a key person. My survival for twenty years as a
professional staffer for the Joint Committee on Printing depended as
much on the good will of other staffers, political and professional, as
it did on the members of the JCP. This included staff from the JCP
parent committees, Senate Rules and House Administration. Usually a new chair would ask staff on the parent committee to evaluate
the staff on the Joint Committee. I handed in my résumé to a series
of chairs and staff at least ten times to see whether I would fit in with
their goals for the committee. At times, the staffer who seemed to
have no power gained it when his or her legislator became the chair.
I found that to accomplish my goals, I needed the support of all
staffers, no matter what their political party or role. I depended on
staff like Faye Padgett of the JCP and William Cochrane, staff director of the Senate Committee on Rules and Administration, to support my goals and convince other staff to support them.

Cochrane and I worked together on the legislation authorizing
law school libraries as depositories. He told me his secret to an almost forty-year career on the "Hill": "Never be better known than
the chair of your committee. Your job is to make the chair and committee look good, not yourself." He graciously introduced me to
staff on the Rules Committee as well as on the Committee on House
Administration. I worked with Dave Sharman, staff director, and
Dean Costen, a special staffer on the Committee on House Administration. Costen and I shared memories of the exciting early days of
working for the Environmental Protection Agency. Earning the trust

of those staffers not only helped me accomplish my goals but on at least one occasion saved me my job.

Never assume that all the people who work for a policymaker agree with each other. In the privacy of a staff briefing of the policymaker, staff may disagree and force the policymaker into making his or her own decision. Or perhaps the staffer who said nothing may be more influential. For example, when Representative Augustus Hawkins (D-Calif.) chaired the Subcommittee on Printing of the House Committee on Administration, his wife Elsie, a staffer on the subcommittee before their marriage, sat in on all the meetings about the revision of the *United States Code*, title 44. One could assume that she briefed him on the meetings held in his absence and shared her opinions with him.

There is a fine line between a political and a nonpartisan staffer. A long-term nonpartisan staffer may be related to a member of Congress, elected officer, or political staffer. Though they are nonpartisan, they will still have influence on a policymaker through their personal relationship. Since much of legislative activity depends on the good will of policymakers, it is wise not to disparage any of the players, particularly within earshot of staffers. Some bills have gone down because of animosity among the players. No matter how much you may dislike a policymaker's actions in other areas such as the environment or welfare, always assume that the policymaker supports the value to the democratic process of the public's access to information and libraries. Always remind the policymaker that everyone, no matter where they are on the political spectrum, needs information to argue their position.

When the policymaker changes, new staff are often put in place. The former staff are people that you may have educated, known on a first-name basis, and counted on to get to their bosses. Suddenly they are gone. This is particularly true if a different political party in Congress takes over. In some cases, a staffer can survive, perhaps on the same committee or by moving to the staff of another policymaker. Even if this staffer moves to a position outside government, she or he may still have influence with policymakers in the institution left behind.

Political Staff

Members of most legislative bodies are able to hire any staff they want for their personal offices and for the committee on which they serve. The number of staff is determined in the appropriations process. The number of staff they are allowed to hire for the committees on which they serve also depends on committee rules and their seniority on the committee. They are able to hire this staff on a political basis. By political, I mean they do not have to advertise jobs based on certain publicly established and monitored criteria and can hire whomever they like. They hire staff who worked on their campaign, people from their own political party, people from their own state or geographic area, people they went to school with, the children of their supporters, and so forth. When they are named to a committee, they are authorized a certain number of staff that can be hired in a similar manner. This is accepted practice, because a legislator wants staff that she or he feels will carry out his or her wishes, shares similar philosophies and goals, and is someone whose advice and information they can trust.

Funding for staff comes through the budget and appropriations process for members' personal offices, committees, and support offices. The sums allocated to each entity are voted on by the entire legislative body. In most instances, a certain sum is allocated for staff and the member, committee, or support office can decide on the number of staff and the pay level for those staff. Sometimes the amount of money allocated and the top number of staff that can be hired is based on the size of the member's district or state. Staff for U.S. senators' personal offices is based on their state's total population—the more population the more staff. U.S. representatives get equal amount of staff and money because most districts are about equal in the number of people represented. Some members may opt to hire a few highly qualified staff at top salaries, whereas others may go for more staff at lower salaries.

Nonpartisan Professional Staff

Most legislatures also have a category of staff called *professionals* who are hired on a nonpartisan basis because of their professional skills and background. They usually have professional degrees, extensive technical training, or experience with the executive branch, newspapers, or other organizations. These staff work for committees and support offices. Titles vary, but in the U.S. Senate, the title *professional staff* means staff hired for their professional expertise. They can only be fired for specified reasons agreed to by the U.S. Senate.

The fact that the Senate or any other body says that they hire and fire on this basis does not mean that they always keep their word. They may create an excuse for firing professional staff who have been hired by a chair from a different party. They may say they are downsizing or reorganizing or give some other reason. But on the whole most professional staff survive much longer than political staff. They survive because they master the legislative process or a particular operation of Congress, like budgeting and appropriations, or technical oversight of programs and agencies. They know how to make things work. Savvy legislators realize they cannot do their job without knowledgeable staff helping them.

Funding for nonpartisan staff is determined after committees and support offices present a desired budget. Then it is reviewed and approved during the budgeting and appropriations process. The final sum for each committee and support office is approved by the entire legislative body.

Designated Legislative Staff

Most members of a legislature will have designated legislative staff on his or her personal staff who are assigned subject areas. Depending on the number of staff to which a member is entitled, the number of areas that this staffer is responsible for will vary. If the legislator is on a committee and entitled to committee staff, his or her personal staff may refer constituents to the member's committee staff.

Sometimes the personal office legislative staff may disagree with the committee staff. If that is the case, you as the constituent need to find that out. It is wise to talk to both personal and committee legislative staff because usually the committee staff are more familiar with the technical aspects of legislation and the plans for hearings, markups of bills, witnesses, questions, and related issues.

Administrative/Secretarial Staff

Never underestimate the power of the administrative/secretarial staff. Often they, too, are political and may have worked on the legislator's campaign or come from his or her home state. You cannot afford to make them unhappy. Treat them with great respect. They often know more about what is really going on than staff assigned to the subject. That is because like professional staff, they often are the ones who have been around the longest. Unlike many legislative staff, they are not using their job as a stepping stone to something better, although some of them are.

Titles can be deceptive. One of the staff directors that I worked for started out as a secretary. She continued to type letters for the chair of the committee so other staffers would not know what was happening until the letter was sent.

These are the staff who know where the committee publications and files are. If you are nice, they may find them for you. They are the ones who can fit you in for a visit with the legislator or will know where the legislator is so you can track him or her down and get in a good word. Many a wise lobbyist send candy, wine, a fancy calendar, or other gifts to the legislator's secretary.

Support Offices and Agencies Staff

To provide organized support for the legislative process, both the United States Senate and the House established a variety of support offices. The staff of those offices play an important role in the legislative process. Legislatures have majority and minority leaders as well as majority and minority whips who deal directly with congressional members concerning how they will vote. More details about the offices, staff, and responsibilities can be found in such publications as the *Congressional Directory*.

The Senate established the Office of the Secretary of the Senate to provide ongoing support for the legislative process. *Secretary* is a traditional title given to a staffer who holds considerable power. This person is chosen by the majority leader of the Senate and is then confirmed by vote of the Senate. The secretary controls many of the offices that provide direct support for the enactment of legislation. Those offices include the legislative, enrolling, bill and journal clerks, official reporters of debates, the parliamentarian, the documents room, office of printing services, the librarian, historian, archivist, financial clerk, keeper of the stationery, bookbinder, curator, public records superintendent, Senate gift shop, and the Senate Page School.

In the House of Representatives, the clerk of the House provides many of the services that support the legislative process. The clerk reports directly to the Speaker of the House and oversees the chief legislative clerk, official reporters of debates, general counsel, documents room, the librarian, and the archivist. Other support services are provided by a parliamentarian, sergeant at arms, chief administrative officer, Office of General Counsel, Office of Legislative Counsel, Office of the Law Revision Counsel, House Information Systems, Office of Inspector General, and majority and minority printers.

The entire Congress is supported by large agencies such as the Congressional Budget Office, the General Accounting Office, the Library of Congress, and the Government Printing Office. These agencies also provide services to other parts of the government as well as to the public.

State, county, and city legislatures vary in how they organize support offices. Some provide services in a nonpartisan manner with all staff working for both parties, while other states provide separate support to the majority and the minority. There are some county and city legislative bodies elected on a nonpartisan basis, and they usually share staff support.

Interns

Interns are usually college or high school students, paid or unpaid, who work for a legislator for the summer or a year. Selected by the legislator, they may be chosen because they worked on the legislator's campaign or someone in their family contributed to or worked on the campaign. Some legislators hold contests and ask students to compete for the post. Others ask teachers to recommend students interested in the political process. Some interns initiate a request on their own in person or by mail.

Interns are paid in a number of ways: by the legislator's office or a committee, by their home institution, or by grant or other funds. They plan to return to school, graduate work, or employment. Interns can be a blessing to a short-staffed office. Interns often run errands, make copies, answer phones, and do basic research for the legislator and his or her staff. Sometimes an intern gets to work on a worthwhile project and may play an important role in legislation or policy decisions. You really cannot afford to assume that an intern is doing busy work. Even if that is the case, she or he may have significant influence with the legislator, and if you treat interns badly, they may just let their patrons know.

Interns who have a good experience are often inspired to pursue political office. President Bill Clinton started as an intern for Senator William Fulbright (D-Ark.). (President Clinton could tell us a lot about the dangers of underestimating the power of an intern to influence events, since his affair with an intern at the White House almost cost him the job that he had worked all his life to attain.) A young intern may be the relative of someone you want to influence or may have worked on the legislator's campaign writing speeches, think pieces, and answers for questions raised at news briefings. So even if an intern is not important while working for a legislator, he or she may be important in the future. Some regular legislative staff do not welcome interns because it means more work for them in organizing meaningful work for the interns. Occasionally, an intern may return to the legislative office as a staffer or even as a member of the legislature, so even legislative staff need to treat interns with respect.

Sometimes professionals will take a sabbatical and work for a legislator for a year or two on a special project. These professionals may be paid by their institution, the member, or a committee out of funds set aside for temporary staff. When these professionals return to their universities or offices, they will have a certain amount of influence with the legislator. If you know anyone like that, you should think of them as a link to the person you want to lobby. While they are on sabbatical, you should make a point of offering them assistance and keep up with their activities.

If you are a former intern or professional who worked on a temporary basis for a legislator or other public official, do not let that policymaker forget you. Send a note updating your activities; stop in to see that person when you are in town. You never know when you might want to lobby your former patron.

While I was a staffer at the Joint Committee on Printing, two librarians spent their sabbaticals as members of the staff. Beth Helmbold and Cynthia Bower were both assigned to work with me, and together we designed projects that were of interest to them and benefited the work of the committee. Their work influenced policies in the area of services to libraries.

Beth Helmbold

Beth Helmbold, a library assistant for the Public Affairs Service at the University of California at Los Angeles (UCLA), decided that she wanted to spend some time working for the Joint Committee on Printing before she returned to work in a library. She persuaded UCLA to support her internship. She applied to the Joint Committee, and we were happy to welcome her as an unpaid staff assistant.

Helmbold spent much of her time working on ways to improve the Library of Congress/Government Printing Office International Exchange Program. She helped organize the International Conference of Government Publishers, Printers, Librarians, and Users at Saratoga Springs, New York. Many of the librarians who participated in the conference were from libraries that participated in the International Exchange Program overseen by the Joint Committee on Printing.

Cynthia Bower

Cynthia Bower, head of government documents at the University of Arizona Library, applied for a position on the Joint Committee on Printing as a publications distribution specialist in 1984. When the Appropriations Committee declined to appropriate the requested funds and the position was eliminated, she proposed that she be allowed to spend her sabbatical working for the Joint Committee on Printing. She developed a sabbatical proposal that would suit the needs of her university and JCP. Two years later, the university agreed to pay her salary while she worked for JCP. She wanted to investigate the reasons why "fugitive documents" were not being distributed to federal depository libraries and make recommendations about how to bring those documents into the program. The JCP was delighted to welcome a talented new staff member without having to pay her, and Bower found a way to pursue a cause dear to her heart.

Bower's sabbatical did not turn out quite the way she and her university had expected, however. In her summary of her sabbatical, she explained:

It was clear from my first day at work on the "Hill" that the focus of my efforts on behalf of the Joint Committee on Printing would be different

from that outlined in my sabbatical proposal. There were several reasons for this, primary among which was the fact that at the time of my
arrival the Public Printer and the Joint Committee were embroiled in a
fierce battle over continuation of dual format distribution to depository libraries. I was immediately called upon by the Committee to assist in gathering information in support of its position, and to investigate alternative means of achieving significant cost savings. Although
the results of these efforts were extremely positive, they did not con-
stitute the central aim of my proposal.[4]

Bower's experience shows how someone on sabbatical can influence a committee's work. Bower explained that in the area of her
proposal, the identification and analysis of the fugitive documents
problem, "I was permitted to function as a regular member of the
JCP professional staff, with the full authority of the Committee behind my efforts."[5]

In 1991, Bower's experience on JCP and later work in the field of
fugitive documents allowed her to further influence public policy by
testifying at a Joint Committee on Printing hearing entitled "Government Information as a Public Asset." Her testimony covered
practical advice on how to improve operations in government publishing agencies as well as at the Government Printing Office to improve access to government information for the public through libraries. She supported the use of automated systems to help track
government publications as well as creative ways to encourage
agencies to comply with the law requiring that they work with GPO
to provide government information to the public.[6]

Formal and Informal Groups of Legislative Employees

Legislative employees are members of formal and informal
groups. Some of the groups cross political lines, such as the Administrative Assistants Association (*administrative assistant* is the title for
the top staff person in a member of Congress's personal office), Legislative Assistants Association, Congressional Black Associates, Congressional Hispanic Staff Association, and the Congressional Staff
Club. Others are political, such as Association of Democratic Press
Assistants, Republican Communications Association, and Democratic and Republican Women of Capitol Hill.

EXECUTIVE BRANCH OF GOVERNMENTS

Elected Officials Such as Presidents, Governors, and Mayors

On the national, state, and local levels, the chief executive is usually elected. These elected officials include the president of the United States, governors, county executives, and mayors. On the national level, only the president and vice president are elected. All other officials are nominated by the president and confirmed by the Senate or are hired by the president either through patronage or the civil service system. On the state level, governors and lieutenant governors are elected. In some states, other officers such as secretary of state, attorney general, state auditor, and superintendent of public instruction are also elected. The number of officials in state government appointed by the governor varies from state to state. County executives and mayors are usually elected, although some of them are appointed by county and city commissioners.

The major responsibilities of these elected executives on all levels is to uphold the Constitution, carry out the laws enacted by the legislatures, appoint or nominate other officers of the executive branch, and prepare and send budgets to the legislatures. They also play a key role in the legislative process by preparing their own versions of law, which are accepted, modified, or rejected by the legislature. They address the legislatures in order to persuade them to enact laws favored by the executive and in some cases call the legislature into special session to address a special concern. If all else fails, they have the power to veto bills. Most governors have the power to veto parts of bills. The president of the United States does not have that power. Unless the legislature overturns that veto with another vote, the bill does not become law.

A good source for information about state government activities is *State Legislatures,* the national magazine of state government and policy. A 2001 editorial pointed out the effects of an election on government at several levels:

> When the new President is a governor, the trip to Washington can have a dramatic impact on state legislatures. Not just in federal policy as it affects the states, but in who is in charge at the state house. In Texas, that man is Senator Bill Ratliff, who because of a provision of the Texas Constitution, was catapulted into the most powerful lieutenant governor's

office in the nation when Governor George W. Bush was elected President Bush. In New Jersey because of a quirk in the constitution, Senator Donald Di Francesco is not only President of the Senate, but acting governor of a state with one of the strongest executive offices in the country because former Governor Christine Todd Whitman is the new EPA Administrator.[7]

Senator Warren Rudman (R-N.H.) in his memoirs, *Combat: Twelve Years in the U.S. Senate,* says that he voted for confirmation of Clarence Thomas for Supreme Court Justice to preserve his ability to influence the president in other matters of importance to his state. He explained, "I had no doubt that if I voted against Thomas my ability to go to the White House and obtain federal funds and projects for New Hampshire would be at least temporarily crippled, along with my hopes of gaining the president's support for several lawyers who I believed would make outstanding federal judges." He went on to say that bargaining for a vote among senators is rare, that bargaining for a vote with the White House is more likely.

On the local level, the races for county and city commissioners are the ones that will most affect our daily lives. All of these executive branch elected officers are approachable, particularly when they are running for office or when they have just been elected or reelected. They are still in the mood to listen to all of the voters and not just to select voters. In some states, these elected officials are very approachable. In states with smaller populations, elected officials are more like family and want to hear from other members of the family. Act like a member of that family.

For example, a group of Montana librarians were on a tour of the Capitol building of Montana, and as they walked through the governor's area, they ran into Judy Martz, lieutenant governor–elect. She later was elected the first woman governor of Montana. A friendly politician, she stopped to chat with the group. During the chat she revealed that she has many teachers in her family and that she was impressed that the school where one of them taught was using electronic services. She remarked that younger teachers were going to have to use electronic services even more to help students. One of the group took this as an opportunity to ask her to support the expanded provision of electronic access to citizens through libraries. When she said that budgets were tight, this same librarian pointed out that more money spent on libraries would be preventive medicine for keeping people from going to prison, which would save money. A few days earlier the governor had submitted a budget to the legislature asking for a budget increase of $100 million for prisons, an increase of 53 percent. By contrast, the librarians were asking for a modest $340,800 to establish a Montana Access Program that would provide electronic information services to citizens all over the state through public and academic libraries. In spite of the librarians' bill being introduced by a member of the legislature, it did not pass in the 1997 legislative session. The librarians changed tactics and lobbied the governor and lieutenant governor, and the governor agreed to include the program in the Montana State Library's budget request for 1999. The legislature agreed to give the State Library almost $400,000 to establish and fund the program for the next two years.[8]

To influence the president, you need to know how the White House is structured. Bradley H. Patterson Jr., in his book *The White House Staff: Inside the West Wing and Beyond*, describes what the almost six thousand people in some 125 offices do. But of most importance to you as a lobbyist is to understand how the White House lobbies Congress. The White House has an Office of Legislative Affairs in the West Wing run by an assistant to the president with a staff of about thirty-five, counting federal employees, interns, and volunteers. The organization of the staff depends on the president in office, but the work is usually divided up between those who work with the Senate and those who work with the House. On the Senate side, a lot of the work revolves around getting the president's nominees confirmed by the Senate. The vice president is key in working with senators because of his or her special role as president of the Senate and tie breaker of close votes. On the House side, much of the work revolves around the budget and appropriations process since those types of bills are initiated in the House.

White House staff spend a lot of time on the Hill getting to know members of Congress and staff. They do a lot of vote counting so they can pressure members who may be planning on voting against the president's wishes. They can then decide when and whether it is appropriate for pressure to come from the White House chief of staff, members of the president's cabinet, or the president.

White House legislative staff work with other units in the White House to lobby legislators to support the White House position on bills and budgets. Perks that are available for persuasion are invitations to

White House state dinners, picnics on the White House lawn, tickets to the Kennedy Center president's box, a seat on Air Force One during international trips or trips to the legislator's district or state, presidential letters praising an activity of the legislator to be used at conventions and meetings, special tours of the White House such as at Christmastime for legislative staff and family of legislators, and special briefings on issues for constituents of members of Congress. Presidents also will campaign for members up for election by attending a function in their district or even holding a fund-raiser for them.

Sometimes a president's staff organizes an event to promote goodwill between presidential and congressional staff and that attempt ends up doing the opposite. For example, President Carter's new congressional liaison, a former staffer for Representative Frank Thompson, organized a special visit to the White House for congressional staff. Congressional staff were not impressed. They were expecting refreshments, music, maybe even a quick word from the president or some high-level staffer; instead, they groaned, "This is simply a glorified tour like the ones we provide for our member's constituents." Because one of the JCP staffers was a friend of the congressional liaison, we got a behind-the-scenes tour of his office and a can of "Billy Beer," so it was not a wasted evening for us.

On the other hand, First Lady Rosalynn Carter invited all the members of the District of Columbia Library Association to a reception at the White House on November 9, 1978. She served tea and cookies, provided music, and spoke to the librarians for a good fifteen minutes. That event was initiated by Judy Sessions, president of DCLA and a former resident of Georgia. The contrasting events illustrate the need to understand those you are attempting to influence.

Sometimes it is not clear who is lobbying whom. During the presidential race of 2000, staff of the American Library Association Washington office and the White House arranged for a briefing of influential members of the library community at the Old Executive Office Building several weeks before the election. White House staffers Laura Efurd, deputy assistant to the president and deputy director of public liaison, and Bethany Little, associate director of the White House Domestic Policy Council, ran the meeting. The briefing included (1) information on the Clinton–Gore administration accomplishments and the current efforts to influence appropriations bills; (2) an update on the status of the Gore/OMB/GSA private/

public sector project FirstGov (a website providing online access to many government data bases) by Thomas Freebairn from the GSA Office of Governmentwide Policy; (3) an update on efforts to change the intellectual property laws by Peter Fowler, chief of staff, U.S. Patent and Trademark Office, and (4) an update on the Freedom of Information Act and privacy by Richard Huff, codirector, Office of Information and Privacy, Department of Justice.

Nancy Kranich, the president of ALA, and other librarians asked the White House to oppose the latest filtering bill attached to an appropriations bill and to support libraries and public rights in the area of intellectual property. In spite of the glamour of a briefing at the White House by White House staff, the president did not veto the filtering bill, and ALA was faced with another expensive court fight. Vice President Gore did not win the presidential election, so the librarians must persuade President George W. Bush to consider their concerns important enough to warrant a special briefing at the White House. President Bush's wife, Laura, is a librarian and let the world know that when she sponsored an inaugural event featuring authors. Mrs. Bush has encouraged the administration to support a program to provide money for educating new librarians. She has sponsored several book festivals in conjunction with the Library of Congress.

There has been a long competition between the White House and the Congress about who can operate with the fewest employees. This competition intensifies every time the budget comes out and the press writes stories about the cost of running Congress and the White House. One way both entities make it appear that it takes fewer staff than it does to handle their work is to depend on detailees from departments and agencies, interns, and volunteers. The White House has about two hundred interns and a pool of about a thousand volunteers. There is intense competition in securing one of the intern and volunteer positions. Interns work all over the White House. Volunteers sort and answer mail, give tours, manage meeting rooms, and provide support of all kinds.

Two of my friends worked at the Clinton and Bush White House as volunteers. Anne Heanue, a retiree of the American Library Association Washington office with a lot of experience lobbying Congress, was assigned to the Legislative Affairs Office, where she drafted letters from President Clinton to senators and representatives. Most of the letters she drafted were to accompany printed and red-lined copies of bills sponsored by a member of Congress and signed by the president into law. Victoria Buckley, a retiree from the Detroit Public School System, was assigned to the White House Conference Center on Jackson Place, where she welcomed attendees to meetings sponsored by the White House. All volunteers were asked by the Bush team not to show up for work after the 2000 election. Later Buckley and Heanue were recalled as volunteers for the Bush White House at the White House Conference Center. Without the work of talented and experienced volunteers, a lot of work at the White House would go undone.

Both the president and the vice president are lobbied by members of the cabinet, other federal employees, members of associations and institutions, and the public. Vice President Gore was very accessible to federal employees, members of associations, and others interested in promoting electronic publishing and dissemination of government information. His position concerning who should control some of the aspects of government publishing changed when he went from the Senate to the executive branch and was put in charge of reinventing government. He was lobbied and convinced by staff running the National Performance Review (NPR) that publishing, printing, and disseminating government information and publications should be decentralized and no longer channeled through the Government Printing Office.

Gore supported the expansion of the role of the National Technical Information Service at the Department of Commerce to include private-public publishing efforts. He used NTIS to publish the NPR report, although as a member of the Joint Committee on Printing, he would have insisted that it be published through the Government Printing Office. Although he had supported NTIS for years when the secretary of commerce announced in August 1999 that NTIS would be abolished and its assets transferred to the Library of Congress, he did not disagree. The secretary of commerce justified the abolishment of NTIS by citing the trend to free access to government information on the Internet and financial losses at NTIS, which had caused NTIS to ask for $2 million in appropriations. Commercial supporters of NTIS immediately established a website advocating the continued existence of NTIS. The library and public interest associations scrambled to enunciate their position and issue statements.

In January 2000, the ALA Council passed a resolution advocating that NTIS be transferred to GPO and that the scientific and technical publications be made a part of the Depository Library Program and therefore available at no charge to the general public.

The National Commission on Libraries and Information Science (NCLIS) conducted a review of the proposal by the secretary and held a series of meetings inviting stakeholders to give advice on the future of NTIS. NCLIS issued a report to Congress and the president arguing that NTIS continue to be funded as part of the Department of Commerce until NCLIS could conduct a study to determine where it should be on a permanent basis.

In June 2000, Senator John McCain (R-Ariz.) wrote to NCLIS stating that the Senate Commerce Committee had held hearings on the reorganization of the National Technical Information Service. He asked NCLIS to

> undertake a review of the reforms necessary for the federal government's information dissemination practices. At a minimum this review should include assessments of the need for proposing new or revised laws, rules, regulations, missions, and policies; modernizing organization structures and functions so as to reflect greater emphasis on electronic information planning, management, and control capabilities, and the need to consolidate, streamline, and simplify missions and functions to avoid or minimize unnecessary overlap and duplication; revoking NTIS self-sufficiency requirement; and strengthening other key components of the overall federal information dissemination infrastructure.

He requested that the study be completed by December 15, 2000.

NCLIS conveyed its *A Comprehensive Assessment of Public Information Dissemination* to the Senate Commerce Committee and the president on January 26, 2001. NCLIS strongly supported citizen access to government information with the following statement:

> Proactive dissemination of government information to citizens in all walks of life is the key that enables them to have a voice in public affairs, enables them to hold public officials accountable for their actions, prevents their rights from being trampled upon, and empowers them to better meet their personal, family business and job-related needs and goals, including matters pertaining to their health, safety, security, and enriching the quality of their lives.

NCLIS argued that access to information would be furthered by 1) government adopting the national goal that public information be considered a strategic resource and that an information dissemination budget be established for all agencies; 2) merge NTIS and the Superintendent of Documents in a new executive branch agency called Public Information Resources Administration; 3) establish a Congressional Information Resources Office and a Judicial Information Resources Office to take over the printing and publishing now performed by GPO for the courts and Congress; 4) Congress provide funding for the public good functions of NTIS and other comparable information service agencies rather than requiring them to be self supporting.

In May 2001, the General Accounting Office issued its report GAO-01-490 on NTIS, *Information Management: Dissemination of Technical Reports*. It had been requested by several members of the U.S. House Committee on Government Reform and Committee on Science. The conclusion was that much of the information available through NTIS is available nowhere else.

As of 2001, NTIS was still alive. The future of NTIS was addressed in S. 803, the E-Government Act of 2001. OMB was directed to convene an interagency task force to make recommendations on "which agency or agencies should develop and maintain databases and a website containing data on federally funded research and development." The membership of the task force includes the agencies now contributing to the NTIS database. It was passed by the Senate and the House in 2002 and signed by the president.

Political Appointees

Presidents, governors, county executives, and mayors are allowed to nominate or appoint the heads of their departments and agencies. On the national level, those nominations must be confirmed by the Senate. In states, counties, and cities, the practice varies. Once those department heads are confirmed, they in turn can appoint a certain number of staff without having to go through the usual hiring procedures. These staff usually have some connection to the political party of the elected officials and department heads. On the national level, those jobs are listed in the *U.S. Government Policy & Supporting Positions*, nicknamed the "Plum Book" and available in paper and on the GPO Access System. ("Plum" refers to special jobs, not to the color of the book. The Congress publishes most of its books in conservative green or brown, believing that publishing in more colorful shades is a waste of the tax dollar.) The Plum Book is published alternately by the Senate Committee on Governmental Affairs and the House Committee on Government Reform. Practically all staff working for a member of Congress's personal office or on a committee are also listed in the Plum Book. The first time I saw my position listed in the Plum Book, I was convinced that I would lose my job. I did have to hand in my résumé each time, but I was one of the fortunate few who survived twenty years and five listings in the Plum Book.

Political appointees are committed to enacting the philosophy of elected officials. That is why they are hired. People who worked on the presidential, gubernatorial, and mayoral campaigns are often selected for jobs in the executive branch. You probably know some of these people; they may even be related to you. Ask your friends and relatives whether they know anyone who works for the president, the governor, the county executive or the mayor, a department, or an agency. If you work in an academic library, some of your former students may now be working for an elected or appointed official. When you are in Washington, D.C., the capital of your state, the county seat, or downtown near the mayor's office, drop in to see the people you know. They may be homesick. Bring them a little memento from their hometown. Ask them to explain their agency and job to you. When you need them, you will know where they are and what they do, and they will know you.

On the national level, a number of key officials in the area of information and libraries are nominated by the president and confirmed by the Senate. They include the librarian of Congress, the public printer of the United States, the archivist of the United States, the secretary of education, the director of the Institute of Museum and Library Services, and the chair of the National Commission on Libraries and Information Science. Depending on the holder of the office, these officials spend considerable time interacting with members of the library and information community.

Traditionally, the librarian of Congress is one of the most active supporters of libraries and librarians. The librarian sends staff to the meetings of most library associations and often attends those meetings. LC works closely with the American Library Association in developing national standards that affect cataloging and other services provided by LC to libraries all over the world. LC has a booth at library association meetings, where its services are demonstrated and explained to attendees. Daniel Boorstein, librarian from 1975 to

1987, and James Billington, librarian from 1988 to present, spent many hours courting and persuading business people and others to contribute financially to projects at the library, including restoration of the buildings and digitization of the collections. They also were successful in lobbying Congress for more funds. Billington lobbied Congress to increase LC's ability to publish and partner with private sector publishers in order to increase revenue and the visibility of the library. Both librarians saw the potential in electronic publishing and the need to use technology to preserve and provide access to the vast collections at LC. In 2001, Billington succeeded in obtaining $100 million from Congress for the digitization of many publications in LC's collection.

Until the tenure of Michael DiMario, it was unusual for a public printer to attend library association meetings. Most public printers have given their attention to printers and paper and equipment producers. Not until the creation of GODORT and the rebirth of the Depository Library Council did GPO make a practice of sending staff to library association meetings on a regular basis. DiMario actively supported public access to government information and expanding the depository program to include electronic information. He expressed his appreciation to the library community for their support of the Federal Depository Library Program by hosting luncheons where he invited the leaders of associations to meet with him and staff to discuss issues and services and by inviting librarians to special events at the Government Printing Office.

After failed attempts by the library community to get legislation passed to mandate permanent public access to government information, DiMario set up the Permanent Public Access Working Group to consider how key players might voluntarily cooperate in assuring such access. He convened a series of high-level meetings with legislative and executive branch officials, including congressional staff and representatives from the Library of Congress, the National Archives, the National Agricultural Library, the National Library of Medicine, the Energy Department, the National Commission on Libraries and Information Science, the Defense Technical Information Center, other agencies, and the library and user communities. As I have suggested a number of times, if legislation fails, try other means to affect public policy.

Under Title 44, the public printer is authorized to appoint the superintendent of documents. The library and information community are most familiar with this appointee because he or she runs the federal depository, sales, and bylaw distribution programs. Most superintendent of documents have been very responsive to the library community and have attended the Depository Library Council meetings and library conferences.

As a chair of the American Library Association Government Documents Round Table and a professional staffer on the Joint Committee on Printing, I worked with all of the superintendent of documents serving since 1970. In 1973, I served with Carper Buckley, superintendent of documents in the 1950s and 1960s on the reborn Depository Library Council. Robert E. Kling recommended my appointment to the Depository Library Council by Nick Spence, public printer in 1973. While at the Joint Committee on Printing from 1974 to 1995, my primary assignment was oversight of the superintendent of documents operations. I worked with Wellington Lewis, Carl LaBarre, Raymond Mason Taylor, Michael DiMario, Donald Fossedal, and Wayne Kelley. In 1997, Francis Buckley, the first professional librarian and a member of the ALA Governing Council, was appointed superintendent of documents.

The director of the Institute of Museum and Library Services attends library association meetings and works directly with librarians all over the country to strengthen libraries and museums. The institute provides funding and other support to "help libraries to use new technologies to identify, preserve, and share library and information resources across institutional, local and state boundaries and to reach those for whom library use requires extra effort or special materials."[9] The director's job alternates every four years between individuals with special competence in library and museum service. In 2001, Robert Martin, a member of ALA's Governing Council and interim director of the Texas Woman's University School of Library and Information Studies, was nominated as director of the institute by President Bush and confirmed by the Senate.

In 1996, most library programs were moved from the Department of Education to the Institute of Museum and Library Services; therefore, the attendance of the secretary of education and his or her staff at library association meetings has been greatly reduced. The secretary is still active, however, in working with the various educational associations on all levels.

The chair and members of the National Commission on Libraries and Information Science are frequent attendees and speakers at library

144 Chapter 5

association meetings on all levels. All of the commissioners are nominated by the president and confirmed by the Senate. Commissioners come from a variety of information related backgrounds. Most of the commissioners are not librarians, although a number of them have served as library trustees or members of library foundations. NCLIS advises both the president and congress on the implementation of national policy pertaining to the library and information needs of the nation. Its members and staff work with the library and information community to identify policies that need review.

NCLIS organized and ran White House Conferences on Libraries in 1979 and 1991. In late 1974, the staff director of the JCP sent me to sit in the staff gallery of the House of Representatives to monitor the progress of the bill authorizing the first White House Conference. Representative John Brademas (D-Ind.), a member of the JCP, was one of the sponsors of the bill. The idea of a White House Conference was first advocated in 1957 by a library trustee, and it took seventeen years to get it authorized and another two to get it funded. This is another example of why passing legislation depends on the persistence of its proponents. I was an official observer at the conferences in 1979 and 1991 and a delegate to the Federal Pre-White House conference in November 1990. I remember the 1979 conference well because the library community persuaded President Carter, his daughter Amy, and Governor Clinton of Arkansas to attend. They were enthralled with the then-emerging technology being used to support access to information. Later President Clinton would go on to promote access to the Internet to all libraries.

As a professional staffer at the Joint Committee on Printing, I worked with a series of NCLIS chairs and executive directors on policies affecting publishing and disseminating of government information. Chairs Charles Benton, Jeanne Hurley Simon, and Martha Gould were all longtime champions of libraries and the public's access to information.

I knew many of the staff directors before they became director since we had worked together on projects, committees, and issues. Our ongoing interaction over the years made it possible for us to work well together when they assumed the role of executive director. It illustrates my point that you never know when an old friend or friendly adversary may move into a new arena where he or she can help you achieve your policy goal. It also shows how professionals move in and out of government and that those who have a variety of experiences often make the best policymakers.

The first NCLIS director I worked with was Alphonse F. Trezza, former director of the State Library of Illinois. The Illinois secretary of state carries the actual title of state librarian. Trezza, one of my key supporters in starting the ALA Government Documents Round Table, was an adroit librarian and convinced Illinois politicians to strongly support the state library and public libraries. He found it much harder to convince the Congress to give NCLIS enough funds so it could be effective. Toni Carbo Bearman was a strong supporter of the depository library program before and after she came to NCLIS. Peter Young and I had been friends since meeting in 1975 at a workshop on government documents held at Rice University in Texas. He went from Rice to the Library of Congress and then to NCLIS and back to LC and is now director of the National Agriculture Library. He understood the role of federal libraries in assuring the public's access to information and made sure that there was a Federal Pre-White House Conference. Robert Willard, current executive director (formerly with private legal information publishers and the Information Industry Association), and I were friendly adversaries in the struggle over whether government publications should be micropublished by GPO. Judy Coffey Russell, NCLIS deputy executive director, served on the JCP Ad Hoc Committee on Depository Library Access to Federal Automated Data Bases. While a key staffer at GPO, she worked with JCP staff in setting up the GPO Access System.

Permanent Nonpartisan Staff of Departments and Agencies

The majority of the staff in executive branch departments and agencies are nonpartisan professional or clerical staff. They are often referred to as civil service employees. They are selected in a competitive manner under well-defined guidelines. They must have skills and education to suit the position.

There is a practice in many governments of converting political staff to nonpartisan staff. This happens usually when a political party sees that they are not going to win the election and so start moving their people into nonpolitical positions. This tactic can make it hard for the incoming political party to get their philosophy and policies accepted and their programs implemented. You may be lobbying the

same people, but they will have different titles and new responsibilities, and they still will be important in helping you get what you
want from an agency.

Don't make the mistake of ignoring the new political staff. They
are going to be the most important people in the agency, at least until the next election. Find out who they are. Ask to meet with them
as soon as possible. Offer to provide them with information and to
introduce them to other people they will need to know. Usually
those who meet the new people first are remembered.

Most governments at all levels publish directories or manuals that
list agencies and their purposes as well as both nonpartisan and political staff. Many of those directories are now on the Internet. The
Government Printing Office Access System provides online access to
many of the directories compiled by government. There are also privately published directories of legislators and their staffs and the officials of the executive and judicial branches of government. Some
nonprofit groups also publish guides complete with names, telephone numbers, and addresses of elected officials.

The truly nonpartisan staff are important because they usually
last the longest and have long-term memories of how things work.
They can be your greatest allies. They are the ones who are most
dedicated to the mission of the agency, and if they think you are also
interested in the mission, they will do their best to help you.

There is one group of nonpartisan professional staff that will always
be happy to see you. These are the librarians in departments and agencies. They need you as much as you need them. They are the ones who
will know about policies that affect the public's access to information.
They work with everyone in their agency. They struggle, just as you
do, to get information from everyone else in their agency. They struggle to get their library program recognized and supported.

Another group of professionals who will usually be on your side
are the agency authors, editors, publishers, and public affairs officers. They want their information out to the public. They may not
recognize librarians at first as their allies, but, after you educate
them, they will.

Formal and Informal Groups of Government Employees

Government employees, whether political or nonpartisan, come
together in formal and informal groups to attempt to influence poli-

cies and programs. Formal groups generally need the formal support of their agencies, including formal recognition, financial support, and scrutiny by the agency. Informal groups are not officially part of their agencies, although agencies authorize members time off to attend meetings and support them in their work.

Federal employees are members of a number of groups organized to improve government publishing and access to that information. They are the (1) National Association of Government Communicators (NAGC) organized in 1975 by Henry Lowenstern, Associate Commissioner, Office of Publication, Bureau of Labor Statistics; the (2) Federal Publishers Committee (FPC) organized in 1980 by Robin Atkiss at the Department of Health and Human Services and June Malina of the National Archives, (3) Interagency Committee on Printing and Publications Services (ICPPS); (4) CIO Council and its Federal WebMasters Forum; (5) Federal Geographic Data Committee (FDGC); and (6) CENDI. Federal librarians organized a group called the Federal Library Committee in 1965 that evolved into the Federal Library and Information Center Committee.

National Association of Government Communicators

Henry Lowenstern was inspired to form the National Association of Government Communicators (NAGC) after a visit to the Joint Committee on Printing in 1974 when he confided in me that government publishers had little to say about the JCP, OMB, and GPO regulations and policies. I suggested that he organize a group to represent their interests. He invited public affairs officers, editors, writers, and publishers in the federal government to join him. NAGC got the attention not only of JCP and OMB but of administrators in the agencies. NAGC holds an annual conference and monthly meetings where influential government communicators, reporters, and others are invited to speak. President Carter's Public Affairs Officer, Jody Powell, was one of the first speakers.

NAGC led a successful fight to change the policies governing how the federal publications sales program at the Government Printing Office was structured and how prices for those publications were established. NAGC persuaded JCP to include pricing as a separate issue in the attempt to revise the printing and dissemination laws in 1979. Lowenstern was included as a member of the Ad Hoc Advisory Committee on Revision of Title 44 Subcommittee on Pricing of

Government Information as a representative of NAGC. Later he served on a GPO committee that developed a new pricing formula.

Federal Publishers Committee

The Federal Publishers Committee (FPC) was organized as an informal, unofficial forum for agency publishers. The *FPC Handbook of 1993* states, "In 1980, a group of Federal employees engaged in publishing and information dissemination formed a voluntary association to support and improve these activities in the Federal Government, through information and problem sharing, advocacy, and improved communications with the Government Printing Office, the Joint Committee on Printing, and agency printing officers."[10] FPC started with a handful of members and grew to over five hundred members. Robin Atkiss and June Malina were the force behind FPC.

Since it was informal, FPC was free to invite speakers who were involved in the latest burning issues, such as the effort by the Reagan administration to eliminate or privatize many publications. The members were good at asking important and provocative questions. FPC was so successful in attracting speakers, generating advice, and representing the interest of federal publishers that OMB ended up recognizing it as an official voice of the federal publishers. FPC worked closely with others such as the library community to protect public access and to encourage compliance with the Federal Depository Library Program.

Interagency Committee on Printing and Publications Services

The Interagency Committee on Printing and Publications Services (ICPPS) is composed of representatives of most of the departments and agencies. Those representatives are usually staff who work on a daily basis with the publishing and printing operations of their agencies. ICPPS has been around the longest of any of the groups working on government publishing concerns. It works very closely with the Government Printing Office, the Joint Committee on Printing, and others in the federal government in developing standards, guidelines, and educational programs for those in the federal government engaged in publishing and printing activities. It serves as a sounding board for solving problems in the arena of printing and publishing. ICPPS's latest publication is *Guide to Federal Publishing*, which gives advice on traditional as well as electronic publishing and dissemination practices.

Chief Information Officers Council

The Chief Information Officers Council (CIOC) was formed as a mechanism to allow chief information officers to coordinate and share information about their responsibilities with each other and the Office of Management and Budget. CIOC works closely with the Office of Management and Budget. It has not spent a lot of time on dissemination of government information issues, although it was involved in the work of setting up the FirstGov system, a website providing online access to government databases. CIOC set up a Federal WebMasters Forum to discuss the issues involved in going from a paper-based information system to an electronic one. The forum is addressing the lack of coordination and standardization for agency websites, the issue of multiformat publications, and how to decide what should be included in an electronic system and which older publications need to be converted to an electronic format.

Federal Geographic Data Committee

The Federal Geographic Data Committee (FGDC) is an interagency committee established in 1990 according to OMB Circular A-16. FDGC is composed of representatives from seventeen departments and independent federal agencies. One of its projects is the National Spatial Data Infrastructure, which is used to set policies, standards, and procedures for cooperatively developing and sharing geographic data. FDGC also works cooperatively with similar organizations on the state, local, and tribal level. Much of the data incorporated into federal databases is collected by agencies on the state and local levels. The consolidated data is then used by all types of governments, research organizations, universities, and others.

CENDI

CENDI is a voluntary interagency committee established after the Committee on Scientific and Technical Information (COSATI) was abolished. The name CENDI is based on the original membership of

Commerce, Energy, National Aeronautics and Space Administration, Defense, and Interior. CENDI has members from nine major government agencies involved in research, publishing, or the collection of scientific and technical reports. These agencies are the major suppliers of sci/tech reports to the National Technical Information Service for dissemination to the public. CENDI operates as a coordinating and advisory group for the collecting, cataloging, and dissemination of technical reports. It maintains and updates the COSATI cataloging standards. CENDI is supported through member contributions.

Federal Library and Information Center Committee

The Federal Library and Information Center Committee (FLICC) was created in 1965, and its members include the Library of Congress, National Agriculture Library, National Library of Medicine, National Library of Education, federal libraries in all three branches, and information centers like NTIS, DTIC, and DOE. Representatives from the Superintendent of Documents and the National Commission on Libraries and Information Science are also invited to attend meetings.

Each member agency contributes financial support so that FLICC has its own staff to assist the libraries in such endeavors as cataloging, joint purchasing of services and publications, and education of the staff of member libraries. FLICC operates the Federal Library and Information Network (FEDLINK). It influences policy by organizing and publishing the proceedings of seminars with key players as speakers who interact with members of the audience. FLICC's seminars often cover government information issues. FLICC writes standards and works to persuade other agencies, such as the Office of Personnel Management, to adopt those positions or standards.

NONPROFIT SECTOR

Associations

The same associations that lobby are often the associations that you as an individual or an association will want to lobby. Nonprofit associations include those that represent publicly owned institutions such as libraries, museums, and archives and those who work for those institutions. They include associations set up to represent public interest issues such as civil liberties, the right to read, write, create works, and publish them without threat of censorship, such as the American Civil Liberties Union and the Freedom to Read Foundation. Other public interest associations represent a variety of groups such as the homeless, those on welfare, the disabled, and retired.

Nonprofit Institutions, Think Tanks, and Advocacy Organizations

You will also want to lobby non-profit institutions, think tanks, and advocacy organizations that hand out money to those who engage in research, lobbying, and advocacy. I have already discussed many of those groups in the chapter on who lobbies.

Coalitions

It is important to convince coalitions to support your cause. You do not have to belong to a coalition to convince it to get interested in your cause. You need to provide information and updates on issues to coalitions in your field of interest.

Unions

Since unions are a tool used by workers to organize themselves to improve their working conditions, wages, and benefits, it is not unusual for librarians and information professionals to organize themselves into unions. Unions differ from professional associations in that they concentrate on making life better for individuals rather than for institutions. Not only do unions work to better the working conditions of their members, but many work to better society. Library associations like ALA have units that work with unions to identify common concerns.

During the Great Depression, Congress passed legislation promoting unions as a means of lifting workers out of poverty. In 1935, the Wagner Act was passed to support workers' rights to organize their own unions and not be forced to join company-run unions. The National Labor Relations Board was established to oversee collective bargaining practices.

Michael Zweig in the *Working Class Majority* argues:

> Congress passed the Wagner Act not just because of economic calcula-tions having to do with recovery. Some congressmen and senators de-fended this intrusion on corporate rights and power by calling on eth-ical considerations as well: fairness, dignity, democracy. Growing inequality in the distributions of income and wealth suggested that workers needed more power to be able to share fairly in the wealth of the country. Supporters of the Wagner Act understood that a worker acting alone to confront a large corporate employer could not win; col-lective strength was essential. Whether dealing with wages or work rules or arbitrary treatment by management, unions were seen as a means for the worker to approach the employer as an equal. A collec-tive bargaining agreement could provide the dignity of fair treatment in the daily life of the union member.[11]

Unions of all types are interested in access to information so they can inform and educate their membership. Build on that need to ed-ucate their membership by inviting their members to attend library workshops and participate in programs. Ask them to recommend books and services to be added to the library's collection. Invite them to sponsor and attend fund-raisers for the library.

Some unions take partisan political positions and campaign for candidates. Some stay neutral and ask all parties to support policies that are good for workers. When it comes to support for libraries, li-brary activists should assume that union members will support pub-lic libraries since libraries serve all members of a community. Li-brary activists should ask unions to help get out the vote for library levies, lobby for funding for libraries and support unfettered and eq-uitable access to information for citizens through libraries.

A good example of librarians organizing through their unions is the history of the struggle of the San Jose (Calif.) Public Library staff to gain equal pay for comparable work. Since the library field is dominated by women, library staff are often paid less than men who hold jobs deemed "men's jobs." This was the case in San Jose where library staff were paid less than employees in other jobs even though their work was equally complex and their levels of responsibility were comparable.

Joan Goddard was one of the leaders in the fight for pay equity. She worked twenty-seven years at San Jose Public Library, primarily as a supervisor of a series of branch libraries. She was an officer and board member of the Municipal Employees Federation, a chapter of Local 101 of the American Federation of State, County, and Municipal Employees, from 1978 to 1988. She was a member of the contract negotiating team during the historic eight-day "pay equity" strike in July 1981. It was the Municipal Employees Federation with the support of AFSCME and AFL-CIO against the City of San Jose. The strike resulted in significant pay equity salary increases for "women's work" jobs over the next ten years. The victory for the union, including the library staff, required patience and persistence.

Preparations for the pay equity negotiations and strike included

- a presentation to the City Council by City Women for Advancement, assisted by the Municipal Employees Federation;
- lobbying of City Council members and the first female mayor of a large U.S. city;
- working on neighborhood petition campaign of an African American woman who was appointed to the City Council and who later helped assure that the pay equity study was handled well;
- working on several City Council members' election campaigns to assure that communication channels would be open when needed;
- a sickout by City Hall clerical and administrative staff on the same day the police had the "blue flu"—which led to the inclusion of nonmanagement, non-sworn-public-safety city jobs in a job classification and compensation study that the city manager had requested for management staff only. Union staff insisted that the study include internal salary comparisons, not just the region's public jurisdictions labor market;
- strong involvement of union members in the study and the job analysis to show the complexity and importance of "women's work" jobs;
- organizing of union members against the city's "brick wall" resistance to appropriate salary increases beyond a minimum level; and
- support from local area women's rights organizations and the South Bay AFL-CIO Labor Council, including strike sanction, and refusal to cross picket lines by AFL-CIO and Teamsters members.

Goddard is a past member of the ALA Council and its Pay Equity Committee. She is the founder and cochair of the Coalition for Equal Pay, which creates local area activities for Equal Pay Day, a nation-wide observance and action day to underscore the problem of the women's wage gap and the need for legislative and other efforts to improve women's and families' income. Equal Pay Day is sponsored by the National Committee on Pay Equity, a coalition of union, pro-fessional, and women's organizations, including ALA. ALA president-elect Maurice Freedman invited Goddard to serve on a Better Salaries and Pay Equity Committee to help him fulfill his action pri-orities. The committee plans to have recommendations ready to im-plement during Freedman's term (2002–2003).

Librarians attending the American Library Association conference in San Francisco in 2001 got an in-person education regarding how unions operate when they believe their rights are in jeopardy. ALA chose the Marriott Hotel as its headquarters although ALA staff had been warned that there was an ongoing contract dispute between Union Local 2 and Marriott management. The union and their allies, Local 790 Librarians Caucus, the San Francisco Public Library Com-mission, dozens of organizations, and local San Francisco area pub-lic officials, including Mayor Willie Brown, urged ALA to move its headquarters. When that form of lobbying failed, the workers and their supporters marched in a picket line in front of the Marriott chanting slogans asking librarians to honor the boycott.

Months before the conference, alert librarians took the warning on the ALA hotel registration form about the contract dispute seriously and requested rooms in other hotels. Many units of ALA moved their events to other locations. Some units' requests to be moved were not honored by ALA staff since they feared financial repercus-sions. The Social Responsibilities Round Table Coretta Scott King Book Award Breakfast was canceled at the request of King and SRRT members. King reminded librarians that her husband, Martin Luther King Jr., had supported hotel workers in their fight for fair pay and good working conditions.

Getting moved to another locale seemed to depend on how much lobbying clout you had within ALA. If there was a lot of money in-volved where Marriott would demand compensation, ALA was re-luctant to honor the request. On the other hand, units realized that if enough of their members refused to cross the picket lines that there would be no meeting. A number of ALA members refused to attend the annual banquet, including several award winners and the president-elect. The ALA Council debated and referred a resolution directing that "be it resolved that all hotel contracts, those to be negotiated and those to be finalized, will contain both a strike and a boycott clause, providing the flexibility to void contracts where labor bodies have endorsed either type of organized action" to the ALA Conference Committee and asked it to report back to the council at the midwinter meeting in 2002.

The National Writers Union, a trade union for freelance writers, is affiliated with the United Auto Workers. Its 6,500 members and seventeen local chapters work to improve the economic and working conditions of freelance writers. The Union filed a lawsuit against the *New York Times* claiming that the newspaper violated writer's constitutional rights by forcing writers to give up their copyright protection when it comes to republishing their work electronically. The writers want to be paid for the reuse of their work. The writers have gained the support of the American Library Association and the Association of Research Writers.

Political Parties

Political parties are the way that citizens can actively influence who will run for office and what policies governments will adopt if their party wins the elections. An election year is a good time to identify and assist library supporters to win public office. To influence political parties, librarians and public interest champions need to be active in the political process. Pick a party and participate. Serve as a party precinct captain, chair a county central committee, volunteer to work for a candidate, provide information to candidates and parties, or run for office yourself. Go to town meetings and ask the candidates what they plan on doing for libraries and access to information if they get elected. If you, your party, or candidate win the election, you have a good opportunity to influence government policies affecting the public's access to information.

More and more librarians are running for office. Representative Major Owens (D-N.Y.), the first professional librarian elected to Congress, not only represents his Brooklyn district but the public's right to information. Representative Owens persuaded another Brooklyn librarian to run for and win his former seat in the New York Legislature. Linda McCullough, a school librarian and representative in the

Montana House, sponsored bills supporting libraries which were enacted into law in 1999. She won the Democratic nomination for Montana superintendent of public instruction and was elected in November 2000. Margaret Crennen, a retired high school librarian who served on the Helena City Commission, and Ilen Egger Stoll, a retired librarian from Montana Tech, ran for the Montana House in 2000. Crennen lost in the primary, and Stoll lost in the general election.

Other librarians have volunteered to work in campaigns, stuff envelopes, drop literature at voters' doors, sign signature ads for newspapers, hold fund-raisers, and give money. Several have even served as campaign managers. If your candidate wins, he or she will not forget you when you ask that policymaker to sponsor or vote for a bill or policy that helps libraries.

One librarian persuaded the local chapter of a political party to hold a fund-raiser for the public library, pass a resolution urging the city and county commissions to increase the public library's funding, and work to get out the vote for a levy increasing funding for the library.

Library associations and libraries have set up minilibraries at political conventions where they provided the delegates with information. This is a practical way to educate politicians about the role that libraries play in assisting public participation in the political process. In the 2000 elections, the American Library Association wrote a letter to all the presidential candidates asking them to make support of libraries part of their campaigns.

Librarians often belong to the League of Women Voters, the Chamber of Commerce, and service clubs as a way to educate members about libraries and to get them to support policies that help libraries. Some of them have used their membership as a stepping stone to getting appointed or elected to library boards and commissions on the local, state, and national levels.

If you do not participate in politics, keep track of librarians and public interest advocates who do. Ask them to carry the word about libraries to the officials they have helped get elected. It would be helpful if librarians and their supporters were active in every political party, so no matter who gets elected, we will have officials who care about libraries.

Once the elections are over and the winners are determined, librarians need to make sure that the newly elected and reelected public officials know about the library and its needs. Send the newly elected politicians a note of congratulations and invite them to visit the library. Hold an open house for all newly elected office holders.

Send a note to the losers and thank them for their public service. This is particularly important if they have supported legislation, programs, or policies that support libraries. You never know—they may run for another office and win the next time. They may become lobbyists or take a position in the for-profit or nonprofit sector where they can be of help to the library.

Once elections are over and the winners are determined, librarians need to act quickly to influence the newly elected public officials. This includes officials who have been reelected. After a campaign, everyone is ready for a new start. In Helena, Montana, one of the candidates for city council who lost helped with the campaign to get a levy for the library. He helped organize the yard sign effort. Those who become lobbyists can help. Include officials on all levels of government—city, county, state, and national.

When you hold an open house for newly elected officials, issue a news release announcing it. Public officials love publicity. Invite the mayor, city and county commissioners, governor and state legislators, your district's representative to the U.S. Congress, and your senators. Be sure and invite the members of your board and the Friends of the Library organization. Demonstrate the services that you can provide for the officials and their constituents. Make the open house festive with music, food, an exhibit, and new bookmarks or brochures.

An appropriate bookmark or brochure would emphasize the government resources available at the library and through the library from the Internet. Include such information as whether the library (1) provides tax forms and booklets; (2) has information such as census data, government manuals and phone directories, consumer, safety and health government information; (3) is a depository for any level of government information; (4) is able to refer patrons to libraries that do have government information collections; or (5) has a website where the user can go to government information or political sites.

Set up an exhibit on the political process. Include posters or photos of campaigns. You could contrast campaigning by train, like Roosevelt and Dewey, to the campaigning by bus, like Clinton and McCain. Include political books, buttons, bumper stickers, newspaper ads, videos of TV ads, and debates. Include memoirs about campaigns, such as the one written by Jeanne Hurley Simon about her experiences when her husband Senator Paul Simon ran for the presidency. Her book is called *Code Name Scarlett: Life on the Campaign Trail by the Wife of a Presidential Candidate*. Include information about presidential libraries. Most of these libraries have websites. The National Archives can supply you with brochures. If you have memorabilia or the papers of local political officeholders, include them in the exhibit and consider providing a bibliography of what is in the collection.

Visit the local office of your congressional and state legislators, and talk to them about what your library does for your community. Brief them on any bills in the works or bills you would like to see introduced that will help your library serve the public better. If you have a bill in mind, ask the legislator if he or she would introduce, cosponsor, or support it. Offer to be a witness at hearings on library issues. If the legislator has a website, suggest that it be linked to the library's site so constituents are aware that they can get information needed to participate in the democratic process at their library.

If your library collects and preserves public papers, ask the official to consider depositing his or her papers with the library. Offer to help the official plan on how best to organize the papers for transfer. Public papers preservation agreements are a good way to assure that the officials will keep the library in mind when policies affecting libraries are being developed.

When the balance of power in a newly elected government is a narrow one, as reflected in the federal elections of 2000, it is more important than ever to get to members of both parties and public officials in both branches of government. It is important also to cultivate champions on both sides of the aisle. The elections of 2000 illustrate the importance of being part of the electoral contest. This was an election where the presidency itself was disputed for weeks and the balance of power in the U.S. Senate was held by virtue of a few seats. Since the Senate was evenly divided between Democrats and Republicans, the chairs were held by Republicans because the vice president, a Republican, held the tie-breaking vote. When Senator Jeffords (I-N.H.) became an independent and aligned himself with the Democrats, power shifted to the Democrats. Jeffords was rewarded with a chairmanship. Even with his move, the balance of fifty-one to forty-nine could still be altered by the death or resignation of another senator. Not having a clear idea as to who is really in control of the committees and the danger that control could tip the other way during the session is added worry for lobbyists. It means more work with more elected officials since committee members and chairs may be playing musical chairs during a Congress. You need to have a strategy for getting to all the players on a regular basis.

FOR-PROFIT SECTOR

Associations

Many associations represent the for-profit sector. In the field of information and publishing, the American Association of Publishers (AAP) and the Software and Information Industry Association (SIIA) are two of the most active. Librarians work with these associations and attempt to influence them to support policies good for libraries. Library associations work with for-profit associations on issues where there is agreement such as protection of the right to read and the promotion of literacy. But there are other issues such as copyright and government information policy where they sometimes end up on opposite sides.

American Association of Publishers

The American Association of Publishers (AAP) represents some three hundred publishers. AAP hired a former member of Congress, Patricia Schroeder, in 1997 to serve as president and to lobby for them. As a member of Congress, she was known as a wit and attracted a lot of press attention. When AAP held its annual convention in February 2001, Schroeder told Linton Weeks, a reporter for the *Washington Post*, at a party for attendees that publishers are terrified of librarians. Weeks explains it as follows:

> No joke. Of all the dangerous and dot-complex problems that American publishers face in the near future—economic downturns, competition for leisure time, piracy—perhaps the most explosive one could be libraries. Publishers and librarians are squaring off for a battle royal over the way electronic books and journals are lent out from libraries and over what constitutes fair use of written material. Grossly oversimplified: Publishers want to charge people to read material; librarians want to give it away. "We," says Schroeder, "have a very serious issue with librarians." "Publishers have to figure out a way to charge for

electronic material," Schroeder says. "Markets are limited. One library buys one of their journals. They give it to other libraries. They'll give it to others. If everyone gets a free copy," she says, "the publisher and the writer and others involved in making the book go unpaid." "Libraries have spent all this money on technology," says Pat Schroeder. "They don't have any money left for content."[12]

Nancy Kranich, president of the American Library Association, begs to differ.

"The reason we're in a bind," says Kranich from her office at New York University, "is that the price of some of the materials has skyrocketed, without any explanation." In principle, librarians believe that patrons should have free and easy access to all information. In Kranich's mind, library-goers should be able to duplicate limited amounts of information for educational purposes. Suppose you want to copy a journal article, quote a section of a book or use a line from a poem, she says. "That is all permitted under the fair-use provision of the copyright law. In the digital arena, fair use has been narrowed to the point of disappearing." "The publishing community does not believe that the public should have the same rights in the electronic world," Kranich says. The AAP is looking for ways to charge library patrons for information.[13]

"Politically," Schroeder says, "it's the toughest issue. Libraries have a wonderful image." No one, she says, wants to go up against libraries.[14]

Software and Information Industry Association

The Information Industry Association (IIA) was founded in 1968 and merged with the Software Association to form the Software and Information Industry Association (SIIA) in 1999. IIA was established to promote private information companies and to convince government and others that information is a commercial product to be marketed and sold, just like any other product. SIIA argues that nothing should be done by government in the distribution and dissemination of information that the private sector can do.

In the early 1980s, Anita Schiller, librarian at the University of California at San Diego, investigated the role of IIA in information production and dissemination. She attended IIA conferences and interviewed congressional and executive branch staff about attempts by IIA to convince policymakers that government should confine itself to the collection and management of information and then turn it over to the private sector for sale. Then Anita and Herbert I. Schiller warned, "With almost no public notice, the national stock of information, created through heavy public expenditures over the years, is steadily being removed from government custodianship and transferred to private ownership and control."[15]

Corporations, Think Tanks, and Advocacy Organizations

Institutions such as for-profit corporations, think tanks, and advocacy organizations supported by corporation's funding play an important role in policies affecting libraries and the public's access to information. To protect the public's interests, it is to our benefit to lobby these entities. We lobby these entities all the time although we may not think of it in those terms.

We are particularly active in trying to influence the policies of publishers and vendors of services and equipment needed to support libraries. We lobby them by

- inviting them to exhibit and participate in our professional meetings and conferences;
- serving on their advisory boards to help them develop products that will serve our libraries needs;
- working with them to support common interests such as freedom of speech and reading;
- asking for financial support for library schools' scholarships, awards for excellence in the library and information field, and receptions and meal functions;
- forming coalitions with them when it suits our common interests;
- being judicious in what we buy from vendors;
- being published by them in their journals, newsletters, and books; and
- giving awards to publications and services that we as professionals deem worthy of praise and support.

Librarians lobby for-profit and nonprofit publishers and services companies (including those in government) to provide publications and services that librarians believe will assist them in serving the users of libraries. Many publishers and vendors produce publications and services that support libraries because they believe in libraries. Often it is difficult to know who is lobbying whom or where the original idea for a publication or a service springs from. The lobbying back and forth is like a community gathering to design and sew a quilt. Each participant adds a square to the quilt. Often the publishing project would not succeed without the cooperation and support of librarians because the collections of publications to be indexed, filmed, and/or turned into electronic databases are those that were collected and protected by librarians.

Sometimes members of the public do not agree with the librarians' and publishers' decisions on how to protect the long-term access of the public to information. Novelist Nicholson Baker launched a crusade to dissuade librarians from converting publications from paper to microform and digital formats without saving the paper originals. He argued that libraries need to keep the originals because they are more complete, have details that can not be reproduced in the copies and in many cases last longer than the copies. He chose to lobby for his cause by writing *Double Fold: Libraries and the Assault on Paper*, giving television and radio interviews and confronting librarians at library meetings. He was successful in forcing the library community to look at the issue and question some of their long-held policies.

In the area of government publications, it is librarians who persuaded the governments to send those publications to libraries on a regular basis. It is librarians who have expended the public and private dollars to collect and care for the publications. It is librarians who realize that the public pays for the publications but often does not know that they exist and so cannot benefit from their tax dollars. Librarians know from talking to government editors and publishers that even though the agency has the money to publish as required by law, it does not have the money to provide support services such as indexing that will help the public access the information. Agencies do not have the money to publicize the publications. Only after librarians realize that they and government publishers need help in getting information to the public do they turn to for-profit publishers for assistance.

Once a publisher agrees to undertake a project, many librarians volunteer or are recruited to serve on publishers' and vendors' advisory committees and boards at no compensation in order to influence the shape of the publication. They may want to influence such aspects as the selection of publications indexed, the terms used to index them, and the format of the indexes.

Even though the process of publishing often starts out as a community affair conducted as much for the good of society as for profit, sometimes the publishers end up selling their company to larger publishers or corporations who are in the business primarily for profit. Sometimes that leads to (1) higher prices for the publications and services than libraries can afford, (2) a reluctance on the part of the new owners to take chances on projects advocated by librarians, (3) the termination of publications loved by librarians but not popular enough to bring in enough profit to suit the new owners, and (4) the reluctance of librarians to spend their time and money assisting publishers.

Following are examples of collaboration between publishers (for-profit and government) and librarians in the field of government publishing where I have personal knowledge of the origin and the outcome of the projects. It was always a delicate dance between aiding publishers and not undermining the policies that we believed in such as the right of government publishers to publish and disseminate in microform and over the Internet.

Librarians Work with MARCIVE to Clean Up Government Publications Cataloging Records

The Government Printing Office started using the Anglo American Cataloging Rules and LC subject headings in 1976 in cataloging government publications. The Library of Congress sold the *Monthly Catalog of United States Government Publications* cataloging records on tape and libraries put the records up in their online catalogs. Problems developed because between the time that GPO cataloged a record into OCLC, an online cataloging utility and the tape of the records was sold by LC, errors had been found and corrected by GPO but not included in the tape sold by LC.

In 1980, Judy Myers and Kathleen Lewis Jackson of the University of Houston conducted a study of cataloging records for government publications produced by GPO and LC and discovered an average of two errors per record. At that time, LC corrected the errors in its records before selling them to libraries, but GPO did not. Thanks to Myers and other librarians, GPO began providing cleaned-up records in 1983. Myers, Jan Swanbeck at Texas A&M, and Carol Turner at Stanford, as part of a grant, developed a proposal to clean up the cataloging records generated between 1976 and 1983 and presented that proposal in 1984 to the Depository Library Council and the GODORT Cataloging Committee.[16] The proposal was supported by both groups. Myers wrote a very persuasive article in 1985 about how such a cleanup could be done as a cooperative project between GPO and librarians. James Plaunt of MARCIVE promoted the use of electronic records in his article "Cataloging Options for U.S. Government Printing Office Documents" in 1985.[17] GPO agreed that the work needed to be done but said it did not have enough money to do a retrospective cleanup.

That is when Judy Myers, Barbara Kile, Jan Swanbeck, and Myrtle "Smittie" Bolner[18] turned to MARCIVE for help. The librarians cornered Plaunt at a reception at an ALA conference and persuaded him to enlist MARCIVE, a cataloging services company, in a cooperative effort with several university libraries to clean up the database. Between 1987 and 1989, Barbara Kile at Rice University, Smittie Bolner at Louisiana State University, and Jan Swanbeck and Laura Salas Tull at Texas A&M University cleaned up cataloging data, and Judy Myers provided expertise. MARCIVE provided the computer processing and the support of staffers Richard Smith and Janifer Meldrum. MARCIVE made good money, and the librarians got clean records for their catalogs.[19] It was a good trade. Years later, GPO bought the cleaned-up cataloging records from MARCIVE and used them in setting up their own online database.

Redgrave Information Resources Corporation

Herb Cohen, president of Redgrave Information Resources Corporation, and Bob Aselon, Xerox University Microfilms, were always on the outlook for new publications that would serve libraries. In 1975, they invited librarians and professors to meet with them during an ALA conference to advise them on a proposal to micropublish and index state publications. State publications at that time were difficult to track down and acquire and few of them were cataloged. Redgrave called their index the *Checklist of State Publications*. That title was very similar to the Library of Congress's *Monthly Checklist of State Publications*. LC had been collecting and listing the state publications that it received since 1910. It discontinued its list in 1994, arguing that it was no longer needed since LC was including many state documents in their cataloging database. Agnes Ferruso, a longtime LC staffer in charge of state publications, was key in getting the documents into LC's catalog. Redgrave listed almost twice as many state documents as LC listed by including titles in checklists issued by state documents clearinghouses, state libraries, and historical societies. Redgrave's checklist was later bought by Information Handling Services and renamed *State Publications Index*.

Information Handling Services

After Herb Cohen joined Information Handling Services, he asked me to advise him and his chief indexer Judy Russell concerning how to make an index to title 40 of the *Code of Federal Regulations (CFR)* useful to those in the environmental field. Title 40 is a compilation of federal environmental regulations and is treated like the Bible by litigants and defendants in the area of environmental enforcement. As librarian at the Environmental Protection Agency Region 7, I provided daily help in locating relevant regulations in the *CFR* to enforcement lawyers, biologists, engineers, and the public. The official index to the *CFR* was difficult to use. I not only was able to help shape a useful index for my library's users but made several lifelong friends. The index was later sold to Capitol Services and then to the Congressional Information Service.

READEX

READEX, another company that works closely with the library community, was started by William Boni with the simple premise of publishing all the government publications listed in the *Monthly Catalog of United States Government Publications* on microcard. READEX had an agreement with the Library of Congress whereby LC loaned all the publications cataloged by the Government Printing Office to READEX for filming. In return, LC received a complete set of microcards for their collection. GPO received nothing. READEX sold the microcard sets to libraries. Even depository libraries bought the sets since GPO did not send every requesting library a copy of every publication indexed in the Monthly Catalog because GPO could not get enough copies of all titles.

Boni worked closely with the Government Documents Round Table to promote his product. He attended GODORT meetings and sponsored receptions and suites for GODORT. In spite of that close

relationship, GODORT supported GPO producing the same publications in microform for depository libraries.

When I started working at the Joint Committee on Printing, I discovered that the collection of documents being filmed was the property of GPO and was sent to the National Archives for permanent
preservation. After the National Archives informed me that many of
the documents arrived at the Archives damaged from the filming
done by READEX, I informed the staff director of JCP and the public printer. The Library of Congress was told to find another source
of documents for READEX. READEX found another library willing
to loan their documents for filming in return for a set of the microcards. READEX now uses a process that does not damage the documents while they are filmed.

READEX later became part of NewsBank and developed other
publications like AccessUN where United Nations publications are
indexed and the indexes are available on CD-ROM and through the
Internet access. The service provides URL links to the actual full text
documents. One of READEX's creative marketing strategies is to
hold education retreats for librarians at their conference center in
Vermont. The seminars bring librarians and experts on the contents
of the publications together to exchange information.

Greenwood Press

Greenwood Press launched an ambitious effort in 1971 to identify, index, and film documents issued by 153 cities and twenty-
five counties, called the *Index to Current Urban Documents*. Tracking down urban documents is not an easy task. Greenwood
undertook the project with the help of David Beasley, coordinator,
Bibliography Program for City and County Publications at the
New York Public Library (NYPL). He asked his own library and
NYPL's bibliography partners in libraries in other municipalities
and counties to send copies of their publications to the editor for
filming and indexing. In return, libraries received a free silver microfiche copy of every publication they submitted and a discount
on the purchase of the index and the fiche from other urban centers. Greenwood sold the fiche in 1972 as a complete set and as
partial sets covering specified cities and counties. Twenty-nine
years later, the index is available in print, on CD-ROM, and on-

line. Access to the publications is sold by subscription over the Internet in an Adobe Acrobat PDF format.

Aaron L. Fessler, former chief librarian of Bard College, signed on as editor. Beasley served as consulting editor. Greenwood, on the advice of its editors, invited respected librarians in the field of government documents to serve on an advisory board. They included Bernard Fry, dean of the Library School at Indiana University; William Smith, chief librarian at the National League of Cities/U.S. Conference of Mayors; Donald Wisdom, assistant chief of the Serial Division at the Library of Congress; Elsa Freeman, director, Library at the Department of Housing and Urban Development; Joseph Benson, librarian, Joint Reference Library, Chicago; Joyce Malden, librarian, Municipal Reference Library, Chicago; Eugene J. Bockman, director, Municipal Reference and Research Center, New York City; Joyce N. Watson, head, Municipal Reference Library, Toronto, Canada; and me, then the library director at EPA, Kansas City Region.

The librarians participated in the project because their users needed urban documents and it was difficult for libraries acting alone to collect and index them. The editor was paid but the librarians on the board were not (unless you consider sandwiches and drinks at two meetings a year pay). The librarians believed that the benefit to their libraries was worth their efforts. They were successful in lobbying the publishers to provide a service that they could not afford to provide by themselves.

I also worked with Rochelle Field at Greenwood to critique a project it was working on with the Senate Library and a number of congressional committees. Greenwood produced a *Bibliography and Indexes of United States Congressional Committee Prints* covering the Sixty-First through the Ninety-First (1969) Congress. They filmed some four thousand committee prints published during that period. Until 1976, depository libraries were getting very few committee prints. Depositories started receiving most of them after I was assigned by the staff director of the Joint Committee on Printing the task of persuading congressional committees to authorize GPO to distribute prints to depository libraries. Only the Senate and House libraries, Library of Congress, and the National Archives were getting prints, and they were not getting all of them. The Greenwood project worked because government librarians believed that their institution and the public were well served by cooperating with a commercial publisher.

Infordata International Incorporated

One of the more interesting collaborations between commercial publishers, librarians, and government publishers was the production of the *Index to Government Periodicals* by Infordata International Incorporated. Many, but not all, federal government periodicals were sent to depository libraries and sold by the Government Printing Office. Infordata planned on microfiching the 150 periodicals in its index and selling them as a set. Of the 150 titles, some 100 were not indexed in any standard library indexing tool like the *Periodicals Index*. In 1973, Allen Carpenter, editor of the index, and Ivan Waters, publisher of Infordata, wrote to documents librarians describing the proposed reference tool and included a list of the periodicals to be indexed. Librarians were asked whether they supported the project, whether the periodicals chosen were the ones that should be covered in the index, and whether they had other titles to suggest. They were told, "Your response will be helpful in making this publication of the greatest possible reference and research value."

Once Infordata received an enthusiastic response from the survey, well-known documents librarians were invited to serve on an editorial advisory board. At least one of those asked to serve had been active in lobbying Infordata to produce such an index. The board in 1974 included Joe Morehead, School of Library Science at the State University of New York, and a columnist and author of books on documents; Margaret Chisholm, dean, College of Library Science at the University of Maryland; Julia Dees, head, Sociology and Business Departments at the Denver Public Library; Marion Howey, government documents librarian at the University of Kansas; Edwin Johnson, director, Government Documents at Valpariso University; Giles Robertson, head, Public Services Division, University of Illinois Chicago Circle Library; and me, then librarian at the Environmental Protection Agency. As members of the board rotated off, the board continued to attract well-known documents librarians to serve on the board. The board believed that government periodicals were a very under-used resource and that could be remedied by access to a good index.

In 1977, Infordata lobbied the publishers and the editors of the periodicals as a means of assuring their ongoing support of the index. They brought together the editors of some 150 government periodicals with librarians and others for a day-long meeting in Washington, D.C. I moderated the panel that included John C. Boger, director, Office of Information for the Armed Forces, Department of Defense; Sandra Coleman, head of the Reference Department, Library, University of New Mexico; and Henry Lowenstern, Bureau of Labor Statistics, Department of Labor. R. Gordon Hoxie, president of the Center for Study of the Presidency, made the introductory remarks covering the importance of government periodicals as a source of information about a vast number of subjects. The editors of periodicals in attendance were introduced and after the panel presentations there was a spirited discussion about the obstacles government publishers and librarians faced in getting the word out about government periodicals. They all agreed that an index to the periodicals was a valuable aid in promoting their use by the public.

Corporations Fund Think Tanks and Advocacy Organizations

Corporations give money to think tanks and advocacy organizations. In return, the think tank can promote the interests of the corporation by taking a public position that supports the position of the corporation, whereas if the corporation spoke, it would seem self serving. According to a story in the *Washington Post*, "While corporations are prohibited from contributing directly to political candidates, there are no restrictions on their giving to nonprofit organizations such as CSE whose advocacy may help their interests. And though lobbyists representing corporations must register publicly, nonprofit groups are not required to identify the corporations financing their lobbying work."[20] Citizens for a Sound Economy (CSE), founded in 1984, established a foundation that can take tax-deductible contributions and its board voted in 2000 to set up a political action committee with the goal of raising $1 million for candidates. Why should we worry about these think tanks in regard to information policy? One good reason is the lobbying efforts by CSE to convince Congress to limit the Justice Department's budget for antitrust enforcement after receiving $380,000 from Microsoft.[21] And though Microsoft itself set up a foundation to help libraries and others, we must remember that corporations look after their own interests first and those of the public second.

Not all think tanks conceal the names of their contributors, and others are careful not to appear to be controlled by those giving them their money. Others do not engage in outright political activism such as that practiced by CSE.

Coalitions

For-profit institutions and associations form coalitions. For example, during the 1980s a fight over an attempt by the Joint Committee on Printing to revise its regulations to address the use of new technologies, a number of trade and professional associations formed the SPIRIT Coalition (Sensible Policy for Information Resources and Information Technology). Members of these groups were involved in publishing, telecommunications, computer manufacturing, higher education, and business in general. The SPIRIT Coalition issued a statement in 1984 laying out its objections to the proposed regulations:

> The SPIRIT Coalition believes that the interests of economy, efficiency and diversity in the provision of information resources will best be served by reliance on the private sector. While government is necessarily limited to a broad, generalized approach to the creation and dissemination of information, the private sector is uniquely suited to the development of a diversity of product choices tailored to the specialized needs of submarkets. Should the incentives that drive this "free market in ideas" be lost or compromised—for example, by the extension of a subsidized, monolithic government information provider in competition with the industry—the present diversity of information systems could be lost. As a result, the public would lose the benefit of the creative organizational, marketing, and training enhancements added to basic information by various entrepreneurs in the industry, as well as the diversity of ideas inherent in such information—a diversity which is critical to the functioning of our free society. This is a consequence to be avoided at all costs. To that end, SPIRIT submits that the GPO should be confined to its primary role as the Congress' printer, and the Federal Executive Agencies should be permitted to exercise their traditional authority to control their own procedures, including the publication of information, subject, of course, to Congress' continuing authorization, appropriation and oversight.[22]

The SPIRIT Coalition also argued that "an expansive reading of the scope of material that is to be made available to depository libraries could lead to federal expenditures of hundreds of millions of dollars."[23] The coalition further argued that "[t]he proposed limits on government agencies' freedom to contract with private publishers is another area where the guidelines could have a major impact on the public access to government information and on private sector information companies."[24] SPIRIT urged that a comprehensive review of the underlying statutes be initiated and that the "constitutionality of the legislative scheme establishing GPO and the scope of GPO's jurisdiction"[25] be explored.

SPIRIT's dire prediction that expanding the depository library program would cost the government hundreds of millions of dollars did not happen. On the contrary, the entire depository library program, including the dissemination of some 170,000 electronic publications, cost less than $30 million a year in 1999. That sum included other services such as cataloging, training, inspections, and provision of publications in paper, microforms, CD-ROMS, and floppy disks.

MEMBERS OF YOUR OWN GROUP

You must learn how to lobby the members of your own group. That group may be the institution you work for or your professional association. You must understand the power structure of the groups that you are part of in order to influence them. Figure out where in that group you are best able to influence policies.

When I moved from a university library to the executive branch of the federal government, I had to learn a whole new structure. In 1970, I was hired to start a regional library for the Department of Interior Federal Water Quality Control Administration (FWQA). I attended ALA and in the middle of the conference my new job started, so I crossed out my former institution and wrote in my new one. One of the Department of Interior Headquarters librarians spotted the change and told me that she had heard that I had been hired and advised me to work with the personnel officer to make sure that I reported to as high a level as possible, preferably the regional administrator, a political appointee of President Lyndon Johnson. She said the usual practice was to have the librarian report to the head of administration, and at that level I would have little power. I took her advice and lobbied the personnel officer to make my position report directly to the regional administrator. I got the next best thing, reporting to the deputy regional administrator. Being on the same level as all other department heads, I was part of the policymaking team.

I used that position to influence agency wide policies in the area of library service. Several months after I started, all field librarians were sent to Interior headquarters in Washington, D.C., for a week-long workshop. We were surprised to learn that the decision to make FWQA a part of the new Environmental Protection Agency and fold other parts of the Department of the Interior into the new National Oceanic and Atmospheric Administration had precipitated a struggle about what resources would be transferred to the new agencies. Interior's headquarters' library director in D.C. seized the opportunity to transfer staff he did not want to the new agencies but was reluctant to break up the headquarters library collection. We soon-to-be EPA librarians were dismayed to learn that the librarian designated to be our headquarters' librarian was not strong enough to wrest away our fair share of the headquarters library. We later heard that one EPA laboratory director was so determined to have a good library that he and other staff went to their former parent agency library on the weekend and kidnapped the collection, taking it to the new EPA location. When lobbying doesn't work, some people take more direct action!

We soon-to-be EPA librarians decided that one way we could have a say in the new EPA and its policies was to start our own EPA-wide library automation committee. Jean Circiello, the San Francisco regional librarian, and I agreed that what we were able to do at the national meeting was not enough to ensure that our new agency had a good library and decided to do a little lobbying of our own. When we got home, we asked our regional administrators to ask the EPA administrator, William Ruckelshaus, to hire a good librarian for the EPA headquarters. As a result, Sarah M. Thomas (later Kadec) was persuaded to come home from a sabbatical in Israel to take over the headquarters library.

Thomas learned that since she did not control the regional and laboratory librarians and could not tell us what to do, she would have to persuade us. She was quite good at getting us to agree on policies and programs. She knew that when people agree on a policy, they usually work hard to implement it. The committee that we librarians had started at that first joint meeting of EPA librarians showed her that we were capable of creative thinking and taking the initiative. Working together and lobbying the automation staff at EPA allowed us to create an EPA-wide electronic catalog that included the collections of all the libraries. We were one of the first agencies to create such a catalog.

Thomas made sure that the automation staff participated in our meetings and that the programmers and librarians worked together to develop the system. Since most of the programmers were men and the librarians were women, we had a bit of a communication problem at first. We solved that during one of our first marathon working sessions. Seeing a long night ahead of us, the automation staff ordered a case of beer, expecting to take most of it back to their rooms, but after our session there was no beer. The automators were impressed with our ability to drink as well as our knowledge about what makes up a good database. Every group, in order to work well together, needs a catch to help them recognize each other as equals so they can work well together. As librarians we needed something to break the image that the automators had come into the meeting with so they would recognize us as worthy of their trust. Together we created a good automated catalog.

Once the catalog was established and available to EPA users, Thomas persuaded EPA to hold a National Environmental Information Symposium in September 1972. She chaired the committee that designed the program and selected the speakers. The symposium brought together more than 1,700 representatives of industry, government, universities, libraries, professional and trade associations, the press, and citizen action groups. The purpose was to "outline and clarify the difficulties of interchanging information in the myriad forms now available, to present the user of environmental information with a review of the services available, their location, accessibility and cost, and to describe some of the solutions being formulated."[26] The participants met together and in user groups (citizen action, press and publications, industry and trade associations, academia, research organizations and professional societies, and government).

We librarians took the opportunity to lobby all the participants, particularly EPA administrator William Ruckelshaus, about the value of libraries in making environmental information available to the staff of EPA, other government agencies, industry, and the public. We convened an evening meeting of some fifty librarians and formulated recommendations that became part of the final report. We made sure that we had librarians in all the user group sessions so we could answer questions about user access to environmental information.

The final report summarized the access to information concerns of the attendees:

> Much discussion centered around the user fee or other charges levied by organizations, specifically the Federal Government, for information. One user group felt strongly that the Government is obligated to

provide information cost-free to all comers, regardless of levels of detail and volume. However, it was more generally agreed that referral services, accurately directing the potential user to sources of information, should be cost-free, even though some reference services may charge for their services. Regional information centers and libraries could play a role in making the information available free to local users.[27]

One result of our work on the symposium was strong support from the EPA administrator for EPA libraries and librarians. This meant increased financial support for our libraries, paid travel so we could plan and implement our automated systems, and attendance at educational seminars on automation, micropublishing, and cataloging. We were also encouraged to participate in professional library association conferences.

A series of presidents of the American Library Association have lobbied ALA members and other librarians to use the library as a vehicle for shaping public policy issues. Those issues include advocacy and coalition building for community support of libraries, sustainable communities, and democracy. All three issues are of worldwide interest as indicated by a call from IFLA members in 2001 to set up groups to discuss the issues. Sarah Long, former ALA president, put it well when she launched her campaign to encourage libraries to help build sustainable communities:

> People today are hungry for community. Since libraries of all types are often at the geographic center of the communities they serve, they are naturally positioned to be community gathering places. Couple this advantage with the other usual librarian talents: tolerance for diversity of opinion, facilitation skills, familiarity and comfort with new technology, and you have an organization poised to be integral to every community decision. Librarians need to take the next step and act as a catalyst to get people to the table when community decisions are made."[28]

THE MEDIA

The media includes newspapers, journals, television and radio, electronic communications, and specialty publications of all kinds. Using the media is one way of educating the public, legislators, and policymakers about your issue. It is the easiest way to reach a lot of people. It is a way to convince policymakers that many more people than you, your organization or association care about an issue. It is a way to ensure the support of legislators who say they are supporting your position but may have signed on as a sponsor of a bill in order to appear like they are supporting your position, but they have no intention of actively working for the bill. Publicity may encourage them to give your bill more than lip service. On the other hand, you may want adverse publicity to kill a policy or bill that may harm your constituency or issue. Press coverage gets your group known and gives it more clout with the policymakers of your community.

Issue press releases when you testify, when you want to comment on an issue, a bill, regulation, or appropriations request, and when you give a speech. Include a call for action in your press release.

Issue press releases in time for the evening or morning edition of the newspapers, radio, and television news shows. Issue press releases when there is little other news to compete with your news— for example, on weekends or over a holiday.

Hold press conferences during the week. Make your press conference or other activity visual so it will provide a photo opportunity for the newspaper or lively footage for television. For example, a librarian serving in the Montana House asked the House to pass a proclamation declaring March 2 as "Read across Montana Day." She was joined on the floor of the House by a life-sized "Cat in the Hat," a character created by Dr. Seuss to help children learn to read while having fun. She was rewarded with a large photo in the local paper and a spot on the evening television news.

Write a press release as if you were the reporter. Write an opening headline that sums up your story. Write simple short sentences. Keep the release to one page. Type it in an eleven- or twelve-point font and double-space between lines. Refer to your group in the third person. Write for sound bites. The press may only use a part of your press release. Start with the most important part of your story. The first paragraph should include the who, what, where, when, and why information about your news. Clearly identify your group, including the address and phone and fax numbers. Include the name, title, phone number, and e-mail address of a contact person so the reporter can follow up with questions and write the story accurately. Many newspapers now prefer that press releases be e-mailed to them. It makes it easier for them to incorporate the information into their data base. Follow up with a faxed or mailed copy, referring to the e-mail, because sometimes e-mails get lost.

When a reporter calls, first determine whether you are the right person to do the interview. Have a policy about who answers what kind of questions. Determine who answers routine information questions, who discusses policy, and who answers the really difficult questions like "Did you know that your financial officer was stealing from the library?" Determine whether the interviewee should be the chair of the library board, the library director, or the public affairs officer.

Always make the basis of your discussion with a reporter clear from the beginning. Are you going to be on the record, off the record, on background, or on deep background? *Deep background* means that the reporter will not even refer to you as a source connected with a certain office or identify you in any way. If you are leaking information or asking that something be kept off the record, make sure you can trust the reporter to keep your name out of the paper. Reporters do not usually honor requests for off-the-record comments. Some reporters will tell you anything to get a story. They do not care what happens to your relationship with your employer or what effect the story may have on your cause or your job.

Once you agree to an interview, determine what questions you will answer, what questions you will not answer, and why. If you are not going to answer a question, such as "What did the patron read in your library before he set out to mail a letter bomb?" and your library has a policy that patron check out records are private, then be prepared to hand the reporter a copy of the library's policy. If the policy is based on a local ordinance or state or federal law, then provide the legal citation to the law. Write down what you want the reporter to know. Try to limit yourself to three or four key points. Return to those points several times during the interview. Summarize your statement at the end of the interview by returning to the key points. If you are dealing with an aggressive reporter, stay on your topic. Do not allow the reporter to get you to say something you do not want to say. Avoid characterizing another organization's position on an issue because the reporter may misunderstand and report the position as your own. Expect some reporters to misquote you, no matter how much you attempt to educate them. If at all possible, ask to see the story before they print it. This is usually not going to happen, so limit what you say or offer to give them a quote in writing. Do not go off the track in the interview since you risk the reporter emphasizing the side story instead of the one you want covered. Accuracy is essential for your credibility, so if you don't know the answer to a question, offer to find the information and call the reporter back.

If you are being interviewed and taped for radio or television, make your comments concise and be prepared to answer several questions. Usually the reporter will talk to you about the event before the taping or filming starts but will save the actual specific questions for the taped interview. This keeps the interview spontaneous, not canned. If the reporter does not conduct a preinterview, ask for one so you know what the reporter will ask while you are being taped. The taped interview may last for three to ten minutes, but what appears on television could be as short as fifteen seconds.

You can also write letters to the editor. For example, during the struggle to save the federal depository library funding from cuts by the Congress for fiscal year 2001, a depository librarian persuaded one of the board members of the League of Women Voters to write a letter to the editor of the *San Bernardino Sun*. Her letter argued for a multiformat program:

> Just as congressional staff still need to use paper copies for a variety of reasons, constituents still need paper copies of basic federal publications. Books and other print publications are easy to use, are more permanent, cannot be altered by unauthorized people and cannot be damaged by computer viruses. There is a valid place for both paper and electronic copies of government documents. A drastic cut in funding will disrupt the smooth transition to a largely electronic depository program, which provides Internet access to 170,000 federal titles. People are downloading 21 million publications every month—more than 500,000 retrievals per congressional district this year. Increased public use of electronic government information requires more support for libraries, not less. Will our government reduce our opportunity to scrutinize their activities and bury publications and research paid for by our dollars, or will we demand access to these materials through a fully funded GPO and FDLP?[29]

If you have a good human interest angle, call the feature editor. Or call the editor and ask him or her to write an editorial about your issue. Make sure you give the editor enough information so the editorial will be written to favor your position. This approach could backfire since the editor may send a reporter out to interview those who hold the opposing position. Better yet, write an editorial yourself and see whether your paper will publish it.

I got a good lesson in how newspapers decide what to publish from Randall Jesse, public affairs officer at EPA, with whom I shared an office. Knowing about his close relationship with the staff of the *Kansas City Star*, I asked him to get a story about ALA executive director Robert Wedgeworth's visit to Kansas City into the paper. He declined, saying he was not going to use his chits with the paper. He suggested that I ask someone else to contact the paper. I thought that the news about Wedgeworth was worthy of coverage because not only was he a former resident of the Kansas City area but the first black named to his post.

Newspapers

Newspapers are interested in current news, so contact them when an issue is hot or something important has happened. Newspapers are under the control of a publisher and an editor. Newspapers employ different types of writers, including reporters, investigators, columnists, and cartoonists. Some of their reporters write just for that newspaper or all the newspapers in a chain of newspapers. Some reporters may be nationally syndicated and do not work for any particular paper, but their column appears in many papers. Writers employed by one newspaper or a chain have restrictions placed on them by their editors and may not be as free to write what they want as freelance writers and columnists.

Build a long-term relationship with the editorial board and the reporters so when issues arise, they know you and have a positive image of your institution or association. Try to influence all of them. In 1973, I called Mike Causey at the *Washington Post* and told him about government documents distributed to depository libraries being recalled by the government. He told me that it was a "sexy" story and mentioned it in his regular column "The Federal Diary" in the *Washington Post*. I called him because allies in D.C. had been sending me articles he had written on problems with documents distribution at the Government Printing Office. Several of them had called him and given him information about problems with the depository library program.

The Editorial Board

Every newspaper has an editorial board, usually composed of the publisher, managing editor, and other editors depending on the size and organizational structure of the paper. It is important to establish an ongoing friendly relationship with the editorial board. Call the publisher or managing editor and ask him or her to meet with you so you can brief him or her on the activities of your library, Friends of the Library group, or whatever organization you are representing. When a story, positive or negative, breaks, the paper will know whom to contact. The paper also will be more likely to think about your organization in a favorable light. This is particularly important when a negative event occurs.

For example, when the Friends of the Lewis & Clark Library in Helena, Montana, decided to hold a big fund-raiser for the library, they met with the editorial board of the local newspaper. The newspaper included their project in "Celebrate 2000," gave them the centerfold of the weekly events section of the newspaper, and covered the series of events as news stories ending up with a front-page photo of the mural painted by five cartoonists and hundreds of schoolchildren. When the Friends met with the board, they came prepared with a letter outlining what they would like the paper to do to support the fund-raiser. They also gave the board an update on the library's needs and what the money would do for the library. It took follow-up calls and visits to make sure that most of the requested stories were published. The Friends also issued press releases to keep the media up-to-date on events as they occurred.

General Reporters

General reporters must write about a lot of subjects and are not necessarily experts in any of them. Reporters usually write a story on one event and have a short turnaround time. They interview people connected with that one event. Be prepared to provide background information and answer questions. Be sure you give them in writing as much factual information as possible. Your news must be timely and newsworthy, but the paper will decide what is newsworthy. It helps if there is some kind of conflict between opposing viewpoints and you can provide the names of people from both sides who will provide information and quotes. Reporters are people and should be treated with respect. They are more likely to listen to you and take the time to understand the story if you treat them well.

If you have a story, go directly to the reporter who usually covers your issue or organization. The reporter can then take credit with his or her editor for the idea and is more likely to write a positive story. A reporter covering your area may be more likely to understand the issue. If this reporter consistently covers your issue in an unfriendly manner or gets the facts and quotes wrong, then try to find another reporter.

Two stories covering the proposed 62 percent cut to funding for federal depository libraries in fiscal year 2001 are good examples of librarians going to reporters and persuading them to cover a current story. In the first story, reporter Erwin Seba in the June 1, 2000, edition of the *Lawrence* (Kans.) *Journal-World* interviewed librarians in four depository libraries and staff of two Kansas members of the U.S. House, and he gave a brief sketch on the number and services of federal depository libraries in Kansas. He quoted Donna Koepp, librarian at University of Kansas: "I'm afraid we're headed for a new Dark Ages. Public access to government information goes to the core of democracy. Thomas Jefferson must be rolling over in his grave." Koepp was well prepared with a sound bite. This article was circulated to others in Kansas, including the University lobbyists.

In the second story reported by Tom Guarisco in the *Advocate ON-LINE: Capital City Press*, May 19, 2000, Baton Rouge, Louisiana, the headline was an eye-catcher: "Librarians blast federal plan to cut records program." The reporter interviewed several librarians and the chief of staff of the chair of the House Appropriations Committee. Even though the chair had sponsored the cuts and pushed them through the committee, his staffer was already backtracking with the following statement:

> The cuts are still proposals, and are far from becoming final. Taylor said, "This is round two of a 10-round fight." Congress is considering the cuts because the committee responsible for drafting the House budget was under a resolution to cut overall Legislative funding by $94 million, or about 5.5 percent. For the cuts to pass they would have to survive House and Senate debate. There is a good chance federal documents funding will be restored by Oct. 1, when the budget is done.

The reporter then added, "Still, librarians are taking no chances. They have peppered their congressmen with e-mails and letters urging them to fund the federal documents program."

I doubt that the chair of the Appropriations Committee's staffer would have made such a statement without the librarians lobbying to change the representative's mind. Getting a call from a reporter from her or his local newspaper sometimes influences a member to rethink her or his position. Writing letters to the legislator and then getting the press to follow up with questions is a good two-pronged strategy.

Investigative Reporters

An investigative reporter is usually covering an issue rather than one event and has several weeks to as long as a year to complete the story. An investigative reporter interviews many people and reviews documentation. These reporters often use freedom of information laws to uncover information. Most work for a newspaper, but some of them are independent freelancers who write a story and then try to sell it to a newspaper or some other type of media outlet.

Investigative reporters may develop their own ideas, or they may be assigned an issue by an editor. Reporters tend to listen to all types of conversations, always looking for a story or hoping to hear something that will help them with their current story. Some reporters concentrate on uncovering corruption and corrupt officials, while others concentrate on issues.

During my time on the Hill, I was approached by several investigative reporters asking me to give them inside information about the members of Congress for whom I worked. These reporters approached me because we hung out at the same restaurants, had mutual friends, or attended the same parties. I refused to provide that information for several reasons. First, it was not ethical to reveal details about the personal lives of members for whom I worked, particularly while I was working for them. Second, much of the information that I had was secondhand, told to me by other staffers who worked for those members, and I had no way of verifying the truth of those statements. Working closely with other staff on a committee can lead to the sharing of secrets about the member of Congress who appointed them to the job. Sometimes other staffers are the only ones who can understand what is going on and why. It is wise to keep those secrets. If you violate another staffer's trust, it is unlikely that he or she will help you when you need support and it could jeopardize his or her job or even your own. Once a staffer confided in me about the activities of his boss during a campaign and said he wanted to talk to the reporter investigating his boss. He then changed his mind because he was afraid to talk and made me promise that I would not give his name to anyone. I did not reveal his name to the reporter. Another staffer with whom I shared an office was hounded by reporters trying to get her to talk about the member who appointed her. I did sometimes use the reporter's request as an opportunity to lobby them on behalf of free public access to government information and the depository library program.

Columnists

Columnists can take a longer look at issues, and you can take more time in educating them. They have deadlines but are probably working on several columns at the same time or at least thinking about future ones.

You may become a columnist yourself. You can write a guest column about a particular issue. When the Fund Our Library's Future Committee wanted to get information about the campaign to convince the voters to support an emergency mill levy for the Lewis & Clark Library into the newspaper, its chair, Tracy Velazquez, wrote a "Your Turn" editorial for the *Helena Independent Record (IR)*. She did such a good job that she was quoted by Stephen Ambrose when he gave a lecture on his book *Citizen Soldiers* at a fund-raiser for the library. He particularly liked her argument "A great library sends a message: this community cares about its future, and it cares about the quality of life for the people that live there. We need to be sending this message to those that we depend on for our city's continued prosperity and health. A vote for the library this November will be a vote for our library's—and our community's—future."[30]

Molly Ivins wrote a powerful column in the *Star Telegram* about the controversy over providing the e-rate to libraries and schools. Under the e-rate program, phone companies would give libraries a lower rate than other institutional users. The following paragraphs will give you a flavor of her message, which I am convinced helped save that program:

As though determined to prove that the film *Bulworth* has not an ounce of exaggeration in it, the powerful telecom lobby is now putting pressure on members of Congress who owe it a lot to get the industry out of the only redeeming feature of the *1996 Telecommunications Act*. The phone companies are trying to weasel out of a commitment they made in '97 to subsidize the cost of connecting schools and libraries to the Internet.

The industry said the act would promote competition and lower cable rates, among other joys. As you know, it touched off a tidal wave of communications company mergers and has resulted in higher cable rates than ever, phone slamming and other noxious practices. In that horror of a bill was one bit of redeeming social value: the E-rate to help connect schools to the Net. But now the long-distance firms, such as AT&T and MCI Communications Corp., are claiming that the program—funded by fees collected by the Federal Communications Commission—is too expensive, and they intend to pass the charges on to the consumer.

We know what's wrong with the phone companies: greed. But what so addles our elected representatives that they would deliberately harm schools, libraries and rural health centers in their own districts?

This is a singularly disgusting example of corporate greed, made more disgusting by the fact that some of our elected representatives are going along with it. I do hope the ones who are doing so get very large campaign contributions from the industry; maybe it will make them feel better about selling out their constituents.[31]

Journals

Library and information associations, commercial publishers, and governments are responsible for most journals published for librarians and information professionals. The American Library Association and its divisions and round tables publish many of the journals for librarians. They include *American Libraries, Public Libraries, Information Technology and Libraries, Journal of Youth Services in Libraries, Library Administration and Management, College & Research Libraries, Choice, RBM: A Journal of Rare Books, Manuscripts, and Cultural Heritage, Library Resources and Technical Services, Reference and Users Services Quarterly,* and *Meridian*. The Progressive Librarians Guild publishes *Progressive Librarian: A Journal for Critical Studies & Progressive Politics in Librarianship*. Journals published by commercial publishers include *Library Journal (LJ)* , *School Library Journal (SLJ)*, *Government Publications Review,* and *Government Information Quarterly*. Both *LJ* and *SLJ* are available online.

Scholarly journals feature articles that have been reviewed and critiqued by other specialists in the field. If these journals do not ordinarily cover issues of importance to you or your group, you should lobby them to do so. You might even have to agree to write the articles or provide the information on a regular basis. Lobby the chief editor as well as the reporters and columnists for these journals.

The Government Documents Round Table in 1978 was concerned that *Library Journal*, one of the key selection tools for librarians ordering material for libraries, seldom reviewed or publicized government documents. GODORT convinced *Library Journal* to publish an annual list of notable government documents nominated by documents librarians. Publication in this well-read journal helps publicize government documents, encourages publishing agencies and their staff to publish documents of value to libraries, and publicizes the work of GODORT.

Association and Special Niche
Newsletters and Other Regular Publications

Newsletters published by associations and institutions are used to get information out quickly to their members and others interested in the work of those groups. They are published more frequently than journals. Many of these newsletters are available in paper and electronically. Seldom do articles published in these newsletters undergo peer review, although they are edited by the editor. Many newsletters publish the schedule, agendas, and minutes of meetings. They publish the reports of units, including speeches given at programs. They are often used to alert members when lobbying is needed and to educate them about issues and the organization's policies.

Libraries and Friends of the Library groups publish newsletters as well as annual reports, brochures, and news releases. Sally Gardner Reed, in *Making the Case for Your Library: A How to Do It Manual*, argues:

> It occurred to me then that librarians who are already very savvy at marketing their services were just one short step away from using these same vehicles to promote the importance of libraries in a powerful, ongoing way. We are already designing, developing and publishing materials for our public. Why not use these same materials to be more politically effective? Instead of just focusing on increasing use, why not focus on increasing support as well?[32]

Reed gives lots of examples of effective newsletters, brochures, and other materials in her book as well as advice on promotional campaigns of all types.

The American Library Association publishes *ALA Washington News* monthly and make it available on their website, but for urgent and late-breaking news it issues *ALAWON* via e-mail. ALA also issues news releases in paper and through e-mail. During ALA conferences, attendees publish *Cognotes*, a daily newsletter covering programs, speeches, controversies, and vendors.

Most of the units in ALA also publish newsletters. Some of them are comprehensive enough to almost qualify as journals. *Documents to the People (DTTP)*, published by the Government Documents Round Table, is an example of a newsletter that also carries special articles, bibliographies, and other material more often found in a journal. GODORT uses *DTTP* as an educational and advocacy tool. A series of dedicated and creative editors have educated librarians, publishers, government officials, and the public about the documents world—a world that before *DTTP* was considered pretty much a mystery and best left to the experts. *DTTP* editors learned that they could influence the course of policy by (1) reporting about events, meetings, resolutions, programs, people; (2) documenting policy development efforts; (3) providing a forum for opposing opinions; and (4) advocating for positions adopted by GODORT. At times *DTTP* published information about government activities that an investigative reporter would have envied.

Base line is published by the ALA Map and Geography Round Table (MAGERT) six times a year. It provides current information on cartographic materials, other publications of interest to map and geography librarians, meetings, related government activities, and map librarianship. A recent issue of *base line* summarized the presentations by government agencies made to the Cartographic Users Advisory Council meeting in Washington, D.C. A more memorable and amusing aspect of each issue is the cartoon "Great Moments in Map Librarianship," created by Jim Coombs.

Within the library profession, a number of librarians cover meetings of librarians and others, and their reports are published in library newsletters. Since many newsletters come out some time after the event, these reporters often share their reports on electronic discussion groups allowing those not attending meetings to learn quickly about current issues. The whole community can discuss the issue and take prompt action in order to shape the outcome. LeRoy Schwartzkopf and Susan Tulis were very good at capturing the essence of meetings in an objective and interesting manner.

Many government agencies publish newsletters. Most of them are intended for internal audiences but some agencies who have extensive interaction with the public publish newsletters for their constituents. A good example is *Administrative Notes: Newsletter of the Federal Depository Library Program* published by the Superintendent of Documents Library Programs Service at GPO. It is available in paper, microfiche, and through the Internet. It contains news about GPO and other government agencies activities and programs, reports of the Depository Library Council to the public printer, requests for information, testimony given by GPO officials to Congress, appropriations requests, and other information of interest to the depository library community.

Other newsletters concentrate on special subject areas such as information policy, library activities, and news affecting libraries and library policies. *The Unabashed Librarian*, *Library Hotline*, and *News from Nowhere* are examples of newsletters geared primarily toward librarians. *Electronic Public Information Newsletter* is an example of a newsletter geared to the whole information community. The Corporate Library (update) and News Briefs are online resources that help libraries keep track of the activities of corporations and those bodies that monitor them.

The *Unabashed Librarian* subtitled "how I run my library good" letter is published four times a year and is intended to help those running libraries. Topics range from advice on how to keep up to date with what is on the Internet, to librarians self censoring library collections, and to how to lobby. *Unabashed* encourages its subscribers and others to contribute news and articles of a practical nature. Maurice Freedman, the current publisher and editor, is building on the work of the late Marvin Scilken, beloved creator of the newsletter. There are also several contributing editors who write regular columns.

Library Hotline is the weekly newsletter published by *Library Journal* and *School Library Journal*. It publishes news too hot to wait such as recent library contracts, lawsuits, levy elections, donations to libraries, current legislation, and disasters.

Electronic Public Information Newsletter covers policies, legislation, regulations, and programs dealing with electronic government information. Each issue also contains an opinion piece meant to influence policy written by the editor or a guest editor. In the October 1996 issue, the editor commented on the Government Printing Reform Act of 1996 (H.R. 4280), a bill introduced by Representative Bill Thomas (R-Calif.) to decentralize federal printing and procurement and to change the way depository libraries receive information:

> But we don't believe the Thomas bill provides enough safeguards to assure the continued free distribution of government information. If electronic information can be made readily available to the nation's depository libraries, the same is true for the nation as a whole. The Thomas bill needs to be strengthened to make it clear that the Superintendent of Documents, and hence, Congress, intends to create a robust dissemination system of government information not only for depository libraries but for the public at large via the Internet. The report prepared by the GPO on the transition of the depository library program to an electronic format grasped this central fact. It would be well for Thomas and his Committee to reread that study.[33]

The Hightower Lowdown is a newsletter that covers politics, including how information policies and programs influence politics. Jim Hightower not only produces a newsletter but covers events such as the World Trade Organization (WTO) protests in person through his radio program and writes about them later in his newsletter. In his newsletter, he answered the question as to what the protests in Seattle over the WTO meeting achieved:

> For starters, the light of public awareness was shined for the first time into the dark cave of the WTO and into the blinking eyes of its startled corporate creators. They will never be the same. Like my cab driver, the general public has now heard of the WTO and is at least generally aware that there is something so wrong with it that tens of thousands of people would go out of their way to put their bodies on the line against it. As Seattle showed, people worldwide know that voting, writing to your representative, and other traditional avenues of democratic expression increasingly are exercises in futility, and citizens are not going to be satisfied with anything less than participation in the decision making that affects their lives.[34]

Other types of regular publications keep the information community, including the press, informed about what is happening in the information world. One of the most useful was *Less Access to*

Less Information by and about the U.S. Government compiled and published by the ALA Washington office from 1981 to 1998. The majority of the work on this publication was done by Anne Heanue. She read widely to uncover and summarize actions by government and others to affect public policy in the area of information publishing, dissemination, and access. She had an uncanny ability to recognize trends in policy and actions that were seriously threatening the public's access to government information. Many journalists and others sorely miss her valuable publication.

Independent Writers

Independent writers are those who stand outside the institutional control of the established press and are free to violate the cultural and institutional barriers to telling a story truthfully and completely. Some of course are biased, and it is best to read a number of authors in order to learn about several sides of the issue. Some writers, like Vigdor Schreibman, M. B. Schnapper, and Jim Hightower, become their own publishers. Others, like David Burnham, Donna Demac, Eve Pell, and Anita Schiller, find publishers who will publish what they write without changing it. They write about how information is created, the struggle about who controls it, and the technological means used to create and disseminate it. They write about the role of writers, publishers, libraries, government, educational institutions, corporations, and the public in the ongoing struggle over what and how much information the public will have the chance to read. Writers use whatever means is available to share their ideas, studies, and investigations. They publish books and reports; write articles for journals, newsletters, and newspapers; present papers at conferences and seminars; and give interviews to reporters.

Some authors, like Vigdor Schreibman, do most of their publishing over the Internet. One of the first online investigative reporters, Schreibman started out as co-publisher of the *Electronic Public Information Newsletter (EPIN)*. He covered electronic dissemination and communication technology developments in the legislative, executive, and judicial branches as well as activities of the private sector. He later launched his own independent online news service called FINS. The Executive Committee of the Congressional Periodical and Press Galleries refused to renew his congressional press credentials when he left *EPIN* and started FINS. Credentials are needed to sit in the press galleries of the Senate and the House and get preference for admittance to hearings and press conferences. As I said earlier, it is often difficult to get into hearings unless you are staff or press. The Executive Committee argued that Schreibman no longer met the requirements under sections 1 and 2 of the rules regarding the press galleries, such as working for a profit-making periodical. Schreibman sued but was unable to convince the courts to interfere with a congressional decision. He argued in court that the denial of his credentials was because of his ongoing criticism of the establishment press and the actions of the Congress. His brief gives a fascinating history of who receives credentials to cover the Congress.[35]

Electronic Online Networks Such as the Internet

According to Charles Levendosky, member of the board of the Freedom to Read Foundation and newspaper columnist for the Casper, Wyoming, *Star-Tribune:*

> The Internet is the most democratic medium of mass communication yet invented. . . . The Internet and free access to it in public schools and public libraries gives even the economically disadvantaged in our communities the ability to send their messages across the world. Anyone can be a widely read pamphleteer. . . . The Internet has the inherent ability to overcome the social and economic monopolies of power that often control other media. It guarantees that numerous minority viewpoints in any public discussion will be expressed.[36]

Tim Berners-Lee, inventor of the World Wide Web, explains how the web can be used to lobby:

> The Web is more a social creation than a technical one. I designed it for a social effect—to help people work together—and not as a technical toy. The ultimate goal of the Web is to support and improve the weblike existence in the world. We clump into families, associations and companies. We develop trust across the miles and distrust around the corner. What we believe, endorse, agree with, and depend on is representable and, increasingly, represented on the Web. We all have to ensure that the society we build with the Web is of the sort we intend.[37]

Ralph Reed, in his book *Active Faith*, explains why the Christian Coalition was successful in influencing legislation by using technology:

> Neither Old Right nor New Right, these activists make up the Virtual Right, the electronic grassroots of the future. Rather than walk

precincts and lick envelopes, they surf cyberspace and dispatch e-mail
with the click of a mouse. The entire "leave us alone" coalition is getting in on the act: pro-lifers, anti-tax groups, conservative Christians,
home schoolers, small businessmen, and gun advocates. . . . The Internet and its online bulletin boards and web pages allow conservatives
to express and exchange ideas without passing through the filter of the
press. Because millions of religious conservatives either are stay-at-
home mothers or operate small businesses out of their homes, the computer, fax, and modem are as much a part of their daily lives as the telephone. The blending of those high-tech tools with politics is a natural
evolution. Finally, the information highway gives religious conservatives what they have always lacked: a sense that their movement
represents the future, not a frozen snapshot of the past. . . . The pro-
family movement of today owes more of a debt to Buck Rogers than to
Elmer Gantry.[38]

By using this technology, the Christian Coalition was able to defeat
one bill by activating some two hundred thousand activists within
seventy-two hours who then notified others by phone trees that
generated close to a million messages to the Hill.[39]

Electronic Discussion Sites

Electronic discussion and alerting sites are a very powerful way of
informing supporters of your cause and encouraging visitors to your
site to discuss the issues and take action when needed. It is a fast
way to let people know when to write, e-mail, and fax and to provide them with sample letters, names of people to be lobbied, and
feedback concerning what is happening during the lobbying effort.

There are library and public interest sites on the national, state, and
local levels. Most library associations have sites as do many of their
sub units. Make sure that you keep a list of appropriate sites, and be
prepared to send out your message to as many of them as possible. If
you are not a recognized member of a discussion group, identify
someone on it who will agree to forward your requests for action.

THE PUBLIC

Organizing citizen support for a policy, regulation, bill, or funding is
the most crucial part of lobbying. If you want lasting political clout,

you need an organization of active citizens. If you are lobbying on be-half of a professional association or other group, you will want to cul-tivate citizen groups (e.g., Friends of the Library) to assist you in lob-bying for libraries and the public's access to information. Many of them do not know that they can help assure good libraries and ade-quate and equitable access to information. A widespread chain of ac-tivist librarians and library users is important, so legislators and poli-cymakers know that it is not just a small group of people in the capital city of the nation, state, county, or city who care about the issue.

Citizen support depends on a system for letting citizens know what needs to be done and when. Once we had only telephone trees, but now we have fax and e-mail trees. For these trees to work, a structure needs to be established with people who, when you call them, will actually pick up the phone or send an e-mail or a fax to start the tree growing. It is like the old quilting bee, a group of peo-ple are committed to a project and willing to spend time and energy to complete it. Periodically review who is on your lists and whether they are structured in a way to get your message out to your sup-porters. Encourage your members to establish their own lists of peo-ple not on most lists who will lobby on certain issues if requested to do so by a friend or respected colleague. They can include retired colleagues, family, friends, and other professionals who are not di-rectly involved on a daily basis with your issue.

A telephone, e-mail, or fax tree needs to be organized into units. A tree can be organized (1) geographically on the international, na-tional, state, county, city, or legislative districts level; (2) by subject areas, so that a person who is an expert in the subject will be able to explain the issue to others on the tree or to the policy person; or (3) by organizations. The tree needs a unit leader and a back-up unit leader in case the first person is unavailable.

If the issue is too technical, do not initiate a citizen tree, rely on the experts in your group to make calls to the policymakers. Use a few knowledgeable people who can state that they represent many oth-ers. You can fax or e-mail an explanation to the tree participants to help them understand what to say. Concentrate on one issue at a time. Neither the callers nor the policy people can deal easily with more than one issue. Make sure that the first person on the tree gets accurate information. Some groups have been very successful in putting up information, sample letters, and the addresses of policy-makers on websites. The American Library Association has made it

very easy for people to come to its website, where they can modify
a letter to personalize it and then send it from the ALA web page to
the person to be lobbied. ALA keeps updating these information/ac-
tion pages depending on the issues.

It is important to give tree participants enough information to
speak intelligently about an issue, regulation, or bill. For example, if
the topic at hand concerns a bill, give the bill number, sponsor, a
brief title, summary, status, and how long advocates have to lobby.
They also need to know whether to contact members of a committee, their own elected representative, or the governor. If possible,
give both the regular and e-mail addresses and phone and fax numbers of the policymaker to be contacted.

To set up a tree, you need to canvass the membership of the group
you are asking to help. Find out who is willing to be a unit leader
and who is willing to simply make several contacts. Determine
whether he or she is to be contacted at home or work, what times he
or she is available to receive calls, and how many calls or other contacts he or she is willing to make. Prepare a complete listing of the
members of your tree. Update it on a regular basis. Make sure that
all the unit leaders get copies of the complete listing. Make sure that
everyone on the tree has information about where to get current and
updated information. Publicize the tree in your newsletters and
other publications.

Let your communication tree know the results of the lobbying effort. Ask them to thank legislators and policymakers if they deliver
and admonish them if they do not. This feedback inspires the tree
people to participate the next time, because they know that their
visit, call, e-mail, letter, or fax made a difference. Remember to thank
the people on the tree for their work.

Local

On the local level it is essential to establish a citizen group supporting libraries and access to information. It is too late to do it, in
most cases, when the crisis occurs. The group should meet regularly,
educate itself about the issues, work with professionals, and be organized so it can act when needed.

In most cases, the group that supports the library on a regular basis is called the Friends of the Library. Friends groups provide a fo-
cal point for those who wish to support the library in some manner.

They keep the public informed about the activities of the library, organize educational programs and fund-raisers, publish newsletters, attend library board meetings, testify at budget and appropriations hearings on behalf of the library, and write letters to the newspaper on library issues.

Other groups with local chapters such as the League of Women Voters and the American Association of University Women often will take on library issues as one of their interests. Local service groups will sometimes work on library issues, particularly when a library needs a levy increase or a new building. The League of Women Voters runs DemocracyNet (dnet.org), a free voter information service that covers national, state, and local elections. It is a good source for information on issues, ballot measures, debate between candidates, and candidates.

When aggressive political actions must be taken to assist the library, such as increasing the number of mills levied on behalf of the library, in many states a separate political action committee must be established to do the work of campaigning for the votes of the electorate. Often complicated political practices must be followed to show where the money comes from and how it is spent. Take time before you actually set up the group to learn the rules. It is much harder to backtrack and undo errors than to do it right in the first place. Doing it wrong could even jeopardize the outcome of an election, so check with the appropriate political practices office before you set up a bank account or spend any money. For example, Montana has a commissioner of political practices appointed by the governor and subject to confirmation by the Montana Senate. The Montana campaign finance and practices laws are published in the *Montana Code Annotated* and the administrative rules in the *Administrative Rules of Montana*.

Sometimes a political group's desire to improve library services can lead to the formation or revitalization of a group that can devote its full attention to the library's needs. What happened in Lewis & Clark County, Montana, is a good example of how activism on the part of a political party can set in motion a chain of events that greatly benefits the library and its community of users.

When I moved to Helena, Montana, my cousin Shirley Bachini convinced me to join the Lewis & Clark Democratic Women's Club. At my first meeting, I was elected regional director for three counties and therefore became a member of the State Democratic Women's

Club executive board. Several members of our county club are retired librarians. One of them Margaret Crennan, a retired high
school librarian, and I convinced the club that holding a fund-raiser
for our public library would be a good project. Crennan and I organized a Montana authors book fair and party for the spring of
1996. We convinced local public officials and political candidates to
contribute autographed posters, books, and political buttons for a
silent auction. Rather than thanking the political club for their support, local officials were worried that the public would realize that
they were planning on cutting the library's budget once again in order to fund other priorities. The Lewis & Clark County Democratic
Central Committee supported the women's club with a resolution of
its own urging full funding for the library. The Central Committee
invited the mayor and the city and county commissioners to a meeting to talk about how increased funding could be provided. At the
meeting, the mayor asked why the committee had not invited the
sheriff and the fire chief to testify about their budgets. The Central
Committee members responded that it looked like someone in government was looking out for those departments while the library's
budget had been cut for the last couple of years.

The Democratic Women's Club wanted to go on to other projects
so Crennan and I decided to work with Deborah Schlesinger, the library director, to reenergize the Friends of the Library. The Friends
had not had a membership meeting in several years, and most of the
work was being done by an exhausted chair. After she stepped
down, I was elected chair and Tracy Velazquez was elected secretary
and newsletter editor. Velazquez had a background in fund-raising
and newsletter editing for public interest groups. As Friends, we decided we were not going to waste our time raising money for new
chairs for the deck of a sinking library. Instead, we persuaded the library board, the city and county commissioners, and eventually the
voters of Lewis & Clark County to support a mill increase that dra-
matically increased the library's funding.

As Friends, we waged a political campaign to educate the policymakers of the county as well as the voters as to the fragile state of
the library. Users of the library already knew that reference books,
periodicals, and book collections were out of date; that access to
electronic information was almost nonexistent; that the electronic
support system for the catalog was in desperate need of updating;
and the doors seemed to be locked more often than not. What library

users also needed to know was that as voters they could change that by voting for an increased mill levy, which would result in a library worthy of the capital city of Montana.

As chair of the Friends, I convinced Linda Stoll, a former county commissioner—the only one at that time ever elected twice to that position—to testify with me at the county commission budget hearing on the need for increased funding for the library. It took work to convince her to testify. I showed her that the library budgets for the last ten years had been consistently cut and as a result library services were also cut. The library director had held the library together with grants and good management, but it was harder and harder to get grants. After our testimony, the library budget was not cut, but it was not increased either. Stoll advised me that the only way to get an increased budget was to get a levy increase on the county ballot. The city and county shared in the funding for the library, and the commissioners were convinced that the public would not support additional funds from the general budget for the library.

That is when we as Friends decided to launch our campaign. We first had to convince the Library Board to ask the County Commission to put the levy on the ballot in 1998. State law did not permit a long-term mill levy, only an emergency levy. We Friends later joined the Montana Library Association in convincing the Montana legislature to change the law so a long-term levy could be placed on the ballot.

In 1998, the Friends and the Library Board established a political action committee called Fund Our Library's Future (FOLF) to run a political campaign to persuade the community to vote for an emergency mill levy. Neither the Friends nor the Library Board under Montana law could run a political campaign, but we could volunteer as individuals to work on an action committee. Velasquez and two other young mothers agreed to cochair the committee. The political action committee worked with the Library Board and the Friends to identify the needs of the community for library services and the amount of money needed to meet those needs. The Library Board with the help of the Friends convinced the county commissioners to put the levy on the ballot.

Once the Lewis & Clark County Commission agreed to put the mill levy on the ballot, the Fund Our Library's Future Committee enlisted the help of the community. Stephen Ambrose, author of *Undaunted Courage* and many other popular books, part-time resident of Helena, and frequent user of the library, agreed to be the honorary chair.

The Fund Our Library's Future Committee

- wrote to potential donors of dollars, enlisted a treasurer familiar with the political practices laws, and launched a publicity campaign to educate the voters about the plight of the library;
- wrote a campaign flyer using information from a plan developed by the library board for improving the library;
- enlisted a talented designer, Marty Lord, to develop a striking logo of two children reading and then used the logo for flyers, informational brochures, yard signs, and newspaper ads;
- wrote op-ed pieces for the newspaper, met with the local paper's editorial board, asked people to write letters to the editor, and paid for a newspaper ad listing the signatures of local supporters;
- with library board members, spoke to civic, public interest, senior citizen, parent, and teachers groups to enlist their support;
- thanks to a grant from Art Ortenberg and Liz Claiborne, bought television and radio ads featuring Ambrose and users of the library; and
- ran a telephone bank the weekend before the vote.

The levy passed, much to the surprise of the mayor and the commissioners. In 2000, armed with legislation permitting an ongoing seven-year levy, the Fund Our Library's Future Committee II emerged with just as much determination as the first FOLF to fight for the financial stability of the library. This time the committee could point to the benefits from the passage of the emergency levy, which included new public use electronic terminals, current reference tools, reinstated periodicals, new books, and multimedia products as reasons for voting for an ongoing levy.

FOLF II was again blessed with the honorary chairmanship of Stephen Ambrose, who starred in and partially financed radio and television ads promoting the levy. Art Ortenberg and Liz Claiborne came through with another generous donation. Glenda Bradshaw and I cochaired the committee. It was just as much of a struggle to convince the community of the need for a tax increase as it was in 1998. Many voters assumed that financial support for the library had been secured in 1998 and did not realize that if the 2000 levy did not pass, the library would be forced to drastically cut the hours open to the public, reduce staffing, and stop buying new books and videos. FOLF II used the same committee name and logo because the voters were already familiar with them. Since every statewide office was being contested because of term limits and many people were committed to other campaigns, it was hard to get volunteers. In spite of the obstacles, the levy passed thanks to a committee and a community that believed in their library.

National

There are many activist citizen groups on the national level, but few consider the viability of libraries and the public's access to information their priority. Following is a brief description of several groups who work for libraries and librarians.

The national Friends of Libraries U.S.A. (FOLUSA) provides assistance and information about advocacy, fund-raising, and organization management to local friends of libraries groups.[40] You can read how Friends groups around the country have organized and managed their groups and supported their libraries in *Friends of Libraries Sourcebook* by Sandy Dolnick.

FOLUSA meets in conjunction with the American Library Association. In 2002, Sally Reed, librarian and member of the ALA executive board, became the executive director of FOLUSA. FOLUSA presents an annual award called "Friend of the Year." It also publishes *Friends in Action III*, a bimonthly news update, and fact sheets.

The Freedom to Read Foundation was established "to promote and protect freedom of speech and freedom of the press; to protect the public's right of access to libraries; to support the right of libraries to collect and make available any creative work they may legally acquire; and to supply legal counsel and otherwise support libraries and librarians suffering injustices due to their defense of freedom of speech and of the press."[41]

The LeRoy C. Merritt Humanitarian Fund was established, among other reasons, to provide financial support for librarians threatened with loss of their jobs for their "stand for the cause of intellectual freedom, including promotion of freedom of the press, freedom of speech, and the freedom of librarians to select items for their collections from all over the world's written and recorded word."[42] Since its inception in 1970, the fund has provided over

$80,000 in grants to support librarians in their fight for intellectual freedom and professional integrity. Some of the individuals who received grants include (1) a school librarian who was denied tenure in a small-town district for vague reasons although she believed it was based on her stands for intellectual freedom, (2) a medical librarian who was terminated without just cause, and (3) a public librarian who did not support the library board's request to restrict children's access to the adult section of the library and was forced to resign.[43] The Merritt Fund maintains a website at merritt@ala.org.

Both the Freedom to Read Foundation and the Merritt Fund were established by the American Library Association and share the services of Judith Krug, executive director of the ALA Office of Intellectual Freedom.

NOTES

1. Paul Wellstone, *The Conscience of a Liberal: Reclaiming the Compassionate Agenda* (New York: Random House, 2001), 163.

2. Ronald Kessler, *Inside Congress* (New York: Pocket Books, 1997), 83.

3. Oswaldo Zavala, "Despite Lack of Funding, Congressional Hispanic Caucus Moves Forward," *Kansas City Star*, December 28, 1999, B7.

4. Cynthia E. Bower, "Summary and Analysis of Sabbatical Activities, 9/86–3/87," unpublished manuscript, May 1987, 1.

5. Bower, "Summary and Analysis," 2.

6. *Government Information as a Public Asset*, hearing before the Joint Committee on Printing, Congress of the United States, 102d Congress, 1st sess., April 25, 1991.

7. "When the New President Is a Governor," *State Legislatures* 27, no. 4 (April 2001): 12.

8. Information on bill taken from fact sheet *Montana Libraries Say Yes to the Future*, Fact Sheet One: Montana Access Project (MAP), Montana Library Association, January 1997.

9. Institute of Museum and Library Services 1999 programs pamphlet, 3.

10. June Malina, *Federal Publishers Committee Handbook* (Washington, D.C.: U.S. Government Printing Office, 1993), 1.

11. Michael Zweig, *The Working Class Majority: America's Best Kept Secret* (Ithaca, N.Y.: Cornell University Press, 2000), 120–21.

12. Linton Weeks, *Washington Post*, February 7, 2001, C01.

13. Weeks, *Washington Post*.

14. Weeks, *Washington Post*.

15. Anita and Herbert E. Schiller, "Who Can Own What America Knows?" *The Nation*, April 17, 1982.

16. Judy E. Myers, "The Government Printing Office Cataloging Records: Opportunities and Problems," *Government Information Quarterly* 2, no. 1 (n.d.): 27–56.

17. James R. Plaunt, "Cataloging Options for U.S. Government Printing Office Documents," *Government Publications Review* 12 (1985): 449–56.

18. The affiliations of the librarians were Judy Myers, University of Houston; Barbara Kyle, Rice University; Jan Swanbeck, Texas A&M International University; Carol Turner, Stanford University; and Smittie Bolner, University of Louisiana, Baton Rouge.

19. Myrtle Smith Bolner and Barbara Kile, "Documents to the People: Access through the Automated Catalog," *Government Publications Review* 18 (1991): 51–64.

20. Dan Morgan, "Think Tanks: Corporations' Quiet Weapon," *Washington Post*, January 29, 2000, A1 and A5.

21. Morgan, "Think Tanks," A1.

22. *Statement of Richard E. Wiley on Behalf of SPIRIT Coalition Regarding JCP Proposed Guidelines*, August 8, 1984, 2 and 3.

23. *Statement of Richard E. Wiley*, 3.

24. *Statement of Richard E. Wiley*, 3.

25. *Statement of Richard E. Wiley*, 4.

26. U.S. Environmental Protection Agency, *National Environmental Information Symposium: An Agenda for Progress Held at Cincinnati, Ohio on 24–27 September 1972*, vol. 2, "Papers and report" (Washington, D.C.: Author, May 1973), distributed by the National Technical Information Service, U.S. Department of Commerce, R.I.

27. U.S. Environmental Protection Agency National Environmental Research Center, Cincinnati, Ohio, *National Environmental Information Symposium. An Agenda for Progress, September 24–27, 1972* (Cincinnati, Ohio: Author, May 1973), 5.

28. American Library Association in partnership with Global Learning, Inc., of New Jersey, *Libraries Build Sustainable Communities: Decide Tomorrow Today* (Chicago: Author, 1999).

29. Letter from Marion White Vassilakos, member of the board of directors of the League of Women Voters, to the editor of the *San Bernardino County Sun*, June 2000.

30. Tracy Velazquez, "Why We Should Support Library Levy," *Helena Independent Record*, September 2, 1998, 8B.

31. Molly Ivins, "Lawmakers and Telecom Powers Are Hanging Up on Us," *Star Telegram* (Austin, Tex.), June 10, 1998.

32. Sally Gardner Reed, *Making the Case for Your Library: A How-to-Do-It Manual* (New York: Neal-Schuman, 2001), xiv–xv.

33. James McDonough, "More Work on the Thomas Bill," *Electronic Public Information Newsletter* (October 1996): 71.

34. "The Seattle Tea Party: The Showdown over the WTO Was Not about Stopping Trade," *The Hightower Lowdown* 2, no. 1 (January 2000): 3.

35. Vigdor Schreibman, plaintiff-appellant, versus David W. Holmes, et al., defendants-appellees in the United States Court of Appeals for the District of Columbia Circuit, No. 98-5136, brief for Vigdor Schreibman, January 1999.

36. Charles Levendosky, "Marketplace of Freedom," *Casper Star-Tribune*, republished in *Helena Independent Record*, July 20, 1997, 4C.

37. Tim Berners-Lee, *Weaving the Web: The Original Design and Ultimate Destiny of the World Wide Web by Its Inventor* (New York: HarperCollins, 1999), 123.

38. Ralph Reed, *Active Faith: How Christians Are Changing the Soul of American Politics* (New York: Free Press, 1996), 178.

39. Reed, *Active Faith*, 176.

40. Friends of Libraries, U.S.A., headquarters is at 1420 Walnut Street, #450, Philadelphia, Pennsylvania 19102-4017; phone, (800) 9FOLUSA; website, www.folusa.com.

41. *ALA Handbook of Organization 1999–2000*, a supplement to American Libraries (Chicago: American Library Association, 1999), 139–40.

42. *ALA Handbook*; 140.

43. Letter from trustees of the LeRoy C. Merritt Foundation to prospective members, 2002.

6

A Change in the Life of a Public Official Can Unravel Years of Lobbying

Years of lobbying for a law, regulation, or program can unwind like a spool of thread because of changes in the personal or public life of a key public official. You may be so close to a completed quilt that the hanging ceremony has already been planned, but the fate of one person can undo the work of all the quilters. Sometimes it will be the opposite: The departure of a key person and the replacement of that person by another may provide the final stitches needed for the completion of a quilt worth displaying. In either case, the personal lives of public officials affect the outcome of policy.

A public official, because of personal actions, may be forced to resign, be indicted, go to jail, move to a better position, assume more power, or decide not to run for office again. Changes in their lives affect those who work for them and those who are trying to influence public policy through them. It is wise to plan on unexpected events altering your lobbying in unexpected ways. You may have done everything right and your efforts may still be of no immediate benefit.

The examples that follow are presented in chronological order, and each story is a square in the quilt of the policies governing the public's access to government information. It is the story of several key committees' roles in shaping the policies regarding the public's access to federal government information. Those committees include the Joint Committee on Printing, JCP's parent committees (Senate Committee on Rules and Administration and Committee on House Administration), and the House and Senate Appropriations Committees. It is a story of the people who chaired and staffed those committees and the internal struggle to determine what government information policies would be supported. It is the story of how lobbyists from within and without the government attempted to influence the insiders so policies would reflect their views and not those of their opponents. It is a story that is not over and never will be as long as it is possible to change laws and polices. We who cherish the public's access to government information must prepare ourselves and those who follow us for a permanent struggle to protect the public's access to government information. Now to the stories of some of the people involved in the struggle.

CHAIR HAYS AND ELIZABETH RAY, A WOMAN SCORNED

Wayne L. Hays (D-Ohio) was chair of the Committee on House Administration and chair of the Joint Committee on Printing when he made the mistake of scorning Ray and marrying another secretary. He ended up losing his chairmanships and was forced to resign. When I agreed to accept a job on the Joint Committee on Printing in October 1974, I was unaware of Hays's reputation as both a "bully" and "a savvy legislator and a strong-willed politician who is neither reluctant to use his accumulated influence nor hesitant about confronting his opponents in order to bring about the results he believes to be most desirable." In contrast to his reputation, he had been active in 1970 on a task force that "initiated a series of major reforms which spread power more evenly among House Democrats."[1] I knew him as the committed legislator who helped reform and improve the Federal Depository Library Program by getting the 1962 Depository Library Act passed by the House.

When I told Peter Masely, an assistant editor at the *Washington Post* and a stringer for *American Libraries*, that I had accepted a job at the JCP, he asked me whether I had any idea who I was going to work for. I told him that I knew Hays as a champion of depository libraries. Masely said, "I am sending you several clippings from the *Washington Star* that may make you change your mind." After reading those clippings, I decided that if there was anyone in the House who could get a bill passed that would assure the public's access to government information in microform and electronic form, it had to be Hays. I also realized why it was seemingly so easy for Hays to get money from the Appropriations Committee to hire me and two other professionals. The staff of the JCP had been a small one for many years.

Hays waged a long battle to get the 1962 Depository Act passed. He started out in 1955 by getting H.R. 262 passed, which allowed for an investigation of GPO printing and distribution of government publications. Between 1956 and 1962, he held hearings and introduced depository library bills in 1958 and 1959. Those bills were passed by the House but not by the Senate. Finally, in 1961, Senator Frank J. Lausche of Ohio introduced a companion bill in the Senate, and Hays introduced another bill in the House. On July 30, 1962, both the House and the Senate passed an amended bill. Passage was difficult because it increased the cost of the program by (1) doubling the number of depositories in each state and congressional district from one to two per member of Congress and (2) including publications not printed through GPO but in agency print shops and by agency contractors. The superintendent of documents opposed expanding the program because of the cost. The cost increase was balanced by the savings created by no longer requiring all depository libraries to accept and keep forever the government publications they had selected. Instead, up to two libraries in each state agreed to act as regional depositories, accepting and keeping permanently all publications offered. This meant that selective libraries would select fewer publications because they could borrow publications from the regional.

The most important change in the law was the requirement that non-GPO-issued publications be included in the depository library program. Most of the non-GPO publications, such as contractor reports in the areas of science and technology, were printed in small numbers. Hays realized that getting the law passed was only the first step in expanding the public's access to these non-GPO-produced publications. He knew that in order to get these publications into libraries that GPO needed authorization to replicate non-GPO publications in microform. Unable to unilaterally direct GPO to microfilm publications, he supported a GPO pilot project on micropublishing as a way of convincing the other members of the JCP to support a change in policy.

The issue of whether to authorize GPO to microfilm was very controversial. The Information Industry Association opposed such a program as an encroachment on their right to duplicate and sell government publications, whereas the American Library Association supported microfilming as a way to implement the 1962 law. Twelve years had passed, and ALA saw little fruit from their labors in working for the passage of the 1962 law. As coordinator of the ALA Government Documents Round Table, I lobbied the Joint Committee on Printing to support the microfilming program. I met with Rosemary Cribben and Denver Dickerson, rotating JCP staff directors, and they informed the chair of the JCP of ALA's concerns.

According to a memo written by Cribben to Dickerson about the Government Printing Office Superintendent of Documents services:

> Last year both Appropriations Committees expressed concern about the deteriorating service at the above office. They directed JCP to review statutes and procedures to eliminate inefficiency in the distribution and dissemination of Government publications. Conversations with both committees pointed out that the Members were concerned about service to Congress, to the depository libraries and to the general public. Letters from irate constituents to these Members substantiated the Members' concern. Additional funds were requested for three employees to go into the area generally to pinpoint the problems, thereby giving the Joint Committee some background for directives and suggestions to get this program back on track. We have had several years of promises by the Public Printer and some improvements have been made. However, the letters keep rolling in.[2]

In response to the concerns of the Appropriations Committees and the Joint Committee on Printing about Government Printing Office services to Congress and the public, Chair Hays requested a supplemental appropriation for fiscal year 1975 of $66,000 for three additional JCP positions.

Cribben advised Hays in a memo that one of the positions should be filled by a librarian,[3] arguing that since the Appropriations Committee directed JCP to "review the statutes and the documents distribution program of the Government Printing Office in response to the concern of the Committee of the increasing costs of Congressional printing and binding" it made sense to hire a professional in the field.[4] She added that the librarian she had in mind "has written numerous articles on the depository library program, with suggestions for improved services from GPO, and at some of the meetings I have attended of the Public Printer's Advisory Committee on Depository Libraries, of which she is a member, asks most of the provocative questions there. In other words, she is deeply aware of the poor service being rendered this program and refuses to accept the GPO's promises."

I did not realize when I was hired that Representative Hays was anxious to fill the three positions before the chair rotated back to the Senate in the next session. Otherwise the incoming chair would have the right to hire staff. At that time the chair and the staff director's position rotated each year: The chair became the vice chair, and the staff director became the deputy staff director. The staff directors even switched offices from the first floor main office in the Capitol to the terrace level and back again. Later the chair rotated each Congress between the Senate and the House. Hays was adamant that the chair rotate since for many years the chair had been held by the Senate, and he believed that the House deserved its turn. Senator Carl T. Hayden (D-Ariz.) was chair periodically for twenty-one years, and during that time, he held the post for eleven straight years until Senator Jordan took over in 1969. Several staff directors also served for ten years at a time. Hays insisted on naming his own staff director, Rosemary Cribben. She was the first woman named staff director of a joint committee. A month after I started, the chair and staff director positions switched. I then reported to Senator Howard Cannon (D-Nev.) and staff director Denver Dickerson instead of to Representative Hays and Cribben.

The minority party was also entitled to staff on the JCP. In 1974, the Democrats were in control of both the House and the Senate, and the Republicans were in the minority. Paul Beach was the minority staff director. He was chief clerk/staff director from May 1948 to February 1953 during the time that the Republicans controlled the House and President Eisenhower was in the White House. He served as staff director during the tenure of Representative William E. Jenner (R-Ind.) and Senator Hayden. Beach retired before the Republicans took over the Senate in 1981, and his hopes of once again being staff director were never fulfilled.

In 1974, both the chair and vice chair of the Joint Committee on Printing were Democrats, but there was still tension between them and the staff they had appointed to the JCP. They did not support the same strategy for enforcing the printing, publishing, and dissemination laws. Fortunately, differences could be resolved by a vote of the members of the JCP. I learned early that if I were to succeed in promoting my causes, I had to persuade the staff appointed by both the Senate and the House, whether they were Democrats or Republicans, to see things my way. They in turn convinced the members to support my position although the members did not necessarily know that it was my position. To persuade other staff to see things my way, I had to convince them that it would benefit their member of Congress because the member's constituents supported my position. Adopting my position would (1) increase the member's power in the Congress or in the home district by making them look good; (2) enable the members to fulfill their responsibilities on the committee and in the Congress; and (3) save the government and the taxpayers money, time, and effort.

Three of us were hired and on board by December 1974. Cribben organized us into a team to investigate GPO and make recommendations for improvements to Chair Hays, through her. In 1975, when Senator Cannon and his staff director, Denver Dickerson, took over, Cribben as assistant staff director was assigned as our team leader. In 1976, Hays regained the chair, and Cribben was again staff director.

One of the three staffers hired by Hays was Barbara Jones, a savvy former staffer of Senator Mike Mansfield (D-Mont.), Senate leader. Since I had transferred from the executive branch and saw that the rules in the legislative branch were very different, I turned to her for advice. She advised me that only certain staff worked directly with members and that other staff worked through those staff. The staff closest to the chair were generally political staff and guarded their access to the member, so it was not wise to go around them. There was an unwritten rule that you could communicate directly with members and staff from your own state. Since we were both from Montana, Jones made sure that I met other staff from Montana. She advised me to join the Montana State Society. Every state has a society so people working and/or living in Washington, D.C., can get together and talk about home. I joined both the Montana and the Missouri state societies, being born in one state and having lived many years in the other. Societies have several parties a year, and usually the state's members of Congress and their staff attend. Sharing a birthplace or a relative can help you when you need to get information, gain support for a bill, or save your job.

I met the staff of Senator Lee Metcalf (D-Mont.) working on the Senate Committee on Government Operations at a society reception. I convinced the committee to do a survey of all agencies asking them to list the publications they had issued to the public. We used the results of that survey at the JCP to prove that agencies were not providing many of their publications to the depository library program.

My mother visiting me from eastern Montana used just such a gathering of the Montana State Society to lobby Senator John Melcher (D-Mont.) to protect my job after the Senate had been taken over by the Republicans. Senator Melcher told Mary Gereau, his administrative assistant, to look out for me.

At the final meeting of the JCP in 1974 chaired by Hays, the JCP accepted Representative John Brademas's (D-Ind.) call for a broad survey of how the government disseminates information. William Sudow, Brademas's assistant, briefed our team in January about what Brademas had in mind and we started with a major project. We spent a lot of time learning how GPO and the legislative and the executive branches produced and disseminated their publications so we could advise the JCP on how to improve the process.

At the same time, we conducted a study of congressional committees to learn what support they needed from GPO in the production of their publications. We took the opportunity to explain to committee staff why it was important for them to authorize the distribution of committee prints to depository libraries. We discovered that committee staff thought that when they provided copies of their prints to LC's Exchange and Gift Division Document Expediting Project (DOCEX) that the prints were distributed to depository libraries. DOCEX offered

> a specialized U.S. Government document acquisitions service to subscribers. Publications include those not normally interpreted as falling within the purview of the Depository Library Act and those which, because of their specialized attention, DOCEX can supply on a more timely basis. Included in these selections are documents issued by the various departments of the executive branch as well as congressional materials such as copies of bills and committee prints.[5]

Depository librarians complained about paying a fee for documents that they believed should be free to the depository library program. Committees were giving LC copies out of their own allotment and were happy to learn that if they authorized distribution to depository libraries, funds given to GPO would pay for copies. We persuaded many of the committees to stamp depository distribution on the order so they could be sent to libraries. But this still left many prints out of the program. In 1976, Hays directed GPO to provide all committee prints to depository libraries unless instructed not to in writing by the publishing committee. As I said earlier, the work that Arne Richards did to educate the library and congressional community about the value of committee prints and the public's right to read them paved the way for making their inclusion in the depository program my first project at JCP.

When Hays regained the chair in 1976, he authorized our team to build on our study and launch an aggressive effort to get non-GPO-produced publications into the depository library program. We were allowed to visit agencies such as the Central Intelligence Agency (CIA) that Senator Cannon's staff had precluded. The CIA agreed to provide their city maps to the depository program.

Hays was determined to solve the microfilming controversy. He was aware that the other members of the Joint Committee on Printing were being lobbied to keep GPO from getting the authorization to launch a full-scale program. Representative Brademas was concerned about the microfiche publisher, the Congressional Information Service, led by James Adler. Representative Brademas's staffer on this issue, William Sudow, lived next door to me on the Hill. As neighbors we were able to keep each other informed about the latest events in the controversy. And as I later learned he was also able to keep Adler well informed. So be careful that you confide in the right people.

Chair Hays was ready to sign a letter authorizing GPO to proceed with the microfilming when I innocently mentioned to Adler that the letter was being signed that day. He immediately called Representative Brademas's office and got the letter stopped. I learned a hard lesson that day: Never tell anyone about a decision until it is actually verified with a signature and cannot be undone.

In spite of that setback, staff and librarians were assured that the letter would be signed and government information denied to the public would soon be made available in microform. But promises and years of lobbying could not withstand the furor when stories about Hays's relationship with one of his staff became public. It would not be until 1977, while Senator Cannon was chair, that JCP finally authorized the provision of microforms to depository libraries.

Hays's downfall was also the downfall of his staff and the dreams of those who depended on him to expand the public's access to government information. The *Washington Post* reported on September 2, 1976:

Rep. Wayne L. Hays (D-Ohio) resigned from Congress yesterday, and the House Ethics Committee dropped its investigation of his role in the sex-payroll allegations that led to his downfall. Hays, a 28-year House member and once a power through control of member's campaign funds and office allowances, resigned in a letter which his lawyer, Judah Best, and press spokeswoman, Carol Clawson, handed to House Speaker Carl Albert (D-Okla.) yesterday afternoon. . . .

The ethics committee voted 12 to 0 to drop the investigation it began three months ago into charges by Elizabeth L. Ray that Hays kept her on the public payroll at $14,000 a year solely to be his mistress. After receiving Hays' letter yesterday Albert said he believed Hays quit "to save his family." . . . He married a second time shortly before Ray made her charges in a *Washington Post* article May 23. Hays had been on an accelerating slide since Ray's charges were reported. He admitted a "personal relationship" with her, but denied her charge that she did not do office work.

As the *Post* further reported that even though Hays's constituents had renominated him in the primary with 62 percent of the vote for a fifteenth term, his friends on the Hill were quickly deserting him. He decided not to run for reelection in the general election. "Under intense pressure from House Democrats who found him becoming a political liability, Hays resigned as chairman of the Democratic Congressional Campaign Committee and the House Administration Committee."[6]

Why were other members of Congress, supposedly Hays's friends, reluctant to support him in his time of trouble? In his book *Who Runs Congress?* Mark Green gave one explanation:

Sometimes a congressman abuses his public position with such skill and arrogance that only an incidental scandal can force his colleagues to investigate his conduct. A classic case is former Representative Wayne L. Hays (D-Ohio), a behind-the-scenes House potentate who manipulated three committee chairmanships to control everything from the price of haircuts in the Capitol barbershops to staff salaries and the dispersal of Democratic campaign contributions. "I got where I am because people feared me," he once told reporter Myra McPherson.

Hays' power base though was being challenged well before the sex scandal gave Democratic leaders an excuse to purge him. Democrats uncomfortable under Hays' arbitrary bureaucratic discretion to dispense patronage and services tried to dethrone him as Administration Committee chairman in 1975. Hays not only survived, but he retaliated by creating new bureaucratic structures to reinforce his influence. He created new subcommittees on packing and paper conservation, as well as ad hoc committees to manage House restaurant operations and the computer system. Finally, he created the infamous Oversight Committee to keep an accurate check on what all the other committees were doing.

However influential, his style of intimidation foredoomed his dreams of becoming majority leader. And before the scandal broke, one Hill observer prophesied his demise to author Marshall Frady. "One of these days ole Wayne's going to violate one amenity too many and find he's run out of grace all of a sudden. Then they'll converge on him, and when they're done, all he'll have left of his empire is the stub of his gavel."[7]

When Hays died in 1989, *Roll Call* reminded people how a powerful chair had turned a "panel that was a weak housekeeping panel into a powerful political force":

> The ways in which Hays used the House Administration Committee to enhance his personal power were legendary. Since all perks and amenities passed through his office, he could make a Member's life on the Hill difficult—and often seemed to enjoy doing so. . . . He used the committee to punish his enemies and reward his friends. This discretion was often employed when Hays wanted to influence legislation in other committees.[8]

Additionally, the *Washington Post* acknowledged that Hays's constituents loved him because

> he remained true to his beliefs, which included the need to help the poor of his district, the soundness of the Democratic Party's domestic agenda and the importance of the federal government's efforts to combat communism abroad. In the early 1950s, Hays had a moment of fame as an outspoken opponent of communist "witch hunts" on Capitol Hill, holding his opponents up to ridicule and tying some witnesses in knots. . . . Many of his constituents had led hard lives, living in a hilly land of strip mines, small farms and unemployment, but they at least had a representative who, if not loved, was not ignored.[9]

The *Washington Post* reporters in 1976 did not tell the public how they convinced Ray to unmask the affair or that she did so only after Hays jilted her and had the Capitol police deny her entrance to the Capitol on the day he married another secretary.

The newspaper did not tell the public how much damage was done to the good causes that Hays and his staff supported or that almost everyone on Hays's staff lost their jobs. This included his personal office staff as well as staff on the Committee on House Administration and the Joint Committee on Printing. The *Post* did not tell the public how they pursued his other staff, particularly women. Pursuit by reporters seeking to find women who may have been sexually involved with a member of Congress was not limited to women staffers but extended to the sixteen women members of Congress, even the highly respected and proper Representative Barbara Jordan. Fellow Texan Jim Wright recalls in his book *Balance of Power* how Jordan was asked as she entered the House chamber by a *Washington Post* reporter whether she had ever been sexually propositioned by one of her male colleagues. She responded indignantly with one word: "Absurd."[10]

As a staffer working for Cribben and Hays on the Joint Committee on Printing, my experience was quite different than the story told in the newspapers. I neither witnessed nor heard of any behavior by Hays that was disrespectful to women. I knew that Hays hired women for responsible positions and paid them well. Many of his congressional critics did not give women good jobs or pay them as much as men in the same types of jobs, according to a study by the National Political Women's Caucus (NPWC) in 1975.

I did witness some behavior by others that caused me concern. I attended a birthday party for Hays in 1975 one late afternoon. I was impressed with the lovely room in the Capitol and the guests, who included members of Congress and the chair of the Democratic National Committee, but I was uneasy at the free-flowing liquor and the women in evening gowns. I was told that some members of Congress hired women for their looks and not their skills, unlike the executive branch, where you had to meet certain written criteria to be hired. I was told that the liquor had been donated by private companies and some of them were companies that competed for government contracts for printing and equipment. At least one chairman after Hays refused to accept any liquor from private companies because of the perception that a return favor would be expected.

That same year, a printer at one of the agencies asked me to persuade the American Library Association to support him as the next public printer at GPO. He said if I did, he would get me a date with Hays. I was shocked and told him that I was not interested in a date with Hays, and if I were, I certainly did not need his help. I also told him never to call or speak to me again and that under no circumstances would I lobby ALA to support his candidacy or anyone else's candidacy for public printer. He did not become public printer.

The only other incident that troubled me was one involving a woman friend of mine who was looking for a job on the Hill. We attended a Christmas party at the offices of the Committee on House Administration and the then-staff director suggested to her that she might consider a personal relationship with a member of Congress as a way of getting hired. When we expressed our shock at such an idea, he quickly said that he was just joking. We did not believe him.

In spite of those incidents, I never saw anything but a totally professional relationship between Hays and the staff of the JCP. I am convinced that Cribben had no inkling of Hays's relationship with Ray. She told me that he had asked her, as a friend of the bride, to address his wedding invitations in order to conceal the bride's identity and assure their privacy since the ceremony was being held in the Capitol. The day that the Ray story hit the newspapers, Cribben appeared as surprised as the rest of us. Hays asked her for advice on how to deal with the situation, and she advised him to tell the truth immediately, since it would come out eventually.[11]

The deputy staff director, Denver Dickerson, cautioned me to distance myself from Cribben in order to protect myself and my job. I refused, saying that I was one of the few people she could turn to for support and advice. She took me along when she met with the majority leader of the House, Thomas "Tip" O'Neill (D-Mass.), to ask him to intercede on her behalf with Representative Frank Thompson Jr. (D-N.J.), the new chair of the Joint Committee on Printing. O'Neill told her that a chair had the right to choose his own staff director and that he would not interfere with that right. He told her that he would help her find another job. He kept his word and got her some consulting jobs, but she never worked again for Congress.

What I did not know when Cribben and I went to visit O'Neill is that when Hays asked for his help, O'Neill had replied, "No way. You've disgraced the Congress and you've got to resign from your chairmanships." When Hays responded that Speaker Albert said it would be all right, O'Neill replied, "It may be all right with the Speaker, but it's not all right with me. If you don't resign, I'm going to bring this business before the caucus, and we'll strip you of your chairmanships on the spot."[12]

I was under no illusion that accompanying Cribben during her efforts to keep her job would help me keep my own, but I remembered the offer of help Roger McDonough, state librarian of New Jersey, had made at an American Library Association meeting in January 1975. McDonough warned me that I would soon need his help in order to keep my job. Since I had held the job for less than two months, I was puzzled. He told me that Representative Frank Thompson Jr. (D-N.J.) was going to challenge Hays for the chairmanship of the Committee on House Administration. If he won, Thompson would be chair of JCP and get rid of all of Hays's staff. McDonough was sure that Thompson would win. It was rare at that time for a member not in the line of succession due to seniority to challenge and unseat a sitting chair. Hays survived the challenge in 1975, but when he was forced to resign, I called McDonough. He told me not to worry. He and Thompy, as he called him, had been friends since grade school, and he was going to see him that night at a reception and would put in a good word for me. I asked him to also inquire about Rosemary Cribben since it looked like she would lose her job. McDonough called me the next day and told me that Thompson assured him that "your little girl is all right, but that other woman is a goner."

I later learned through the new deputy staff director, Faye Padgett, that Thompson had heard from enough people and that my job was safe, but if he heard from any more, he might be tempted to fire me just so he would not have to respond to any more phone calls and letters.

It was because of another state librarian, Joe Anderson of Nevada, that I was able to attend the ALA midwinter meeting where Roger promised to help me. When Senator Cannon's staff director took over in 1975, he refused to send me to ALA. I called Joe, who called Senator Cannon, and I was permitted to go to the meeting. I met Anderson at the ALA banquet in Las Vegas in 1973 and instantly liked him because he wore a cowboy hat and boots, which reminded me of my dad. Our friendship grew because he shared my passion for government documents and promised to help me any way he could. I did not forget that promise and neither did he. As I urged before, go to meal functions, and take the opportunity to lobby your table mates for your cause.

Roger McDonough, my patron saint in 1976, was no stranger to lobbying. He was one of the librarians who successfully lobbied for

passage of the 1962 Depository Act. He was a member of the first
Advisory Committee to the Public Printer on Depository Libraries
established as a result of Congress's recommendation to GPO in the
1962 Senate Report 1587 on the bill H.R. 8141. McDonough testified
at hearings in March 1962 before the Subcommittee on the Library of
the Senate Committee on Rules and Administration:

> Picking up what Powell has mentioned about the possibility that li-
> braries throughout the country might be sampled as to their opinions
> on the subject, I believe I mentioned 4 years ago when I testified for
> similar legislation that I thought there was perhaps a need for an advi-
> sory committee consisting largely of librarians perhaps to work with
> the Government Printing Office, the Superintendent of Documents, in
> making annual reviews and determinations about the program. I say
> this, not in any attempt to try to dictate, or whatever, but merely to of-
> fer advisory services based on our experience in the field.[13]

REPRESENTATIVE THOMPSON
ENSNARED IN THE ABSCAM WEB

Representative Frank Thompson (D-N.J.), as chair of the Joint Committee on Printing and the Committee on House Administration,
was going to drastically revise title 44 of the *United States Code* until
he became tangled in the Abscam web and went to prison. He
planned to abolish the Joint Committee on Printing and the Government Printing Office and combine them into an independent agency
with a board representing all the user constituencies.

Title 44 of the *United States Code* brings together most of the printing, publishing, and dissemination laws of the U.S. government. It
defines the responsibilities of the Joint Committee on Printing, the
Government Printing Office and the legislative, executive, and judicial branches of government in the area of government information
production and dissemination.

Since I had already experienced the downfall of one ambitious
chair, I wanted assurances that the new one was a good person and
able to get legislation passed. I checked with other congressional
staffers and reporters about Representative Thompson. They all told
me that he was the man with the white hat. No one knew of any
wrongdoing on his part. I was further assured when Thompson assigned Earl Mazo to the Joint Committee on Printing, and he was

sent to share my hideaway office in the bowels of the Capitol. He was an old friend of Thompson's and had worked on Thompson's election campaign. Mazo told me many inspiring stories about the chairman. Mazo and I became friends, and I am sure that his reports to Thompson about the good work I was doing helped me keep my job.

Mazo had been a reporter since 1935, starting with the *Charleston News & Courier*. He served as a combat reporter for the *Stars and Stripes*, had covered the debates between Nixon and Kennedy in 1960, and while at the *New York Herald Tribune* covered President Nixon. He later wrote a biography of President Nixon.

During Thompson's tenure as chair, many steps were taken to improve services to depository libraries, government, and the public. Thompson worked with Senator Howard Cannon (D-Nev.) and later with Senator Claiborne Pell (D-R.I.) and finally with Senator Charles McMathias (R-Md.) to adopt changes in policies and procedures. Those changes included: (1) negotiating a cost-sharing agreement between the superintendent of documents and the map-publishing agencies that made thousands of maps available to depository libraries; (2) directing the Library of Congress to provide support to the superintendent of documents in the cataloging of government publications such as technical advice on the use of the cataloging rules and the MARC format, a cooperative program for establishing name and subject authority files, and certification of GPO catalogers as meeting the cataloging standards established by LC; (3) saving the Government Printing Office bookstores from closure; (4) studying the JCP regulations for possible revisions; (5) establishing the *United States Congressional Serial Set* Advisory Committee; and (6) attempting to revise the printing and dissemination laws affecting government publishing and dissemination.

Chair Thompson established the Ad Hoc Advisory Committee on Revision of Title 44 to the Joint Committee on Printing in early 1978. The Joint Committee on Printing chose the members of this advisory committee carefully, wanting to cover all political bases. Fifteen organizations were invited to designate representatives and alternates. Those organizations were the American Library Association, Joint Committee on Printing, Information Industry Association, Federal Library Committee, Printing Industries of America, National Association of Government Communicators, American Paper Institute, AFL-CIO, Joint Council of Unions at GPO, the Office of Management and Budget, Defense Department, Commerce Department, the

Government Printing Office, the Committee on House Administration, and the Senate Committee on Rules and Administration.

It was the first serious attempt to include the Office of Management and Budget in the legislative efforts to reform the printing and publishing laws of the federal government. Considering later efforts by OMB to destroy JCP and GPO by declaring them unconstitutional, some say it was a long-term tactical error on the part of Congress.

The Advisory Committee issued a report entitled *Federal Government Printing and Publishing: Policy Issues* after holding thirteen public hearings. The hearings were supplemented by the work done by subcommittees, which analyzed six topics that were then debated by the committee as a whole. The topics included the role of the Government Printing Office, access to and distribution of government information, the depository library system, the impact of new technology, the administration of policy, and the pricing of government information. The report summed up the work of the committee this way:

> The Committee sought to identify issues, explore options, and develop essential questions. The Committee's hearings were not intended to produce specific legislative recommendations nor to present solely official agency or organization positions. The members were encouraged to be a "devil's advocate" when they felt the discussion was not addressing all aspects of a particular problem so as to explore the full range of issues and alternatives.
>
> This report is designed to present a better understanding of the Government's system of printing and distributing information and to highlight problems, alternatives and important policy issues. . . . Although there is no single conclusion or unanimous recommendation in this report, we hope our far-ranging discussions on these important issues will aid the Congress in its consideration of title 44.[14]

The distillation of the many weeks of discussions and work of the subcommittees into the committee's report was done by a team of three JCP staffers led by Faye Padgett, deputy staff director. The team included Roy Breimon, appointed to the JCP by Senator Cannon, and me. We were appointed by different chairs, but because we spent so much time together working with the Ad Hoc Committee, we developed a trust in each other that has lasted long after our departure from the JCP. We later worked as a team in the JCP efforts to keep the GPO bookstores from being closed by Public Printer Dan-ford Sawyer in 1983. We did such a good job that the public printer had his staff calling librarians and others to find out if we at JCP had been lobbying them to protest the closing of the bookstores. Several librarians called to tip us off and said they had refused to answer any questions. The public printer even called the chair of the JCP, asking that the three of us be fired. Thompson laughed and said we worked for him, not the public printer, and we were doing exactly what he wanted.

After extensive public meetings and the work of the Ad Hoc Committee, the senators and representatives and their staff on the Senate Committee on Rules and Administration, the Committee on House Administration, and the Joint Committee on Printing were ready to start their work. Although staff participated in the work of the Ad Hoc Committee, they now had to take the work of others and craft a bill that would make it through Congress. Thompson, in setting up the committee and attempting to contact all interested parties, missed a few. Constituencies that had never been thought of emerged. One of those constituencies saw this as an opportunity to take away some of the union rights of workers at the Government Printing Office. GPO union members under the 1932 Kiess Act have the right to bargain for wages and working conditions. When the union and the public printer cannot agree, the unions have the right to ask the Joint Committee on Printing to intercede and settle the dispute. Since Thompson and Hawkins were strong supporters of workers' right to organize, the efforts by the right-to-work supporters did not persuade them to take away the rights of the workers in the proposed bill.

Representative Thompson, in his dual role as chair of the Committee on House Administration (the legislative committee) and the Joint Committee on Printing (the oversight committee), came up with a bill that he was confident would pass the House. Senator Pell, as chair of the Senate Committee on Rules and Administration (legislative committee) and vice chair of the JCP, introduced an identical bill in the Senate and was waiting for it to pass in the House before the Senate Committee on Rules began its work and took the bill to the floor of the Senate. Thompson, Pell, and their staffs worked closely together and even held joint hearings.

The bill crafted by Chair Thompson and his staff was introduced first as H.R. 4572, while Senator Pell introduced a companion bill in the Senate as S. 1436. Four joint hearings were held in July 1979 by the House and the Senate on the companion bills. Representative Thompson as chair of Committee on House Administration and Representative Augustus Hawkins (D-Calif.), chair of the Committee's Subcommittee on Printing, and seventeen other members introduced a clean bill, H.R. 5424, the National Publications Act of 1979, in September 1979. The bill was marked up by the Committee on House Administration in January 1980 and reported out favorably. The bill was then sent to the House Committee on Government Operations and the House Rules Committee and was reported out with a few minor changes.

Chair Thompson was ready to take the bill to the floor, but he was caught in an FBI sting called "Abscam" in February 1980. He was indicted in June 1980 and then convicted of bribery and conspiracy. He served two years in prison. A federal agent had posed as a rich Arab sheikh asking for help with immigration problems. A month before he was convicted, Thompson lost his election to a Republican challenger. He continued to assert his innocence and unsuccessfully appealed his conviction. Thompson's lawyer argued that he did not take any money and the money was taken by the middleman who had set up the meeting.[15]

Thompson issued a statement in his defense on June 18, 1980:

> My response to these allegations is the same as it was when this story was first leaked: I have committed no crime, violated no law, and breached none of my duties to the people of New Jersey. I am confident that the processes of justice will show that this is so. The true facts have not yet been revealed. At times investigative agencies, and disreputable hirelings in their employ, can act in over-zealous or illegal ways. Here, government agents did not stop with manufacturing the very situations they are now prosecuting. They employed another equally unfair and abusive tactic—they selectively leaked to the media charges which they hope would make their undercover operations seem fair and valid. Attorney General Civiletti has now admitted that the "flood of leaks" was one of the "low points" in the history of the Department of Justice, that these leaks "pervert" justice, "wound the innocent cruelly," and "corrupt and injure all of us." During my 30 years in public life, I have been attacked by political enemies many times. In the 1950's when I championed the rights of labor, I was attacked by some—but today we are all proud of our strong labor movement. In the 1960's when I worked for civil rights, there were others who called me names—but today we know that change has strengthened America.

Once again, I am attacked. But my faith in this country, in the fairness of its people, in its courts and in due process of law, is such that I am confident that when the full facts are presented, I will be vindicated.[16]

During this time, Thompson continued to work on improving service to government agencies and the public. In early 1980, he directed the JCP staff to conduct a series of fact-finding inspections and public meetings to improve the federal printing program and to seek input to update the *Government Printing and Binding Regulations* issued by JCP. Joint Committee on Printing and GPO staff teamed up to hold a series of public meetings in Chicago; Atlanta; New York City; St. Louis; Kansas City, Missouri; Columbus, Ohio; Denver; Dallas; Boston; Eugene, Oregon; Seattle; San Francisco; and Los Angeles. Federal agency personnel, private printing contractors, librarians, and the general public were invited to the meetings. The team also visited GPO, government agency and commercial printing plants, paper mills, GPO and commercial bookstores, depository libraries, book jobbers, and private publishers in each of the federal regions. According to an April 28, 1980, press release the public meetings would address the following topics:

> The role of the Joint Committee on Printing under Title 44, the law governing federal printing and binding regulations; procurement of federal printing from the commercial sector, which exceeds $424-million annually; GPO's contractor compliance program; GPO's in-plant capabilities; new technologies; standards for paper used by the Government; and public access to government documents, including the responsibility of the Superintendent of Documents to oversee the depository library program, documents sales and government book stores.[17]

Thompson believed that sending his staff out into the field to meet with all the parties affected by title 44 and the JCP regulations was a good way to gather information needed to revise the regulations. He insisted that this fact finding be done in cooperation with GPO and agency staff. Spending weeks on the road together, although exhausting, forced JCP and GPO staff to see issues from each other's point of view. It also made the two staffs into a team that worked well together in writing the regulations and in improving services to government and the public. Thompson also saw these public meetings as a way of bolstering the influence of the Joint Committee on

Printing and the legislative branch in the world of government printing, publishing, and dissemination. He sent his staff out to lobby the rest of the government and the public.

REPRESENTATIVE HAWKINS HAD
TO DECIDE WHAT TO DO WITH THE BILL

Representative Thompson's successor, Representative Augustus Hawkins (D-Calif.), feared taking the National Publications Act of 1980 to the floor without Thompson, so the bill was dead for that Congress. He did not withdraw the bill; he simply did not take the steps needed to bring it to the floor of the House for a vote. Another chair and many years of effort were lost because of personal problems. This time staff hired by Thompson were in danger as well as staff hired by other members of the Joint Committee on Printing.

Representative Hawkins, as chair of the Subcommittee on Printing of the Committee on House Administration, had played an active role in the attempted revision of title 44 and knew all the players as well as the staff. Chair Hawkins kept most of Thompson's staff, and as Hays's appointee, I survived once again. Hawkins named the staff director of the Subcommittee on Printing, Richard Olezewski, as deputy staff director of the Joint Committee on Printing. Gordon Andrew McKay, general counsel, became the staff director, and Faye Padgett, deputy staff director, became assistant staff director.

Chair Hawkins decided to enforce the current laws regulating government printing and dissemination of government information through the updating of the Joint Committee on Printing's regulations covering government printing, publishing, and dissemination. He believed that a number of the improvements that had been identified in the legislative process could be implemented by the Joint Committee on Printing without changes in legislation.

A CONGRESS DIVIDED AGAINST ITSELF:
A REPUBLICAN SENATE AND A DEMOCRATIC HOUSE

In 1981, the Senate came under the control of the Republicans for the first time in twenty-six years. According to an article in the *Wash-*

ington Star, about 1,300 Senate employees faced the possible loss of their jobs.[18] It is rather unsettling to read in the newspaper that you and most of the staff on your committee are in danger of being replaced, although the professional staff under Senate rules were considered nonpartisan and to be terminated only for just cause as set out in the rules of the committee. Some senators on the parent committee of the JCP, Committee on Rules and Administration, urged the new chair, Senator Charles Mathias (R-Md.), to fire most of the JCP staff. Senator Mathias decided instead to work with the House and evaluate each staffer to determine whether he or she would be retained or not. Senator Mathias did not fire a single nonpartisan professional or secretarial person on the JCP. He did bring in two of his own people and put them in key positions. In contrast, many of the Republican senators fired large numbers of staffers on committees and in support offices. I remember the Senate cafeteria the day after the election being unusually quiet as mourning and shocked staffers tried to figure out what to do next. Senator Mathias's approach was also in marked contrast to the actions of Representative Newt Gingrich (R-Ga.) when he and the Republicans took over the House in 1995 and terminated many staff.

Thus, a period of divided control of Congress began when the Senate was controlled by the Republicans and the House was controlled by the Democrats. The chairmanship of the Joint Committee on Printing was held by the Republicans during 1981 and 1982. Representative Hawkins decided to work closely with Senator Mathias, the incoming JCP chair. Rather than rotate JCP staff directors every two years, they decided to stabilize the staff and together hired a new staff director, Thomas Kleis, founder and director of the Office of University Publications at Johns Hopkins University in Baltimore, Maryland. Gordon Andrew McKay resigned; Hawkins's aide, Richard Olezewski, became the deputy staff director; and Faye Padgett remained as the assistant staff director. Senator Mathias named Anthony Zagami from his home state of Maryland as general counsel. Later on when Representative Annunzio became chair, he continued the arrangement. As a result, I consider 1982 to 1986 to be the most productive and peaceful of the years that I served on the Joint Committee on Printing.

As I noted earlier, a destructive approach was used in the 104th Congress by Newt Gingrich and Representative Bill Thomas (R-Calif.), chair of the Committee on House Administration and the Joint

Committee on Printing. They terminated almost the entire staff of the JCP with the intention of abolishing the committee. "Termination" is a term used by Congress and implies that staff are dismissed for political reasons rather than for failure to do their job. Thomas retained Gingrich's staff person and named her staff director. The Republican senators on the JCP objected to abolishing the committee and to Thomas's February 1995 testimony to the House Appropriations Committee proposing the elimination of funding for the JCP. The Senate Appropriations Committee did not agree with the House, and a greatly reduced JCP survived.

The Senate Republicans forced Thomas to restore two political positions for the Senate members, one for the vice chair, Senator Ted Stevens (R-Alaska) and one for the ranking minority member, Senator Wendell Ford (D-Ky.). Thomas also agreed to give Representative Vic Fazio (D-Calif.), ranking House Democrat, a staff position. Thus there were four political staff. The chair kept several other staff on month to month for purposes of winding down the work of the committee, but after awhile when he realized that the Senate was not going to support abolishing JCP, Thomas agreed to keep those staff for the rest of the 104th Congress.

In contrast to the chaotic and destructive politics of the Republican-controlled 104th Congress, Representative Hawkins and later Representative Annunzio and Senator Mathias collaborated in a nonpartisan way to strengthen the people's right to know. They directed their staff to cooperate in developing Joint Committee on Printing regulations that would reflect changing technologies and help the government deal with the future. In spite of their close working relationship, the regulations that Representatives Hawkins and Annunzio and Senator Mathias worked on were never adopted. The adoption of the regulations became a political battle. The JCP had issued updates to the regulations over the years but had not attempted a full-scale revision until the early 1980s.

On November 9, 1983, Chair Hawkins sent a draft of the proposed revision of the JCP regulations to the heads of all federal departments and agencies for review. He explained the need for an update this way:

> The Joint Committee on Printing recognizes that since its last regulations were issued in 1977, significant technological breakthroughs have made a sharp impact on the ways in which information is captured, edited, formatted, stored, reproduced and distributed. These technologi-

cal advances offer dramatic new opportunities to "remedy neglect, delay, duplication, or waste" in Federal printing, binding and distribution of government publications, the primary charge vested in the Committee by Section 103 of Title 44, *United States Code.* The revised regulations embrace the new technologies and seek to replace JCP micromanagement procedures with oversight and policy-making functions. In addition, the revised regulations include new provisions concerning publications' distribution, particularly with regard to Depository libraries, indexing and cataloging of Government documents, and the sales of Government publications.[19]

On November 11, 1983, Hawkins published the draft in the *Congressional Record* for public comment and after receiving hundreds of comments issued a revised version on June 26, 1984, for a thirty-day comment period and an open meeting with interested parties. The Office of Management and Budget and some private publishers and equipment manufacturers objected to the JCP's assertion that printing included electronic production of publications. OMB asked the Justice Department in December 1983 to issue a legal opinion on the power of the JCP to enforce these revised regulations. The Justice Department opinion of April 11, 1984, concluded that "the regulations were statutorily unsupported and constitutionally impermissible." Justice Department based part of their argument on the Supreme Court cases *Buckley v. Valeo* and *Immigration and Naturalization Service v. Chada.* Even though the JCP had modified the regulations somewhat to accommodate the Justice Department opinion, the OMB in August of 1984 asserted that the June version was still unconstitutional and by issuing them JCP was making law.

At the request of the GPO unions, attorney George B. Driesen issued a memorandum on March 27, 1985, that disputed the Justice Department opinion. Driesen argued:

> It appears that the JCP's determinations under the printing statutes are not "laws," requiring plenary concurrence of both Houses and submission to the President because the printing statutes relate to the relatively insubstantial internal, governmental housekeeping and support matters and do not purport to establish rights or impose obligations outside the government. Determinations under those statutes, therefore do not contain the seeds of "legislative despotism" or (partly because the JCP does not decide whether documents may be printed) prevent the President from defending himself against the Congress, the evils that presentment and bicameralism prevent. For

these reasons, the opinion concludes, it is probable that courts will not deem the JCP's issuance of Printing and Binding Regulations, or its exercise of power to permit an agency to have matter printed elsewhere than at GPO or to prevent the Public Printer (who heads a legislative agency) from contracting to have work done outside of GPO to be "enactments" of "laws" which require plenary consideration by both Houses and presentment to the President.[20]

Until 2003, no one had challenged the JCP's authority in court so there is no court opinion supporting either side.

The SPIRIT coalition of eleven associations opposed the regulations and issued a statement arguing that there should be a comprehensive review of the statutory framework governing public printing. The coalition objected to JCP's expansion into electronic publishing and dissemination. The American Association of Publishers, a member of the coalition, feared that information generated indirectly by government funds would be subject to being printed by the government. JCP responded that that was not the intention of the regulations.

That version of the regulations was never issued. But on September 23, 1985, Mathias issued an addition to the 1977 regulations requiring that departments and agencies submit an annual comprehensive printing and distribution plan so JCP could perform its oversight mission effectively. Agencies did comply with the new requirement. JCP then turned to the Appropriations Committees for support in enforcing GPO's role in providing for the printing requirements of the government. In both 1987 and 1988, language was inserted in the legislative branch appropriations bills mandating that the majority of printed products and services procured from commercial sources be procured through the GPO. JCP in 1989 reasserted its authority to approve agency plans to buy desktop printing equipment arguing that the JCP did not have to abide by the Justice Department opinion.

This struggle between the Joint Committee on Printing and the executive branch led to a number of legislative proposals to either abolish the JCP or to change its authority. None of those proposals as of January 2003 have been enacted into law. So even though JCP has lost its separate office and most of its staff, the law giving it power remains intact.

The Joint Committee on Printing regulations and changes to those regulations always sparked controversy and opposition from the executive branch as well as from private sector publishers. Chair Hays led the JCP struggle in 1974 to amend the regulations to require committee approval before government agencies could make available to private publishers "for initial publication" any information compiled for publication at taxpayer expense. According to a August 12, 1974, story in *Publishers Weekly*, a JCP memo gave three reasons for the move to assert the committee's authority over government publishing.

> The first was cost. Staffers said private publishers, on the whole, charge more than the Government Printing Office. Second it was asserted that publication by GPO assures availability of materials generated by the government with appropriated funds to depository libraries, mechanisms of international exchange and so forth. The third reason was to assure that materials approved for private publication were handled on a competitive basis.

The article continued that the Association of American Publishers will seek a public hearing "[I]f the regulation is approved and does have the effect of curtailing involvement of the private sector in government publishing."

In spite of the efforts of the Office of Management and Budget and private sector publishers to keep JCP and GPO from providing electronic publications to the depository library program, Senator Mathias took steps to make it happen. He started with a historic speech to the attendees of the American Library Association convention in Philadelphia on July 12, 1982, at the Congressional Information Service (CIS) annual breakfast. CIS gave Senator Mathias an honorarium of $2,000 and took him to dinner afterward. CIS did not know that staff more friendly to depository libraries than to the sale of government publications by private publishers had written the chair's speech. In the speech, Senator Mathias announced the establishment of the Joint Committee on Printing's Ad Hoc Committee on Depository Library Access to Federal Automated Data Bases. He explained, "We have just created a new group composed of representatives from the library community and federal agencies to make sure that information captured electronically in federal agencies will be available to you as you need it, without costly processing or storage fees."

In his speech, Senator Mathias forcefully supported a multiformat depository program:

> I favor all federal publications—except those that are restricted for reasons of national security—being available to the public through

the depository libraries. In recent years, we have moved to bring new classes of material into the program. Although eligible for inclusion, much of the material was simply not being provided by the publishing agency. Maps and titles done under contract are examples of what I mean. Today, I am happy to be able to announce that this Fall the maps of the Defense Mapping Agency and the Geological Survey will be made available to depository libraries as a result of our efforts.[21]

Members of the Ad Hoc Committee were carefully selected from "15 organizations, including federal agencies, which broadly represented the producers, disseminators, and users of Government information."[22] To keep some control over those actually selected, the chair of JCP asked each group to name three people giving the committee some discretion in choosing among each group's nominees.

Chair Mathias signed the letter inviting organizations to participate, but the next chair, Representative Hawkins, selected one nominee from each group to serve on the committee. As the JCP professional staff member for library and distribution services, I was appointed as chair of the Ad Hoc Committee. The committee was asked to determine:

1. What and how much Federal government information is in electronic format?
2. If depository libraries have the ability to access the new formats?
3. What are the costs and benefits of providing information in electronic formats?[23]

The committee was also asked to "identify major policy areas which should be addressed in order to meet the intent of pertinent provisions of Title 44, *United States Code*, to make government information publicly available to citizens at no charge through the depository library system."[24]

Although the committee members represented opposing interests, they adopted the following resolution:

The Committee unanimously supports the principle that the Federal Government should provide access to Federal information, as defined in 44 *U.S.C.* paragraph 1901, in electronic form through the depository libraries system. Recognizing that it is technologically feasible to provide such access to electronic information, the Committee recommends that the economic feasibility be investigated through pilot projects.[25]

The Joint Committee on Printing staff held "An Open Forum on the Provision of Electronic Federal Information to Depository Libraries" (S. Print 99-84) in June 1985 to discuss the Ad Hoc Committee's recommendations for pilot projects. Soon after the forum, JCP staff began working with publishing agencies and GPO to identify possible pilot projects. In April 1987, JCP passed a resolution authorizing a series of pilot projects to test the feasibility and practicality of disseminating government publications to depository libraries in electronic formats. A call went out from JCP to agencies asking them to make proposals for pilots. Sixteen proposals were made, and five of them were selected.

Jan Erickson of GPO in consultation with JCP staff developed a plan entitled *Dissemination of Information in Electronic Format to Federal Depository Libraries: Proposed Project Descriptions* in June 1988. JCP members accepted the plan on June 29, 1988, and distributed it for comments. The pilots included providing census data, EPA's *Toxic Release Inventory* and the *Congressional Record* on CD-ROMs, and the *Economic Bulletin Board* and *Energy Research Abstracts* online. The pilots were managed by Jan Erickson of GPO in consultation with JCP professional staffers and took several years to complete. The final reports analyzing the data gathered from the pilots were published between 1992 and 1994. The Joint Committee on Printing did not wait for all the pilot project reports to be published to direct GPO to start providing CD-ROMs to depository libraries on a regular basis. JCP also decided to pursue legislation to make online government information available to depository libraries.

During this time, the House and Senate Appropriations Committees reviewed the progress toward providing electronic government information to depository libraries at their hearings on the legislative branch appropriations. They questioned the Government Printing Office and Joint Committee on Printing about the pilots during their presentations on their budgets. Katherine Mawdsley, associate university librarian at the University of California, Davis, was a frequent and charming witness at the hearings supporting funding for the pilot projects. The university is in the district of the then-chair of the House Committee on Appropriations Subcommittee on the Legislative Branch, Vic Fazio (D-Calif.). Fazio supported funding the pilots even though later he supported the effort under the Bates bill to require that depository libraries pay part of the costs of electronic dissemination and access.

The Joint Committee on Printing believed it needed additional information to assist GPO in providing electronic services for agency publishers and depository libraries. JCP asked the Office of Technology Assessment and the General Accounting Office to conduct complementary studies. In the fall of 1988, OTA produced *Informing the Nation: Federal Information Dissemination in an Electronic Age,* and GAO produced two reports, *Federal Information: Agency Needs and Practices* and *Federal Information: Users' Current and Future Technology Needs.*

James K. Galbraith, economist and professor at the LBJ School of Public Policy at the University of Texas in Austin, at the suggestion of Roy Breimon, JCP staffer and graduate of the LBJ school, served on the OTA advisory committee. Galbraith's selection gave his doctoral student, Kathleen Eisenbeis, the opportunity to educate him about depository libraries and lobby him to support them as a member of the advisory committee. She had worked as a documents librarian at Duke University. When Jaia Barrett, her former boss at Duke and now a staffer for the Association of Research Libraries, alerted her to Galbraith's appointment, she introduced herself and offered to explain the issues from the point of view of the library community. Galbraith and Eisenbeis worked up an independent study course for her, and she spent the semester reading the OTA committee materials and writing briefing papers for him. Eisenbeis attended an open OTA meeting and witnessed Galbraith putting her work to good use defending the public's right to free access to electronic government information.

After earning her Ph.D., Eisenbeis continued to investigate the effects of government policy on the public's access to government information. In 1995, she wrote *Privatizing Government Information: The Effects of Policy on Access to Landsat Satellite Data* (Scarecrow Press).

Another librarian who played a behind-the-scenes role in convincing policymakers to advance the cause of providing public access to government information in electronic format through depository libraries was Richard Leacy. The Ad Hoc Committee on Depository Library Access to Federal Automated Data Bases would never have existed except for the tenacious and charming lobbying of Leacy, government documents librarian at Georgia Tech. He had been a longtime campaigner for the inclusion of statistical data in all formats in the depository program. He was particularly enthralled with the benefits of having government statistical data available to faculty and students. He pointed out the value of having electronic data that researchers could download and combine or compare with electronic data from other sources. He argued that this would inspire research and inventions. When the JCP staff held a public meeting in Atlanta, he organized a special luncheon for JCP staff and local depository librarians. He took the JCP deputy staff director, Faye Padgett, and me out to dinner and lobbied for the establishment of an advisory committee that would look at the feasibility of providing electronic data to libraries. He made a number of visits to Washington, D.C., where he lobbied other members of the JCP staff and his own congressional delegation to support such a committee.

Once the ad hoc committee was established, Judy Russell and Peyton Neal were key in persuading the Information Industry Association to participate in the committee. Neal is a consultant to commercial publishing companies, including a number who republish court opinions and supporting legal information. He also was a key lobbyist for inclusion of law school libraries in the Federal Depository Library Program while he served as a law librarian in Virginia. As a member of the ad hoc committee, Russell initiated the evening get-togethers for committee members at her home. These parties were an important means for members to get to know each other as people and not just as representatives of their organizations. I am convinced that these informal get-togethers made it possible for the committee to arrive at an unanimous recommendation on the steps needed to bring the depository library program into the developing technological world. The story of how online electronic publications became a part of the program will be discussed under the section about Representative Charlie Rose (D-N.C.) and Senator Wendell Ford (D-Ky.).

VOTERS PULL THE PLUG ON REPRESENTATIVE BATES'S PROMISE THAT LIBRARIES WOULD ACCESS ELECTRONIC GOVERNMENT PUBLICATIONS

Representative James Bates (D-Calif.), chair of the Subcommittee on Printing of the Committee on House Administration, assured Eileen Cooke, director of the ALA Washington office on June 4, 1990, that "I am confident that we will mark up and report a successful bill to the full committee." He was referring to H.R. 3849, the Government Printing Office Improvement Act of 1990, a bill that included depository library access to online government information. An internal ALA memo warned its legislation committee members that "HR 3849 proposes, for the first time in the history of the program, that users and depository libraries would have to pay for access to government information, thus increasing the likelihood of a nation of information 'haves' and 'have-nots.'" Bates went from a draft bill in August 1989 that gave free access to government information in electronic format to depository libraries and the public to a bill in 1990 that required cost sharing by depository libraries and fees for library users, back to a bill that waived user fees but still included cost sharing by depository libraries.

Representative Bates's efforts to write a bill and get it passed is a good example of how the passage of legislation is like a play within a play within a play. The on-stage play revolved around the public struggle between those outside Congress who wanted a bill shaped in a particular way and the legislators who were trying to meet the demands of various constituencies outside and inside Congress. The visible play was complicated by the hidden struggle between librarians divided over whether to agree to cost sharing or to fight for free access. The off-stage play was the hidden struggle between members of Congress and their staffs about whether Bates would be allowed to pass a bill that would give the depository libraries free access to government information in online databases. An even more hidden play was whether the members of the Committee on House Administration would allow Bates to pass any bill to bolster his reelection prospects so he could divert attention from the sexual harassment charges that had been leveled against him by several of his staff members.

Bates hired Ronald Kader as a staffer for the Subcommittee on Printing of the Committee on House Administration to help him create and pass legislation. Kader asked staff at the parent committee and the Joint Committee on Printing for assistance in gathering information on past efforts to revise title 44 and in organizing hearings. The JCP assigned me as a professional staffer to assist him. Four Subcommittee on Procurement and Printing hearings chaired by Bates were held in May and June 1989.[26] In August 1989, Kader drafted a bill for introduction by Bates that gave depository libraries free access to government information in electronic format by simply changing the definition of *government publication* in the current use in title 44, section 1901—from *"Government publication"* as used in this chapter means informational matter which is published as an individual document at Government expense, or as required by law,[27] to "the term 'Government publication' means an information product or service which is published, regardless of medium or format, at Government expense, or as required by law."[28]

When Kader asked congressional staff to get their members to cosponsor the bill, he was surprised to learn that one key House staff member on the Joint Committee on Printing and another on the House Appropriations Committee opposed expanding the current program of free access to government publications to online electronic information. Instead, they thought the government could save money by requiring libraries to cost share. They wanted the libraries to pay for the telecommunication costs of receiving the information. The key house staffer remarked at a JCP staff meeting that he had to get involved with the bill if there was a possibility that the full committee might support the bill. At the same time, Senator Wendell Ford (D-Ky.), chair of the Senate Committee on Rules and vice chair of JCP, testified at the May 23, 1989, hearing in support of continued free access to government information in all formats. This set off an internal struggle between those members and staff who supported free access and those who wanted cost sharing.

Kader invited Eileen Cooke and Anne Heanue of the ALA Washington staff to morning coffee several times. He urged them to be prepared to defend ALA's position on free public access to government information in electronic format as testified to by Sandra McAninch from the University of Kentucky at the hearings. He warned them that there were enemies of free access among members of Congress and their staff. This motivated ALA to conduct a survey in the fall of 1989 to find out what depository libraries spent on staff, space, equipment, binding, and other services to support the program. The sample showed that 86 of the 1,400 depository libraries spent $21,402,922 the previous year. This was more than the $19,905,000 spent by the federal government to support all 1,400 libraries.[29]

At the same time the drama off stage was unfolding, Bates had been accused by several of his staffers of sexual harassment. Kader told me that he had given Bates the names of several good lawyers and was concerned about Bates's future as a member of Congress. Kader was so concerned that he started figuring out how he could get another job. I had shown him a financial analysis done by one of the JCP staff, and he asked whether I thought the staff director would object if he were to point out some errors in the analysis. I thought the staff director would be grateful for the information since this would save the committee embarrassment. Kader used that introduction as a way of convincing the staff director and Senator Ford to hire him as an investigator on the Joint Committee on Printing.

Kader's exit from Bates's committee and a warning given to me by a staffer that there was no way that Representative Joseph Gaydos (D-Pa.), a high-ranking member of the committee, was going to allow an alleged sexual abuser to get a bill passed led me to believe that Bates's bill, no matter how good, had doubtful chances of passage. This was not information that I could share with anyone, neither the librarians lobbying for the bill nor other staffers. I had to proceed as if the bill had a chance. Even if the bill failed to gain passage, it would still set a bad precedent if it included language that libraries would have to cost share and users would have to pay fees for online access to government information. Therefore, I encouraged the librarians to listen to Kader's advice and be prepared to defend their position.

After Kader's transfer to the JCP, Representative Bates hired Kathryn Heyer from his home district in California as staff director of the subcommittee. Bowing to the cost cutters, Bates introduced H.R. 3849, the Government Printing Office Improvement Act of 1990, which included "cost sharing, such as contributions from service users, depository libraries, the issuing components of Government, and appropriations for the depository library program." Vic Fazio (D-Calif.), chair of the Subcommittee on the Legislative Branch of the House Appropriations Committee, was a cosponsor. Hearings were held March 7 and 8, 1990, and Katherine Mawdsley from the library at the University of California at Davis in Fazio's district testified for ALA, opposing charging users or libraries for electronic services. The staff of the ALA Washington office and other library associations were good at providing witnesses from the district of the most influential sponsor of a bill. The librarians knew that the elimination of the requirement that libraries cost-share depended on Fazio, the member controlling the purse strings.

In May 1990, Bates, lamented at his first meeting with the Washington Library Task Force that he had just established "that the subcommittee had received an overwhelmingly negative response from the library communities and he raised the question, 'what does the bill accomplish that is not already in title 44?' The Task Force responded that "this bill is important enough to try and save." They further explained in their summary of the meeting, "We also were in agreement that we did not think that the issues had been adequately discussed by the library community and that we were willing to help define the issues and bring them before our colleagues for discussion purposes."

> Congressman Bates' impression and concern is that, without some attention to cost controls in the bill particularly regarding electronic information technology, the Subcommittee could lose the support of members of the House Appropriations Committee. We all intuitively understood this because this is why we were willing to discuss "cost sharing" in the first place.[30]

The Washington Library Task Force was composed of David Cobb, chair of the Depository Library Council to the Public Printer (DLC); Ridley Kessler, former chair of DLC; Susan Tulis, chair of the ALA Government Documents Round Table (GODORT); and Jack Sulzer, chair-elect of GODORT. Bates assured the Washington office of the ALA, that they would be "speaking from a personal viewpoint and not representing the official views of the council or the round table."[31]

This reassurance from Bates about the role of the task force members was important because GODORT had officially adopted a policy on January 1, 1990, that "be it further resolved, that the American Library Association recommend to Congressman Bates that costs of disseminating information in electronic formats to depository libraries be shared by the issuing agency and the Government Printing Office through appropriated funds and not by depository libraries or users of those electronic services." The Depository Library Council members had been appointed by the public printer and DLC is set up to advise the Government Printing Office, not the Congress. Public Printer Robert Houk supported cost sharing.

The task force noted in its summary of the May 1990 meeting:

> It was understood by all present that we were dealing with a very wide range of interests among the depository libraries and that there are differences of opinions within the depository community. In short, we could make no promises, and that, at this point, we were simply acting

individually as concerned depository librarians. We also told Bates that we believed much of the difficulty with his bill was over the definition of "cost sharing" and that the words carried strong negative connotations among librarians who were dealing with budgets as stringent as those faced by federal agencies and Congress. In addition, arriving at a definition of cost sharing, which would have any degree of general acceptance, would be a very difficult task in light of the fact that we were dealing with so many unanswered questions regarding the technology and logistics of electronic information dissemination.[32]

The task force went on to say:

As depository librarians we do not want to pay any costs; philosophically there is a question of depository libraries paying for tax supported information. However, in a worst case scenario we would be willing to discuss telecommunications costs. If need be, access or service fees should be points of negotiation between GPO, the agencies and the library community. In addition, any access fees must be to cover marginal costs only and in no way related to the "value added" to an information service. We like the wording of a May 15, 1990 memo to ARL Directors from Prue Adler on report language for this particular issue which reads as follows: "the cost of accessing those information services that are not basic government information by depository libraries may not exceed the marginal cost of dissemination."[33]

While the members of this task force were willing to consider the idea of cost sharing for electronic products and services by libraries, they were not willing to consider user fees for the public.[34] The idea of cost sharing was raised again among ALA members at the June 1990 meeting of the American Library Association, but the ALA's official position continued to be opposition to cost sharing and user fees. Richard M. Dougherty, president of ALA, and Patricia Glass Schuman, chair of the ALA Committee on Legislation, conveyed that position to Bates, stating:

The American Library Association supports the inclusion of language stating that GPO shall make available electronic information products and services to depository libraries. . . . However, we also urge that the cost-sharing provisions in HR 3849 be withdrawn. We have a fundamental disagreement with the provisions of the proposed legislation that would impose additional costs on depository libraries to access federal government information. Provisions which seek to impose cost sharing in the form of user fees, marginal costs, and licensing fees are in direct conflict with the historic right of Americans to equitable and free access to government information.[35]

The letter went on to say:

We recognize the seriousness of the budget crisis in the federal government; however, a shortage of resources also exists at every level of library service. New and changing technologies have imposed alternate costs on depository libraries. To maintain a viable depository library program, costs of access and dissemination—and thus an informed citizenry—must be a federal responsibility. Shifting this responsibility to other levels of government and institutions supporting depository libraries can only result in inequitable access for the public.[36]

The American Association of Law Libraries testified at the March 1990 hearings:

However, the American Association of Law Libraries cannot support the bill as introduced. Our objections concern (1) the definitions of printing and Government publications and (2) the uncertain and conditional nature of access to electronic information services afforded federal depository libraries.[37]

There were supporters of cost sharing, including the Information Industry Association and Robert Houk, public printer. The public printer and the superintendent of documents are responsible for administering the depository library program. Houk expressed his disappointment in the next version of H.R. 3849:

Finally, the revised language of this section drops any specific reference to cost-sharing. I was hopeful that the concept of cost-sharing could be used as a means of broadening library access to information services in this period of continuing fiscal constraint, although not necessarily in the form that was included in the introduced version of H.R. 3849.[38]

The Information Industry Association expressed its support for the cost-sharing provisions in the first version of H.R. 3849 with this statement:

Section 5 of H.R. 3849 includes a reference to "cost sharing." This is an important concept and the IIA recommends the development of an appropriate legislative history, through additional public hearings, on the intent and implications of this term. We applaud your willingness to step up to one of the most difficult issues of the emerging information age—who will pay. If our citizens are to truly benefit from the products and services of the information society, we must establish government policies which encourage the investment of private sector and other resources to complement the inherently limited taxpayer dollars. Such policies should also permit alternative financing arrangements, including cost sharing, wherein users and other appropriate parties bear a proportionate share of the cost burden. Continued dependence upon the Federal treasury as the primary financing source is guaranteed to deny our citizens the full panoply of information products and services that can be offered. Towards that end, it may well be time to amend Title 44 to create an acceptable mechanism for participating libraries to pay some of the costs associated with the creation and distribution of new electronic information services such as online databases.[39]

The librarians prevailed and the revised H.R. 3849 withdrew explicit references to cost sharing by depository libraries and service users. An August 31, 1990, letter from the American Association of Law Libraries spoke for most of the librarians: "AALL is also relieved that the cost-sharing requirement has been deleted in favor of a requirement that 'all government publications and government produced information be disseminated in whatever format is most appropriate for the information, most cost effective, and most useful for government agencies, libraries and the general public.'[40]

The librarians prevailed because they went to the members of the full committee to plead their case. For example, the Illinois Library Association sent an October 15, 1990, memo to the library constituents of Representative Frank Annunzio (D-Ill.), chair of the full committee and a candidate for reelection, urging them as follows:

Please write to Cong. Annunzio immediately and tell him you'd like to support him but need to know whether he favors the users of government information be specifically exempted from paying "contributions" (user fees) for access to government information in depository libraries and that he agrees that the costs of disseminating information in electronic formats to depository libraries be shared by the issuing agency and the Government Printing Office through appropriated funds and not by depository libraries or their users of those electronic services.[41]

Bates scheduled a markup of the bill for September 18, 1990. Representative Pat Roberts (R-Kans.), a member of the subcommittee, objected to the markup and asked, "Why is it so important to push this bill through subcommittee without thorough study, complete hearings, without budget analysis and without companion legislation in the Senate?" He added, "I also have concerns regarding H.R. 3849 following correspondence I have received from communications industry representatives. Many concerns regarding the legal definitions currently in H.R. 3849."[42]

Bates postponed the markup. He was not able to convince enough subcommittee members to support a markup before the congressional recess in October. Members wanted to go home and campaign for the November elections. Bates lost his election. The decision about whether title 44 would be revised was up to the next chair of the Committee on House Administration and its Subcommittee on Printing.

In working on a bill, always keep in mind that a subcommittee must send a bill to the full committee where it must be accepted before it can go to the floor of Congress for a vote. Unless the chair of the full committee is onboard, the bill will seldom be enacted. In spite of the support for cost sharing by Bates, chair of the Subcommittee on Printing and Procurement, and Fazio, chair of the appropriations subcommittee on the legislative branch, cost sharing by users and libraries was eliminated in the bill because the chair of the full committee, Annunzio, listened to his constituents.

SILENT HOLD AND PRESIDENTIAL
POLITICS DEFEAT THE ELECTRONIC BILL

Sometimes the ideal sponsor of a bill becomes the kiss of death when the sponsor is a political target, usually for something totally unrelated to your bill. Senator Al Gore (D-Tenn.) introduced the GPO Gateway Act (S. 2813), building on the GPO Wide Information Network for Data Online Act of 1991 (H.R. 2772) (GPO WINDO) introduced by Representative Charlie Rose (D-N.C.) in the House. Both bills would have required all federal agencies to provide their electronic databases to depository libraries through the GPO. The WINDO bill passed the House near the end of the 102nd Congress. Since Senator Gore was running for vice president and Senator Ford preferred to present the bill as nonpartisan, he decided to wait for the WINDO bill to be referred to the Senate rather than call for a vote on the version that he and Senator Gore had introduced. Without Senator Gore's name on the WINDO bill, Senators Ford and Stevens

considered it so noncontroversial that they put it on the consent calendar for easy acceptance at the end of the congressional session.
But a mysterious senator found out about Senator Gore's connection
to the bill and put a silent hold on it. The bill never got voted on by
the Senate and so was not passed. Read the whole story about the
mysterious hold in the later section where I discuss passage of the
GPO Access Act.

Secret senatorial holds started in the 1960s as a way of allowing a
senator to work out concerns about the bill with a sponsor. According
to a story in the *Washington Post* in October 1997, holds were responsible for stalling some forty-two nominations to federal positions. To
place a hold on a nomination or a bill, a senator writes a letter to the
majority leader stating the senator's concerns. Those letters are seldom, if ever, made public "although the Senate has approved a measure offered by Sen. Ron Wyden (D-Ore.) to make them public. That
measure was part of an appropriations bill in a House-Senate conference committee."[43] That bill did not make it out of conference.

According to a story in the Sunday *Oregonian*, Senator Wyden
started his crusade against silent holds when "[a]s a House member,
he found that a bill he had co-sponsored, which had passed the
House, suddenly hit a Senate blank wall in the closing days of the
session. Late one night, he recalls, he and a staff member spent time
traipsing over to the Senate, trying to find out who had a hold on it."

Senator Wyden told the reporter, "To hold something up, you
ought to have to do it publicly. What people are concerned about is
the abuse of the hold, absolving the person who does it from any accountability."[44] In 1999, the silence was shattered when Senate majority leader Trent Lott (R-Miss.) and minority leader Tom Daschle
(D-S.D.) issued a joint letter directing senators requesting holds to
notify the bill's sponsor and the appropriate committees, as well as
the majority and minority leaders. Senator Wyden said, "The Senate
is sending a message that there's going to be some sunshine on the
floor of this body."[45]

REPRESENTATIVE CHARLIE ROSE'S
BEHIND-THE-SCENES WORK TO UNSEAT A CHAIRMAN

Representative Charlie Rose (D-N.C.) defied the tradition of seniority when in 1991 he defeated both Frank Annunzio (D-Ill.), the chair,

and Joseph Gaydos (D-Pa.), ranking member of the Committee on House Administration, to become the committee's chair for the 102nd Congress. This also made him the chair of the Joint Committee on Printing for 1991 and 1992.

Representative Rose's later efforts to acquire more power illustrates the danger of aspiring to too much power and what happens when you lose. Representative Rose decided to run for Speaker of the House in the 104th Congress when it convened in 1995, but when the Republicans won the November 1994 elections, it became a leadership race for the Democratic Caucus rather than the speakership of the whole House. He ran against Representative Richard A. Gephardt (D-Mo.) and lost. Shortly thereafter, the *Washington Post* reported, "Democratic Leader Richard A. Gephardt (D-Mo.) this week deposed Rep. Charlie Rose (D-N.C.) as the top Democrat on the House Administration Committee."[46] Instead, Representative Vic Fazio (D-Calf.) became the ranking member of the House Oversight Committee (new name for the Committee on House Administration). The *Washington Post* reporter speculated that Rose had been punished for his challenge to Gephardt. "It used to be that strong congressional leaders maintained party discipline by punishing errant members, a practice that has been abandoned in this era of independent-minded lawmakers. Or has it? Circumstances surrounding two committee assignments in the House and Senate suggest otherwise."[47]

As a staff member of a committee chaired by Rose, I had a real interest in his ambitions because if he won, the chair of the Joint Committee on Printing would change and staff would once again be in jeopardy. One of Rose's staff actively involved in his campaign told me that he was shocked when Rose lost because he had counted the votes ahead of time and Rose had more than enough to win. He ruefully concluded that they had simply not factored in enough liars.

DEMOCRATS AND REPUBLICANS
WORKING AS A TEAM TO PASS THE GPO ACCESS ACT

During the 102nd and 103rd Congresses, Representative Charlie Rose (D-N.C.), chair of the Committee on House Administration, and Senator Wendell Ford (D-Ky.), chair of the Senate Committee on Rules, rotated the chair of the Joint Committee on Printing. They and their staff worked together to pass the GPO Access Act of 1993 (PL 103-40), which established a system to provide the public with free access to government information in electronic form. One reason they were able to pass the bill is because they included the Republicans, Senator Ted Stevens (R-Alaska), ranking member on the Senate Committee on Rules and Administration, and Representative Bill Thomas (R-Calif.), ranking member of the Committee on House Administration, as full partners in their efforts.

It took a long time and the efforts of many librarians, library associations, public interest lobbyists, and congressional staff to persuade key members of the Senate Rules Committee, the Committee on House Administration, and the Joint Committee on Printing to secure the passage of the GPO Access Act. The key members of those committees would not have pursued provision of online government information to depository libraries without the long-term lobbying efforts of librarians and others in their home states and districts.

Librarians had to convince members of Congress that the arguments for providing free electronic access to libraries were right and the objections to it by others should be ignored. Private sector publishers argued that government should only produce information in electronic format and should then turn that information over to the private sector for dissemination. Government agencies argued that they should control dissemination of electronic information and should be able to charge the public for that access in order to cut the cost of government.

It was very helpful that during the years this legislation evolved and passed a series of presidents of the American Library Association, chairs of ALA's Legislation Committee, and the Government Documents Round Table were from the home states of key members of Congress. A number of the witnesses at the hearings held by the legislative and appropriations committees to explore the shape of the legislation were also from those states thanks to the ALA Washington office, which was often called on to suggest and work with witnesses on their testimony. In preparing for the Joint Committee on Printing's hearings on public access and technology and later on the bills, one of the political staff asked me how so many experts could come from our members' states, and I replied that fortunately these people were experts. Those librarians who testified and lobbied over a number of years to persuade members of Congress to sponsor and pass the bills deserve most of the credit.[48]

Another reason the GPO Access Act passed is because the staff of the Joint Committee on Printing believed in the public's right to free access to government information and convinced the members of Congress, whom they represented on the JCP, that providing electronic government information through the depository library program would strengthen democracy. That belief was held by staff representing both Democratic and Republican senators and representatives. As a professional staffer and librarian, I worked with all of the political staffers to provide them with information to bolster their belief that getting electronic government information into the depository program would benefit the public and Congress. I made sure that political staffers met the officers and staff of the library and public interest associations so they would understand why access to government information was important to their member's constituents. I encouraged those staffers to accept speaking engagements at library conferences and attend Depository Library Council meetings. When they did attend meetings, I made sure that they met librarians from their member's home districts, states, and alma maters. I encouraged librarians and public interest advocates to visit and call the members of Congress and political staff.

Anne Heanue, a lobbyist for the American Library Association, was there every time an attempt was made to provide the public with access to electronic information through libraries. She made sure that members of ALA were called as witnesses at hearings, helped them write their testimony, introduced them to members of Congress and their staff, kept them informed about every step toward the passage of a proposed bill, and encouraged them to lobby and to keep fighting. Every time a bill came unraveled, she was there to encourage the library community to pick up the quilting needle and start all over again.

Heanue and I realized that passage of a bill to provide the public with access to online government information would not happen without the support of public interest groups and others. When Anne met James P. Love of the Taxpayer Assets Project at a hearing, she suggested that we enlist him in our cause. Heanue and I met with Love and told him about librarians' long quest for a law authorizing the inclusion of electronic government information in the depository library program. He agreed to work with us to write a position paper laying out exactly what we wanted. There were three drafts (November 26, December 13, and December 26, 1990). Love's paper laid out a plan that would allow depository libraries and the public access to all government databases. The ALA Committee on Legislation reviewed each version of the position paper as it was being developed and worked on enlisting supporters.

ALA's lawyer, Thomas Sussman of Ropes and Gray, took that position paper and drafted the GPO Wide Information Network Data Online Act of 1991 (GPO WINDO) to fit the vision that we had articulated. Anne Heanue and Eileen Cooke of the ALA Washington office brought the draft bill dated June 20, 1991, to meetings with JCP and GPO staff, where some changes were made. ALA also indicated that the following organizations were also in support of the draft bill: American Historical Association, National Coordinating Committee for the Promotion of History, Organization of American Historians, Public Citizen, Special Libraries Association and the Taxpayer Assets Project.

On June 26, 1991, Heanue and Cooke met with Charlie Rose, chair of the Committee on House Administration, and asked him to introduce the bill in the House. They expected him to tell them that he needed time to review the bill and that he would get back to them. Instead, he shocked them by saying, "I will introduce the bill in the House today so you will have something to take to your national meeting next week in Atlanta." Rose had already been assured by the staff director of the JCP that the staff supported the language of the bill. It was introduced as H.R. 2772.

Chair Rose was well educated in how government publications were escaping the depository library program and was ready to introduce the bill because he had heard from his librarian constituents and held hearings on April 25, 1991, entitled "Government Information as a Public Asset." Witnesses included librarians, public interest advocates, agency publishers, and the public printer. A number of witnesses were from his home state of North Carolina. The first panel explained what government information was not being provided to depository libraries as required by law. Cynthia Bower, government publications librarian at the University of Arizona, suggested that one way to solve the problem of fugitive documents would be to provide an electronic catalog of government documents and allow libraries to download the full text of those documents into their own system. Ridley Kessler, regional federal documents librarian at the University of North Carolina at Chapel Hill, and Sandra McAninch, head of government publications at the University of

Kentucky Library, agreed with Bower that electronic technology could help solve the problem. A second panel discussed how current information dissemination practices affected the users of government information. Panelists included James Love of the Center for Study of Responsive Law, Joan Claybrook of Public Citizen, and Jeanne Isacco from Chapel Hill, North Carolina, and director of U.S. government publications for Readex. A third panel composed of agency publishers and printers discussed what agencies could do to improve the public's access to government information. Witnesses included James Billington, librarian of Congress; John L. Okay and Ronald N. De Munbrun of the Department of Agriculture; and Alvin M. Pesachowitz of the Environmental Protection Agency. Robert W. Houk, public printer of the United States, was the final witness.

Before the introduction of the WINDO bill, librarians and others lobbied for or against the bill. Faye Padgett, assistant staff director of JCP, and I met with Eileen Cooke and Anne Heanue, ALA Washington office lobbyists; Patricia Glass Schuman, president of ALA; and Nancy Kranich, the chair of the Subcommittee on Government Information of the Committee on Legislation. Padgett and I also met with the staff of the *Electronic Public Information Newsletter*. They wrote a number of editorials supporting the bill.

After introduction of the bill, JCP staff met with Linda Kennedy, the chair of GODORT; Sandy Morton, lobbyist for the Special Libraries Association; and Patricia Glass Schuman. I had dinner with Arthur Curley, the president of the Association of Research Libraries and asked him why as of October 21, 1991, the association had not indicated support of the bill. Shortly after that ARL signed on. I had lunch with Jeanne Hurley Simon, chair of NCLIS; dinner with Thomas Susman, lawyer for ALA; lunch with Timothy Sprehe of the Office of Management and Budget; and talked to Joan Claybrook of Public Citizen. I also met with Dennis McKenna, editor of *Government Technology Journal*, who later wrote an editorial supporting the bill. James Love invited me to attend a Public Citizen Conference at Georgetown University where he and David Burnham spoke on a panel about access to government information.

JCP staff met with the ALA Committee on Legislation at their retreats before and after introduction of the bill. JCP staff also attended receptions given by ALA for Congressional staff and others. During this time ALA issued press releases supporting the bill and sent letters to all the members of the Committee on House Administration with a copy of the July 1991 ALA resolution supporting the GPO WINDO bill. By that time over a dozen associations were supporting the bill. ALA also sent a copy of the resolution to all the associations supporting the bill.

In the middle of the work on the bill, Faye Padgett and Richard Olezewski, longtime supporters of provision of government information in electronic format to depository libraries, left the JCP. Chair Rose hired John Merritt as his staff director of the JCP and charged him with getting the bill passed. Merritt started work on October 28, 1991, and I met with him on November 19, 1991, to discuss a strategy for getting the bill passed. He asked me to set up a series of meetings with those for and against the bill and also to arrange meetings for him with all the interested groups and brief him on who they were and what they had to gain or lose from the bill. He invited me to accompany him to meetings with library groups such as ALA, Coalition on Networked Information, Depository Library Council, American Association of Law Libraries, and the Medical Library Association. We met with the American Association of Publishers, CENDI, Mitch Kapor and Jerry Berman of the Electronic Frontier Foundation, Printing Industry of America, the Information Industry Association, National Technical Information Service, Office of Management and Budget staff, and the unions at GPO.

We booked Representative Rose as a speaker at the Federal Library Committee's annual Forum on Federal Information Policies on March 17, 1992. Rose told the audience:

> The future of government information is, indeed, highly dependent upon how we, who serve in government, effectively balance and utilize money, management and technology. A major concern I have, which was reflected in my first chaired hearing by the Joint Committee on Printing on April 25, 1991, is that government information remain a public asset. It is evident that a concern continues to exist and that a great deal of information gathered at public expense is not reaching the depository library system.

He discussed the GPO WINDO bill that he had introduced on June 26, 1991, and emphasized the need for congressional action with a quote from President Woodrow Wilson: "The informing function of Congress should be preferred even to its legislative function."[49]

On April 27, 1992, Rose spoke at the Special Interest Group on CD-ROM Applications and Technology (SIGCAT) conference. Merritt asked me to help write Rose's speech and sent me along to brief him on the attendees at SIGCAT. Rose explained his bill to the group. Then he pulled a CD-ROM out of his suit jacket and said that he carried around his own reference library. After the speech, Rose and I were let off at the Capitol. He told me that he was aware that I had been hired by Hays. He said that Hays had been kind to him as a freshman legislator and had helped him through a personal tragedy. He told me not to worry—we were going to get a bill.

We invited Ridley Kessler, regional depository librarian from the University of North Carolina at Chapel Hill, to meet with Rose on April 7, 1992, to explain why the bill would be good for North Carolina. Later that day, Kessler and Gary Cornwell, federal documents librarian at the University of Florida, met with John Merritt and me to discuss details of the bill. Both Kessler and Cornwell were members of the Depository Library Council as well as members of GODORT. On April 22, Cornwell sent a letter to John Merritt praising Representative Rose for his commitment to passage of the GPO WINDO bill. The letter included the draft of a list of concerns regarding the bill and steps that GPO could take in providing electronic information to depository libraries. Cornwell and Kessler met with Merritt and me on April 29 to discuss the draft paper. The paper emphasized, "By definition, depository libraries should be free from costs for government documents" and "telecommunication charges should be picked up by the agency or GPO."

During the rest of 1992, Merritt authorized me to speak about the bill at the conferences of the Association of Public Data Users, EDUCOM, the Coalition on Networked Information, and the Federal Publishers Committee. In January 1993, Representative Rose sent Shirley Woodrow, Senator Stevens's staffer, and me to the ALA midwinter conference in Denver to discuss the bill with GODORT and the ALA Committee on Legislation. Woodrow delivered a message for Rose about the GPO budget shortfall. Rose had received a lot of letters as the result of a November 18, 1992, letter sent to depository librarians from Superintendent of Documents Wayne Kelley outlining cuts to the program. Woodrow explained to the attendees of the conference:

> I was asked to bring you a specific message from Chairman Charlie Rose. That message is a renewed challenge to librarians to acknowledge

a downward trend in funding. That challenge is to recognize there are limits to format and product; to come to terms with the fact that there will be a net reduction in funds for libraries in the next few years unless changes are made. It will be politically impossible to ask for supplemental appropriations for libraries. This is what is known in Washington as a "reality check."[50]

Woodrow went on to say that Chairman Rose wanted the conference to put together a "Blue Ribbon Committee" representing various types of libraries in the depository program "who must have the authority to speak for their constituencies as a whole" and who will "identify and prioritize cost-saving alternatives" and "meet quickly and act decisively to bring a consensus to the Chairman."[51]

Julia Wallace, the chair of GODORT, met with John Merritt, outgoing staff director; John Chambers, incoming staff director; Shirley Woodrow; and myself on February 11, 1993, to discuss GODORT's plans to address the challenge and the bill to provide electronic access to depository libraries. By the middle of February, Rose was no longer chair, and Chambers withdrew the challenge. Discussions were further complicated by the resignation of Robert Houk as public printer and the appointment of Michael DiMario as acting public printer. GODORT decided to address the challenge anyway and organized a group of eighteen librarians, including seven former GODORT chairs and representatives of other library associations to focus discussions on the future of the depository library program.

Once the GPO WINDO bill was introduced, Rose wanted every member of the Committee on House Administration to cosponsor his bill, so I was directed to call the staff of all the Democratic committee members and ask them to ask their boss to cosponsor the bill. The majority of the members responded that if it was Rose's bill, it had to be good, and they signed on. Dan Crowley and Linda Kemp handled getting Republican House members to cosponsor the bill. Of course, without the long-term education by librarians of members of Congress about the value of the depository library program, those phone calls would have fallen on deaf ears.

Once the bill was introduced in the House by Charlie Rose, we needed a companion bill on the Senate side. JCP staff set out to capitalize on the work that librarians in the field were doing to convince Senator Ford and other senators to introduce a bill. We knew that Senator Gore, a member of JCP and the Senate Rules Committee, would be key because of his work in the passage of the High Performance Computing Act of 1991 with its provisions for construction of the National Research and Education Network (NREN), one of the legs of the electronic information superhighway. Senator Gore testified in support of Congress getting on the Internet at the June 1991 JCP hearings on new technology and GPO. I asked James Klumpner, Majority senior economist on the Joint Economic Committee, to help me convince Michael Nelson, Gore's staffer on technology issues, to persuade Senator Gore to introduce a companion bill. Nelson served on the Subcommittee on Science, Technology, and Space of the Senate Committee on Commerce, Science, and Transportation. Klumpner argued that it made economic good sense to use the existing Federal Depository Library Program to deliver electronic government information to the public, and Nelson agreed. Senator Gore introduced S. 2813, the GPO Gateway to Government Act of 1992. Klumpner then persuaded Senator Paul Sarbanes (D-Md.), chair of the Joint Economic Committee, to cosponsor the bill. Lois Mills persuaded Senator Paul Simon (D-Ill.), Sandra McAninch and James Nelson persuaded Senator Ford, and Robert Walter and Duane Johnson of Kansas convinced Senator Nancy Kassebaum (R-Kans.).

On July 23, 1992, Senator Ford, chair of the Senate Committee on Rules and Administration, and Representative Rose, chair of the Committee on House Administration, held a joint hearing on both bills. Opening statements supporting the bills were made by Senators Ford, Stevens, and Gore. Witnesses included Representatives Major Owens (D-N.Y.) and Barbara Vucanovich (R-Nev.); Robert Houk, public printer; Richard West, chair of the Steering Committee of the Coalition on Networked Information and associate vice president of information systems at the University of California; Brian Kahn, Information Infrastructure Project, John F. Kennedy School of Government at Harvard; William H. Graves, associate provost, Office of Information Technology, University of North Carolina at Chapel Hill; James Nelson, state librarian of Kentucky; Penny Loeb, reporter for *Newsday*; Steven Metalitz, vice president and general counsel for the Information Industry Association; and Patricia Glass Schuman, immediate past president of the American Library Association.

To gain the support of the Republicans for the GPO WINDO bill, Chairman Rose agreed to rename it the Government Printing Office Electronic Information Access Enhancement Act of 1992 (H.R. 5983) and it was introduced on September 22, 1992. It was sponsored by

Representatives Rose, Thomas, Roberts, Owens, and twenty-seven other Democratic and Republican members of the House. It was favorably reported out of the Committee on House Administration to the full House on September 23 and passed by the House on September 29. The GPO Access Act bill was referred to the Senate. It was reported favorably out of the Senate Rules Committee and put on the consent calendar.

Senator Ford did not want politics to interfere with passage of the bill although the GPO Gateway to Government Act sponsored by Senator Gore and himself was reported favorably out of the Senate Rules Committee on September 10, 1992. He decided to wait until the GPO Access Act passed the House and was referred to the Senate Committee on Rules and Administration for a vote of the committee. He did this because Senator Gore was running for vice president, and instead of having the bill caught in a political contest, Senator Ford decided it would be better to pass the House version and put it on the consent calendar.

Once the House bill was referred to the Rules Committee and reported out, it was put on the Senate consent calendar because Senators Ford and Stevens were not expecting any objections to the bill. JCP staff were so sure that the bill would pass that we brought champagne to the JCP offices to celebrate. Instead, we ended up spending a terrible night trying to find out the name of the mysterious senator who had put a hold on the bill. The hold was the result of this senator learning of a request by Gore's staffer Michael Nelson for a colloquy between Senators Hollings and Ford. The colloquy mentioned the role that Gore had played in the legislation. Senator Ford did not want such a colloquy, fearing that it would doom the bill. We tried to persuade Nelson to drop the colloquy with the promise that Senator Ford would issue a press release later praising Senator Gore's role in the legislation. Instead, Nelson got Senator Hollings to put a hold on the bill to pressure Senator Ford to allow the colloquy. Word got out and another senator, unknown to us, put a hold on the bill in order to kill it. Librarians, congressional staffers, and even OMB staff called around to find out who had the hold on the bill to try to get him or her to lift it. We never did learn the identity of the mysterious senator. The bill was dead for the 102nd Congress.

The GPO Access Act was reintroduced as H.R. 1328 on March 11, 1993, by Chairman Charlie Rose, Bill Thomas, Newt Gingrich, Sam Gejdenson (D-Conn.), and Gerald Kleczka (D-Wisc.). The new version added a storage facility and was reported out favorably to the full House on March 17. S. 564, a bill identical to H.R. 1328, was introduced by Senators Ford and Stevens and reported out favorably from Senate Committee on Rules on March 18 and was passed by the Senate on March 22. On May 20, S. 564 was referred to the Committee on House Administration and reported out to the House. It passed the House on May 25, and Public Law 103-40 was signed by the president on June 8, 1993.

During the complicated process of introduction, reintroduction, and passage of the bill, the library community continued to lobby key members of Congress in both political parties. Celebrating Freedom of Information Day, March 15, 1993, the Coalition on Government Information awarded the Madison Award to Senators Ford and Stevens and to Representatives Rose and Thomas for their support of the bill. The award was also given to Vice President Gore for his early work on the bill. After accepting the award from the chair of the coalition, Nancy Kranich, Senator Ford said he had never hugged a dean of a university before. Kranich is the one who suggested that they be honored after I complained to her that none of the members of the Joint Committee on Printing had ever been honored by the library community for their ongoing support for the Depository Library Program and the public's access to government information. I also suggested that both Democrats and Republicans be honored since they had all worked so hard for the bill. The members seemed to be genuinely touched by the award, and even though they were already committed to passage of the GPO Access Act, I believe that the award strengthened their resolve. For example, Senator Ford introduced the bill in the Senate just after Freedom of Information Day. Senator Stevens put his award in an honored place behind his desk.

The support for the bills by Senators Ford and Stevens and Representatives Rose, Thomas, and Roberts did not happen overnight. Librarians from their states had educated them and their staff about the Depository Library Program over the years. The librarians visited their offices during the joint ALA/District of Columbia Library Association annual legislative day and when they were in town for the Depository Library Council and library association meetings.

Sandra McAninch, regional depository librarian at the University of Kentucky, and Jim Nelson, Kentucky state librarian, had convinced Senator Ford that providing electronic government information through depository libraries would benefit the state of Kentucky. Nelson had been a speech writer for Senator Ford when the senator was governor of Kentucky.

The University of Kentucky and the State Library developed a depository library pilot project proposal to test how government information in electronic format could be shared with all the libraries in the state. Senator Ford sent me to Kentucky to give them some technical advice on developing their plan. In 1989, the proposal was accepted, and McAninch invited Senator Ford to visit the university library in 1990 to see how the students and faculty were using the government information. The press covered his visit, and his photo appeared in the University of Kentucky newspaper.

Senator Ford decided that passage of the GPO Access bill would enhance distance learning in his mountainous state. Distance learning would make it possible for working people to attend college without having to move to the college town. The Senator worked behind the scenes to assure that the storage facility for electronic publications required by the GPO Access Act would be located at the University of Kentucky in Owensboro. (Owensboro was his hometown.) He believed that having the storage facility would attract economic development to Kentucky.

McAninch worked closely with Senator Ford's press liaison in his Kentucky office. She often consulted him on whom to contact in Washington, D.C. Both McAninch and Nelson attended library legislative days in D.C. and were witnesses at congressional hearings. When McAninch was chair of the Government Documents Round Table, she testified on behalf of ALA at hearings on revision of depository legislation in 1989. Once the GPO access bills were introduced, McAninch invited John Chambers, Ford's key staffer on the JCP, to attend a meeting with librarians in Kentucky to explain the bills. She worked with Sara Jones, general counsel of JCP and a native of Kentucky, on the plans for the storage facility at Owensboro. She kept the librarians in the state informed about the status of the depository library pilot projects, hearings, and the successive bills. She would e-mail, call, or write them when action in support of the bill was needed.

As noted earlier, North Carolina librarians played an important role in convincing Representative Rose to champion depository library access to electronic government information. Those librarians included Ridley Kessler, regional depository documents librarian at the University of North Carolina at Chapel Hill; Dan Barkley, documents librarian at Wake Forest University; Jeanne Isacco at Readex; and Marilyn Miller at the University of North Carolina, Department of Library and Information Studies. Miller was also president of ALA during 1992 and 1993.

Once we knew that the bill would pass, JCP and the legislative committee staffs started work on language for the reports that would accompany the bill. The reports were H. Rpt. 102-933 on H.R. 5983 (September 29, 1992), S. Rpt. 103-27 on S. 564 (March 18, 1993), H. Rpt. 103-51 on H.R. 1328 (April 1, 1993) and H. Rpt. 103-108 (May 25, 1993) on S. 564. Reports include committee action, committee oversight findings, statement of budget authority, Congressional Budget Office cost estimate, committee discussion and consideration of the bill, and a section-by-section explanation of the bill.

I was assigned the job of gathering information for Congressional Budget Office to use in its analysis. I asked Wayne Kelley, superintendent of documents; James Klumpner, Joint Economic Committee; James Love, director of the Taxpayers Assets Project; and Anne Heanue at the ALA Washington office to provide data. ALA and the Coalition on Networked Information started working on gathering data on the cost of implementing the proposed GPO WINDO in early 1992. Love had been working on the possible costs of electronic dissemination since early 1991. The superintendent of documents had the results of the electronic pilot projects and subsequent distribution of CD-ROMs to the depository libraries.

The ALA Washington office staff reviewed the series of reports, and Anne Heanue suggested the addition of the following language to the final report H. Rpt. 103-108: "While this legislation does not require agencies to make Federal electronic information available through this system of online access, the Committee does not intend to relieve agencies of their existing responsibility to provide publications in electronic formats to the Depository Library Program."[52]

After passage of the legislation, the American Library Association passed a resolution on June 30, 1993, thanking the Congress for passage of the GPO Access Act stating, "Enactment of this Act is a splendid first step in establishing a framework that will guarantee the public equitable, free, and easy access to government information in electronic format."

REPRESENTATIVE NEWT GINGRICH
AS THE NEW SPEAKER TAKES CREDIT FOR
GETTING HOUSE DATA ON THE INTERNET

Representative Newt Gingrich (R-Ga.) became the Speaker of the House of Representatives in 1995, the first Republican Speaker in forty years. One of his first priorities was to promote himself as the force behind the public's access to House legislative information over the Internet. In his book *Lessons Learned the Hard Way*, he writes:

> Another example of entrepreneurship was Vern Ehler's remarkable achievement between Election Day 1994 and the day after our swearing-in January 1995. In less than two months' time Vern had worked with James Billington, the Librarian of Congress, to develop an Internet system for the United States House of Representatives. It is called Thomas after Thomas Jefferson, and it allows anyone in the world to access information and House records through the Internet.[53]

He neglected to tell the world that the new system cost almost $2 million to establish and that most of the electronic bills and hearings in it were provided by GPO to LC and were already available through the GPO Access System as required by the 1993 GPO Access Act. Those electronic bills and hearings were keyed in by GPO staff who also provided the electronic information for the GPO Access system. While Gingrich claimed credit for getting House information on the Internet, the senators who had helped get the GPO Access Act passed were using the GPO Access system to provide public access to the Senate's bills and hearings.

Speaker Gingrich did have it right, though, when he exulted:

> [O]ne of the proudest moments in my career came in the summer of 1997, when Bill Archer got up on the floor of the House and announced, "I am now filing the tax bill. Within thirty seconds it will be available to every American through the Internet without having to call a lobbyist or a trade association or pay for a subscription to any service." This is the true grassroots populism of the information age. It was a wonderful moment, and within a few hours over 200,000 citizens had downloaded the tax bill onto their computers. Lobbyists had the experience of getting phone calls from back home in which the clients to whom they were speaking had the bill in front of them and knew as much or more about the details as their Washington "specialists." This was the dawning of a new day in representative self-government.[54]

The librarians had done a great job of lobbying Congress to provide the public with free public access to online government information through depository libraries, but they had not counted on the politicians seeing this as yet another way to cut the cost of the federal government. Speaker Gingrich and his hand-picked chairs of the Committees on House Administration and Appropriations did not miss the import of the new free services available over the GPO Access System. They saw this as a good opportunity to save money by eliminating the paper, microform, and even the CD-ROM versions of publications. They pushed GPO into developing a plan that would transform the depository library program into an entirely electronic program by October 1998. They argued that this would cut the cost of the program in half and thus proposed cutting in half the appropriation for the depository library program. This forced the same librarians who for years had fought for electronic access to now fight for a multiformat program that not only provided for rapid current access to information but also provided for long-term preservation and access to that same information in permanent formats. The librarians argued that it was not yet technologically feasible to preserve online electronic information for future users. Only acid-free paper has been proven to last for hundreds of years. Not even silver microforms have been around long enough to know how long they will last. Thanks to an outcry from the library community and the intercession of Senator Stevens, the chair of the Joint Committee on Printing, the Senate Rules Committee, and a member of the Senate Committee on Appropriations, the Senate restored the funds for the DLP cut by the House Appropriations Committee, and the plan was not implemented. Instead, a plan was adopted that would gradually increase the amount of government information available only electronically.

Senator Stevens's support of the library community was long-term. The librarians in Alaska had worked closely with Senator Stevens and his staff for years and had lobbied him on a variety of library concerns including the depository library program. It was also fortunate that Ann Symons from Juneau, Alaska, was president of ALA during that time. But the real credit to Senator Stevens's ongoing support of the depository program and the public's right to free access to government information is owed to Shirley Woodrow, Senator Stevens's key staffer on the Joint Committee on Printing. Woodrow and the senator loved libraries and understood the need for public access to government information in multiple formats. Woodrow took her responsibilities to represent Senator Stevens seriously. She worked closely with me as a professional librarian on the staff of JCP and with staff of the Superintendent of Documents Office to learn as much about the depository library program as possible. She attended Depository Library Council meetings and met with depository librarians and staff of the library associations. It was Woodrow who negotiated on Senator Stevens's behalf with the staff of Republican senators on the Appropriations Committee to save the funding for a multiformat depository library program.

THE FATE OF SENATOR STEVENS AS A RESULT OF SENATOR PACKWOOD'S RESIGNATION

Even when a legislator moves to a new position because of colleague's misfortune or good fortune, that member may be able to help your cause in his or her new role. Senator Stevens, champion of depository libraries, gave up the crucial position as chair of Senate Rules Committee where he had power over title 44 of the *U.S. Code* and took over as chair of the Committee on Governmental Affairs when Senator Robert Packwood (R-Ore.) had to resign from the Senate because of sexual harassment charges. This new committee assignment enabled him to assist the depository program in another way since he could influence overall information policy. He continued to hold his powerful position on the Senate Appropriations Committee. In the 105th Congress, he became the chair of the Appropriations Committee and used his new power to continue to protect the depository library program funding during the 105th, 106th, and 107th Congresses. As chair of the Appropriations Committee, he was instrumental in obtaining millions of dollars for the Library of Congress so it could develop a digital library.

NOTES

1. Robert Walters, "A Very Complex Chairman," *Washington Star*, April 9, 1974.

2. Memo from Rosemary Cribben, assistant staff director of the Joint Committee on Printing, to Denver Dickerson, staff director, February 19, 1975.

3. Unpublished memo from Rosemary Cribben, staff director of the Joint Committee on Printing to Wayne L. Hays, chair of the JCP, October, 23, 1974.

4. Supplemental Appropriations Bill, 1975, Senate Rpt. No. 93-1255, to accompany H.R. 16900, 93rd Congress, 2nd sess.

5. Letter to Catherine J. Reynolds, Government Documents Division, University of Colorado, from Document Expediting (DOCEX) Project, Exchange and Gift Division, Library of Congress, Washington, D.C., September 1976.

6. "Rep. Hays Quits Seat in Congress," *Washington Post*, September 2, 1976, A1 and A12.

7. Mark Green with Michael Waldman, *Who Runs Congress* (New York: Dell, 1984), 246–48.

8. "Ex-Rep. Wayne Hays, Famed for Power and Scandal Dies," *Roll Call*, February 20–26, 1989, 1.

9. Richard Pearson, "Wayne Hays Dies; Served in House for 27 Years," *Washington Post*, February 11, 1989, C6.

10. Jim Wright, *Balance of Power: Presidents and Congress from the Era of McCarthy to the Age of Gingrich* (Atlanta: Turner, 1996), 242–43.

11. A conversation between Rosemary Cribben and Bernadine E. Abbott-Hoduski on the day that the story hit the newspapers.

12. Tip O'Neill and William Novak, *Man of the House: The Life and Political Memoirs of Speaker Tip O'Neill* (New York: St. Martin's, 1988), 258.

13. *Depository Libraries*, hearings before the Subcommittee on the Library of the Committee on Rules and Administration of the United States Senate, 87th Congress, 2nd sess., on S. 2029 and H.R. 8141, March 15 and 16, 1962 (Washington, D.C.: U.S. Government Printing Office, 1962), 51.

14. Ad Hoc Committee on Revision of Title 44 to the Joint Committee on Printing. United States Congress, *Federal Government Printing and Publishing: Policy Issues* (Washington, D.C.: U.S. Government Printing Office, 1979), v–vi.

15. Joseph P. Fried, "Frank Thompson Jr., 70; Career in Congress Ended with ABSCAM," *New York Times*, July 24, 1989, D11; *New York Times*, November 29, 1981, 6E; Thompson, Dennis F., *Ethics in Congress: From Individual to Institutional Corruption* (Washington, D.C.: Brookings Institution, 1995), 103.

16. News release issued from the office of Representative Frank Thompson Jr., June 18, 1990.

17. *Congressional Open Meeting in Atlanta*, news release, April 28, 1980, issued by Congress of the United States, Joint Committee on Printing.

18. "Senate Jobs under Control of Republicans," *Washington Star*, December 13, 1980.

19. Letter from Augustus F. Hawkins, chair of the Joint Committee on Printing, asking heads of all federal departments and agencies to review the draft of "Government Printing and Binding Regulations," November 9, 1983.

20. George B. Driesen, *Memorandum for the Joint Council of GPO Unions on the Constitutionality of the Joint Committee on Printing's Statutory Authority over Public Printing*, March 27, 1985.

21. Speech given by Senator Charles McMathias, chair of the Joint Committee on Printing of the United States Congress, at the Congressional Information Service breakfast at the American Library Association Conference in Philadelphia on July 12, 1982.

22. Ad Hoc Committee on Depository Library Access to Federal Automated Data Bases, *Provision of Federal Government Publications in Electronic Format to Depository Libraries: Report of the Ad Hoc Committee on Depository Library Access to Federal Automated Data Bases to the Joint Committee on Printing, United States Congress* (Washington, D.C.: U.S. Government Printing Office, 1984), IV.

23. Ad Hoc Committee on Depository Library Access to Federal Automated Data Bases, *Provision of Federal Government*, IV.

24. Ad Hoc Committee on Depository Library Access to Federal Automated Data Bases, *Provision of Federal Government Publications*, IV.

25. Ad Hoc Committee on Depository Library Access to Federal Automated Data Bases, *Provision of Federal Government Publications*, 10.

26. *Title 44 U.S.C.—Review*, Hearings Held before the Subcommittee on Procurement and Printing of the Committee on House Administration, U.S. House of Representatives, 101st Congress, 1st sess., May 23, 24, and June 28, 29, 1989 (Washington, D.C., Government Printing Office, 1989).

27. *United States Code*, title 44, chap. 19, Depository Library Program, sec. 1901.

28. "A Bill to Amend Title 44, United States Code, to Reform the Public Information Functions of the Public Printer and the Superintendent of Documents," rough draft, Bill No. 1, August 2, 1989, 101st Congress, 1st sess. (Bates 107).

29. Letter from Richard M. Dougherty, president of the American Library Association, and Patricia Glass Schuman, chair of the ALA Legislation Committee, to Representative Bates, chair, Subcommittee on Procurement and Printing, Committee on House Administration, U.S. Congress, July 5, 1990.

30. Summary of meeting of Washington Library Task Force with Representative Jim Bates and Kathryn Heyer on May 22, 1990, submitted by David Cobb, Ridley Kessler, Jack Sulzer, Susan Tulis, June 1990.

31. Letter from Representative Bates to Eileen Cooke, director, ALA Washington office, June 4, 1990.

32. Summary of meeting of Washington Library Task Force with Representative Jim Bates and Kathryn Heyer on May 22, 1990, submitted by David Cobb, Ridley Kessler, Jack Sulzer, Susan Tulis, June 1990.

33. Summary of meeting of Washington Library Task Force with Representative Jim Bates and Kathryn Heyer on May 22, 1990, submitted by David Cobb, Ridley Kessler, Jack Sulzer, Susan Tulis, June 1990.

34. Summary of meeting of Washington Library Task Force with Representative Jim Bates and Kathryn Heyer on May 22, 1990, submitted by David Cobb, Ridley Kessler, Jack Sulzer, Susan Tulis, June 1990.

35. Letter from the American Library Association to Representative Jim Bates, chair, Subcommittee on Procurement and Printing, Committee on House Administration, July 5, 1990, signed by Richard M. Dougherty, president, and Patricia Glass Schuman, chair, ALA Legislation Committee.

36. Letter from the American Library Association to Representative Jim Bates.

37. "Statement on Behalf of the American Association of Law Libraries by Cheryl Rae Nyberg, University of Illinois Law Library before the Subcommittee on Procurement and Printing, Committee on House Administration on H.R. 3849, the Government Printing Office Improvement Act of 1990," March 7 and 8, 1990.

38. Letter from Robert W. Houk, public printer of the United States, to Jim Bates, chair, Subcommittee on Procurement and Printing, Committee on House Administration, U.S. House of Representatives, October 1990.

39. Letter from Kenneth B. Allen, senior vice president, Government Relations, Information Industry Association, Washington, D.C., to Jim Bates, chair, Subcommittee on Procurement and Printing, Committee on House Administration, U.S. House of Representatives, March 15, 1990.

40. Letter from Sarah Holterhoff, chair, Government Relations Committee, American Association of Law Libraries, to Jim Bates, August 31, 1990.

41. Memorandum from Debby Miller, Executive Office of the Illinois Library Association, to Congressman Annunzio's library constituents, October 15, 1990.

42. Comments of Congressman Pat Roberts, House Administration Subcommittee on Printing and Procurement, September 18, 1990.

43. Bill McAllister, "Dozens of Nominees on Senate 'Hold,' GOP, and One Democrat, Using Tactic for Protest and Partisanship," *Washington Post*, October 29, 1997, A21.

44. David Sarasohn, "Bartleby the Senator, in the U.S. Senate, Any Member Can Stop Something by Secretly Saying He'd Prefer Not to Vote on It," *Sunday Oregonian*, August 17, 1997, E-4.

45. "Some Senate Sunshine," *Helena Independent Record*, March 7, 1999, 6C.

46. Kenneth J. Cooper, "Straying Lawmakers May Face Revived Party Discipline on Hill," *Washington Post*, December 17, 1994, A5.

47. Cooper, "Straying Lawmakers."

48. Following are some of the people from key states who greatly influenced members of Congress to support a number of bills supporting public access to government information in electronic format in order by key states: North Carolina, Jeanne Isacco, Marilyn Miller (president of ALA in 1992 and 1993), Ridley Kessler, Dan Barkley, William Graves, James H. Woodward; Kentucky, Jim Nelson (state librarian of Kentucky), Sandra

McAninch (chair of GODORT in 1988 and 1989), Cindy Etkins, Larry X. Besant and Bob Johnson; California, Linda Kennedy (chair of GODORT in 1991 and 1992), Kathryn Mawdsley (witness at many appropriations hearings on depository library budget), Gary Strong (state librarian), Mary Martin, Richard West; Alaska, Ann Symons (president of ALA) and Elizabeth Morrissette; Tennessee, James Veatch, Larry Romans, and Roberta Scull (born in Tennessee but a librarian in Louisiana); Illinois, Lois Mills (persuaded Senator Simon to cosponsor Senate bill); Kansas, Robert Walter and Duane Johnson (persuaded Representative Roberta Palen and Senator Kassenbaum to cosponsor bills); Georgia, Richard Leacy, Lynn Walshak; New York, Representative Major Owens (testified at hearings and cosponsored bill), Patricia Glass Schuman (president of ALA 1991 to 1992), Mary Redmond, Barbara Smith, and Nancy Kranich (chair of Subcommittee on Government Information of the ALA Committee on Legislation); Nevada, Martha Gould and Duncan Aldridge (persuaded Representative Vucanovich to cosponsor bill and testify at hearings).

49. "Keeping Government Information Accessible: FLICC Holds Ninth Annual Forum," *LC Information Bulletin*, April 20, 1992, 177.

50. Letter from Julia F. Wallace, chair of the Government Documents Round Table, to Marilyn L. Miller, president of the American Library Association, April 10, 1993.

51. Letter from Wallace to Miller, April 10, 1993.

52. U.S. House of Representatives, Committee on House Administration, "Report on S. 564, GPO Access Act of 1993," H. Rpt. 103-108, May 25, 1993.

53. Newt Gingrich, *Lessons Learned the Hard Way: A Personal Report* (New York: HarperCollins, 1998), 177.

54. Gingrich, *Lessons*, 178.

Conclusion

Senator Paul Wellstone sums up lobbying with this advice:

> There are three critical ingredients to democratic renewal and pro-
> gressive change: good public policy, grassroots organizing, and elec-
> toral politics. Policy provides direction and an agenda for action;
> grassroots organizing builds a constituency for change; and electoral
> politics is the main way we contest for power and hold decision
> makers accountable.[1]

In his book, Senator Wellstone adds another ingredient, seeing
others as human beings. He says he was not able to persuade other
senators to see things his way until he approached them as human
beings. I have tried to tell the story of human beings who wanted to
do good even though sometimes their personal lives interfered with
their efforts. Some of the stories may sound sensationalistic, but they
are there because that is the reality of lobbying. Human beings make
and lobby for laws, and when they make mistakes, a lot of their
work is lost, at least temporarily. Those who keep fighting for good
policies, no matter the hardships, win.

It is the story of how one idea—free access to electronic government information for all the people—culminated in the GPO Access
Act of 1993. The stories also show that the struggle will never be
over as long as there are people who disagree about the fundamental policies underlying the people's access to information. Everyone
in this struggle must encourage others to carry on the fight so that

after they sew their quilt square others will be there to add their squares to the "star quilt" of information policy.

NOTES

1. Paul Wellstone, *The Conscience of a Liberal: Reclaiming the Compassionate Agenda* (New York: Random House, 2001), 207.

Appendix: Library- and Information-Related Associations

American Association of Law Libraries (AALL), in Chicago, was established in 1906; has about five thousand members, regional groups, an annual conference, a website; and publishes *AALL Spectrum*. www.aallnet.org/

American Booksellers Association (ABA), in Tarrytown, New York, was established in 1900; has about six thousand members, regional groups, an annual conference, and a website. www.bookweb.org/

American Historical Association, in Washington, D.C., was established in 1884, has about sixteen thousand members and an annual conference, and publishes *American Historical Association—Perspectives*. www.theaha.org/

American Indian Library Association (AILA), in San Marcos, California, was established in 1979 and has three hundred members and a website. www.nativeculture.com/lisamitten/aila.html

American Library Association (ALA), in Chicago, was established in 1876; has about sixty-three thousand members, state chapters, an annual conference, a midwinter meeting, and a website; and publishes *American Libraries*. www.ala.org/

American Society for Information Science (ASIS), in Silver Spring, Maryland, was established in 1937 and has about four thousand members, national and local groups, an annual conference, and a website. www.asis.org/

Art Libraries Society/North America (ARLIS/NA), currently in Kanata, Ontario, was established in 1972, has about 1,350 members, holds an annual conference, and publishes *ARLIS/NA Update*. www.arlisna.org/

Asian/Pacific American Librarians Association (APALA), in Atlanta, was established in 1980 and has about two hundred members. www.uic.edu/depts/lib/projects/resources/apala/

Association of American Publishers (AAP), in New York City, was established in 1970 and has about two members, an annual conference, and a website. www.publishers.org/

Association of Research Libraries (ARL), in Washington, D.C., established in 1932, has 120 member libraries. www.arl.org/

Catholic Library Association (CLA), in Pittsfield, Massachusetts, was established in 1921; has about one thousand members, local groups, and an annual conference held in conjunction with National Catholic Education Association; and publishes *Catholic Library World and Index to Catholic Periodicals and National Catholic Newspapers.* www.cathla.org/

Chief Officers of State Library Agencies (COSLA), in Lexington, Kentucky, was established in 1973, has fifty members, meets quarterly, and has a website. www.cosla.org/

Chinese American Librarians Associations (CALA), in Sacramento, California, was established in 1973 and has 770 members and regional groups. www.cala-web.org/

Electronic Publishers Association, in Santa Cruz, California, was established in 1993, has one thousand members, regional groups and an annual conference.

Federal Library and Information Center Committee (FLICC), in Washington, D.C., was established in 1965 and has fifty-seven member libraries from three branches of federal government. www.loc.gov/flicc/

Friends of Libraries (FOLUSA), in Philadelphia, Pennsylvania, was established in 1979, has about 2,800 members, meets in conjunction with ALA, and has a website. www.folusa.com/

Information Industry Association (IIA) merged with Software Publishers Association in 1999 and is now called Software and Information Industry Association (SIAA).

International Federation of Library Associations and Institutions (IFLA), in The Hague, Netherlands, was established in 1927, has 1,700 members in over 150 countries. It holds an annual conference in a different country each year. www.ifla.org/

Medical Library Association (MLA), in Chicago, was established in 1898; has about five thousand members, regional groups, and an annual convention; and publishes *Bulletin of the Medical Library Association*. www.mlanet.org/

Mountain Plains Library Association, at the University of South Dakota, Weeks Library, established in 1948, has 920 members, publishes the MPLA Newsletter, and has a website. www.usd.edu/mpla/

Music Library Association (MLA), in Canton, Massachusetts, was established in 1931, has about two thousand members and regional groups, and publishes *Music Library Association—Notes*. www.musiclibraryassoc.org/

New England Educational Media Association (NEEMA) was established in 1918 and has 1,300 members. www.neema.org/

New England Library Association (NELA) was established in 1963 and has 1,500 members. www.nelib.org

Pacific Northwest Library Association (PNLA), in Burnaby, British Columbia, was established in 1908, has 528 members, publishes *PNLA Quarterly*, and has a website. www.pnla.org/

Patent and Trademark Depository Library Association (PTDLA) was established in 1983 and has ninety members. www.ptdla.org/

PEN American Center (PEN), in New York City, was established in 1921 and has about 2,800 members, regional groups, and a website. www.pen.org/

Reading Is Fundamental (RIF), in Washington, D.C., was established in 1966. It is composed of volunteer groups and has a website. www.rif.org/

REFORMA was established in 1971 and has about nine hundred members, twenty-one regional chapters, and a website. It meets in conjunction with ALA. www.reforma.org/

Society for American Archivists (SAA), in Chicago, was established in 1936; has about 3,400 members, an annual conference, and a website; and publishes *American Archivist*. www.archivist.org/

Software and Information Industry Association (SIIA), in Washington, D.C., was established in 1999, has 1,400 members, and holds annual conferences. www.siaa.net/

Southeastern Library Association (SELA) was established in 1920 and has seven hundred members. sela.lib.ucf.edu/

Special Libraries Association (SLA), in Washington, D.C., was established in 1909; has about fifteen thousand members, regional groups, an annual conference, and a website; and publishes *Information Outlook*. www.sla.org/

Theatre Library Association (TLA), in New York City and established in 1937, has five hundred members, holds an annual conference in conjunction with ALA, and publishes *Broadside*. tla.library.unt.edu/default.asp

Ukrainian Library Association (ULA), in New York City and established in 1961, has about 290 members and regional groups. www.uba.org.ua/eng/

Urban Libraries Council (ULC), in Evanston, Illinois, and established in 1971, has 130 members, holds meetings in conjunction with ALA, has a website, and publishes *Frequent Facts Survey Reports*. www.urbanlibraries.org/

Western Association of Map Libraries (WAML), in San Diego, California, and established in 1967, has about 225 members, meets twice a year, and publishes *Information Bulletin*. www.waml.org/

Glossary

Committee print: Committee prints are special reports developed by U.S. congressional committees to support the legislative or investigative process. Many prints are based on reports researched and written by the Library of Congress Congressional Research Service at the request of the committees.

Government Printing Office: The Government Printing Office is a U.S. legislative branch agency responsible for providing printing of government documents and publications for government agencies. GPO is also responsible for acquiring, cataloging, and distributing government publications to the government, depository libraries, and the public.

National Technical Information Service: NTIS was established after the World War II to handle captured scientific and technical reports. It was later expanded to handle scientific and technical reports published by government agencies and their contractors.

Public printer of the United States: The public printer of the United States is the head of the Government Printing Office. He or she is nominated by the president and confirmed by the Senate.

Superintendent of documents: The superintendent of documents reports to the public printer and is responsible for managing the depository library, sales, and international exchange programs at the Government Printing Office.

United States Congressional *Serial Set***:** The *Serial Set* is the bound permanent compilation of the U.S. congressional reports and documents.

Bibliography

Allen, Judy. *Event Planning: The Ultimate Guide to Successful Meetings, Corporate Events, Fundraising Galas, Conferences, Incentives, and Other Special Events.* Toronto: Wiley, 2000.

American Library Association. *ALA Handbook of Organization 1997–98.* Chicago: Author, 1997. A supplement to American libraries.

———. *Libraries and Democracy: The Cornerstones of Liberty*, ed. Nancy Kranich. Chicago: Author, June 2001.

———. *Smart Voting Starts @ Your Library.* Chicago: Author, 2000. A tip sheet that gives ideas on how libraries can be an electoral resource and use the election season to promote library issues.

American Library Association with Global Learning, Inc. *Libraries Build Sustainable Communities: Decide Tomorrow Today.* Chicago: Author, 1999.

Barbato, Joseph, and Danielle S. Furlich. *Writing for a Good Cause: The Complete Guide to Crafting Proposals and Other Persuasive Pieces for Nonprofits.* New York: Simon & Schuster, 2000. The authors give good advice on how to write about your cause in order to obtain money and support and how to create newsletters.

Beckerman, Edwin. *Politics and the American Public Library: Creating Political Support for Library Goals.* Lanham, Md.: Scarecrow, 1996. Beckerman gives advice on how to use politics to gain support for public libraries.

Berners-Lee, Tim. *Weaving the Web: The Original Design and Ultimate Destiny of the World Wide Web by Its Inventor.* New York: HarperCollins, 1999.

Bernstein, Richard B., and Jerome Agel. *Into the Third Century: The Congress.* New York: Walker, 1989. A well-written brief history of the Congress from its founding to 1989.

Besant, Larry X., and Deborah Sharp. "Upsize This: Libraries Need Relationship Marketing." *Information Outlook* (March 2000): 17–22. The authors argue that librarians must change from counting things like the number of volumes to justify their existence to marketing their services, stressing quality versus quantity.

Bike, William S. *Winning Political Campaigns: A Comprehensive Guide to Electoral Success*. Juneau: Denali, 1998. Bike wrote this book to help candidates running for public office, but much of his practical advice will help when lobbying for votes for a library levy, passage of a bill, or adoption of a policy.

Bingham, Clara. *Women on the Hill: Challenging the Culture of Congress*. New York: Random House, 1997. Bingham writes about how four women members of Congress tried to change the culture of Congress so they could influence legislation.

Birnbaum, Jeffrey H. *The Lobbyists: How Influence Peddlers Get Their Way in Washington*. New York: Random House, 1992. Birnbaum, a reporter who covers politics in Washington, D.C., tells how lobbyists for the nation's corporate giants influence the political process.

Black, Allida M. *Courage in a Dangerous World: The Political Writings of Eleanor Roosevelt*. New York: Columbia University Press, 1999. Black has pulled together the writings of Eleanor Roosevelt, which show how she influenced the world in promoting her beliefs.

Broder, David S. *Democracy Derailed: Initiative Campaigns and the Power of Money*. New York: Harcourt, 2000. Broder, a reporter for the *Washington Post*, explains the initiative process with good examples but draws a different conclusion than I would from the data. Unfortunately, big money influences all political activity, but doing away with the initiative process is not the answer.

Brownmiller, Susan. *In Our Time: Memoir of a Revolution*. New York: Dial, 1999. A history of how women changed the world for women through activism.

Burns, James MacGregor, J. W. Peltason, Thomas E. Cronin, and David B. Magleby. *State and Local Politics: Government by the People*, 9th ed. Upper Saddle River, N.J.: Prentice-Hall, 1998. The authors argue that state and local governments flourished on this continent before a government of the United States was even conceptualized. Indeed, the framers of our Constitution shaped the national government largely according to their practical experience with colonial and community governments. What happens today in our eighty-five thousand state and local governments continues to influence the forms and policies of the national government. The reverse, of course, is also true: The national government and its policies have an important impact on local and state government.

Caro, Robert A. *Master of the Senate*. New York: Knopf, 2002. The years of Lyndon Johnson.

Chandler, Yvonne J. *Guide to Finding Legal & Regulatory Information on the Internet*. New York: Neal-Schuman, 1998.

Clotfelter, Charles T., and Thomas Ehrlich. *Philanthropy and the Nonprofit Sector*. Bloomington: Indiana University Press, 1999. A scholarly book on the nonprofit sector and its influence on society.

DeMac, Donna. *Keeping America Un-informed*. New York: Pilgrim, 1984. A comprehensive review of how the Reagan administration suppressed information; attempted to privatize government information production and dissemination; cut support of federal library programs, including changing the personnel standards for federal librarians (which would have led to the hiring of unqualified staff); and eliminated many publications needed by the public.

———. *Liberty Denied*. New York: PEN American Center, 1988. DeMac writes about how in the name of cost cutting and saving of taxes the government during the 1980s made it difficult for the public to access the government information, particularly that collected by regulatory agencies and privatized federal libraries, thus limiting public access, and attempted to censor information produced by government employees and accessed by the public.

Dolnick, Sandy. *Friends of Libraries Sourcebook*, 3d ed. Chicago: American Library Association, 1996. A good source for information on how to organize and manage a Friends group.

Dychtwald, Ken. *Age Power: How the 21st Century Will Be Ruled by the Old*. New York: Tarcher/Putnam, 1999. Dychtwald, a psychologist and gerontologist, analyzes how organizations representing older people are influencing the political process and allocation of resources through effective organizing and lobbying.

Edwards, Lee. *The Conservative Revolution: The Movement That Remade America*. New York: Free Press, 1999. Edwards, a former member of the National Commission on Libraries and Information Service, tells the story of how the conservative movement was created by building grassroots organizations, starting magazines, seizing control of the Republican Party, and following the lead of its leaders, Robert Taft, Barry Goldwater, Ronald Reagan, and Newt Gingrich.

Esman, Milton J. *Government Works: Why Americans Need the Feds*. Ithaca, N.Y.: Cornell University Press, 2000. Esman argues that those who have instilled distrust of government have gone too far and gives reasons and tactics to work on improving the public's confidence in government.

Frantzich, Stephen E. *Citizen Democracy: Political Activists in a Cynical Age*. Lanham, Md.: Rowman & Littlefield, 1999. Frantzich tells the stories of individuals who lobbied for changes.

Frohmayer, John. *Leaving Town Alive: Confessions of an Arts Warrior*. Boston: Houghton Mifflin, 1993. The former chair of the National Endowment for the Arts tells the story of power politics in Washington, D.C., from the perspective of an agency head in the middle of a heated battle over public funding of the arts. He ended up losing his job but not his integrity.

Galbraith, James K. *Created Unequal: The Crisis in American Pay*. New York: Free Press, 1998.

Gingrich, Newt. *Lessons Learned the Hard Way: A Personal Report*. New York: HarperCollins, 1998

Goehlert, Robert U., and Fenton S. Martin. *Congress and Law-Making*, 2d ed. Santa Barbara, Calif.: ABC-CLIO, 1989. A guide for tracing U.S. congressional legislation, including major information sources about Congress. A lot has happened to make it easier to access this kind of information since this book was published, but it is still good for many of the important sources.

Green, Mark, with Michael Waldman. *Who Runs Congress?* New York: Dell, 1984.

Harass, Richard N. *The Power to Persuade*. New York: Houghton Mifflin, 1994. Harass, a former legislative assistant in the U.S. Senate, staffer at the Departments of State and Defense, and employee at the National Security Council, shares his ideas on how to increase the "effectiveness of the individuals working in and with governments and other large, often unruly, organizations."

Harrison, W. Fox Jr., and Susan Webb Hammond. *Congressional Staffs: The Invisible Force in American Lawmaking*. New York: Free Press, 1977. The basic information about the role of staff is still good, but most of the statistics are out of date now.

Hentoff, Nat. *The Nat Hentoff Reader*. Cambridge, Mass.: Da Capo, 2001. Hentoff gives an inside view of politics in chapter 4, "The Beast of Politics."

Herman, Edward. *Locating United States Government Information: A Guide to Sources*, 2d. ed. Buffalo, N.Y.: Hein, 1999.

Hoffman, Elizabeth Cobbs. *All You Need Is Love: The Peace Corps and the Spirit of the 1960s*. Cambridge, Mass.: Harvard University Press, 1998.

Horn, Zoia. *Zoia: Memoirs of Zoia Horn, Battler for the People's Right to Know*. Jefferson, N.C.: McFarland, 1995. An inspiring story of a life devoted to the defense of constitutional and human rights and the people's right to know.

Hundt, Reed E. *You Say You Want a Revolution: A Story of Information Age Politics*. New Haven, Conn.: Yale University Press, 2000.

Jackley, John. *Hill Rat: Blowing the Lid off Congress*. Washington, D.C.: Regnery Gateway, 1992. *Hill Rat* is a term used to describe those who work for Congress. Jackley turned his journal notes into a book that takes you behind the scenes.

Johnson, Dennis W. *No Place for Amateurs: How Political Consultants Are Reshaping American Democracy*. New York: Routledge, 2001. The author shows how professional consultants are taking over political campaigns, including initiatives and referendums. There is a good listing of political consulting firms and Internet resources.

Kessler, Ronald. *Inside Congress*. New York: Pocket Books, 1997.

Kinney, Lisa F. *Lobby for Your Library: Know What Works*. Chicago: American Library Association, 1992.

Kush, Christopher. *Cybercitizen: How to Use Your Computer to Fight for All the Issues You Care About*. New York: St. Martin's Griffin, 2000.

Levy, Reynold. *Give and Take: A Candid Account of Corporate Philanthropy*. Boston: Harvard Business School Press, 1999.

Loeb, Paul Rogat. *Soul of a Citizen: Living with Conviction in a Cynical Time.* New York: St. Martin's Griffin, 1999. Rogat illustrates citizen activism with stories of people working alone and together to change the world.

Malina, June. *Federal Publishers Committee Handbook.* Washington, D.C.: U.S. Government Printing Office, 1993.

Matthews, Christopher. *Hardball: How Politics Is Played Told by One Who Knows the Game.* New York: Harper & Row, 1988. Matthews, former staffer for Speaker Tip O'Neill, discusses how power to influence legislation and policies is used in Washington, D.C.

Maxymuk, John. *Government Online: One-Click Access to 3,400 Federal and State Websites.* New York: Neal-Schuman, 2001.

McCook, Kathleen de la Pena. *A Place at the Table: Participating in Community Building.* Chicago: American Library Association, 2000. The author gives good advice on how librarians can get involved early in community development by demanding a place at the community planning and development table and what to do once they are there.

Munson, Richard. *The Cardinals of Capitol Hill: The Men and Women Who Control Government Spending.* New York: Grove, 1993. The members of the U.S. House Appropriations Committee have been nicknamed the "cardinals." This book tracks how these members of Congress determine what would be in the fiscal year 1992 appropriations bill and who influenced them along the way.

Nanus, Burt, and Stephen M. Dobbs. *Leaders Who Make a Difference.* San Francisco: Jossey-Bass, 1999. A book on how the leaders of nonprofit organizations can assure that their organization will meet its goals. Lots of good ideas that can be used by anyone learning how to lobby for the public good.

Neal, Tommy. *Lawmaking and the Legislative Process: Committees, Connections, and Compromises.* Phoenix: National Conference of State Legislatures, Oryx, 1996. The author is a policy specialist in the Legislative Management Program at the National Conference of State Legislatures in Colorado. He covers the legislative process on the federal and the state levels. Most of his state examples are based on the practices in Colorado.

Notess, Greg. *Government Information on the Internet,* 2d. ed. Washington, D.C.: Bernan, 1998.

O'Neill, Tip, with Gary Hymel. *All Politics Is Local and Other Rules of the Game.* New York: Times Books, 1994. Tip O'Neill distills the secrets of a lifetime in politics. His advice is good for politicians and those who lobby them.

O'Neill, Tip, and William Novak. *Man of the House: The Life and Political Memoirs of Speaker Tip O'Neill.* New York: St. Martin's, 1988.

Patterson, Bradley H. *The White House Staff: Inside the West Wing and Beyond.* Washington, D.C.: Brookings Institution, 2000. A very entertaining and valuable book unlocking the secrets of the White House staff, including numbers, offices, and tactics. A must read for anyone lobbying the federal government.

Pell, Eve. *The Big Chill*. Boston: Beacon, 1984. Pell covers the efforts in the 1980s of the Reagan administration, corporate America, and religious conservatives to subvert free speech and the public's right to know.

Penny, Timothy J., and Major Garrett. *Common Cents*. Boston: Little, Brown, 1995. A retiring six-term congressman reveals how Congress really works and what must be done to fix it.

Perritt, Henry H., Jr. *Electronic Public Information and the Public's Right to Know*. Washington, D.C.: Benton Foundation, 1990.

Phillips, Kevin. *Arrogant Capitol: Washington, Wall Street, and the Frustrations of American Politics*. Boston: Little, Brown, 1994. Phillips tells us why Washington, D.C., is out of touch with the rest of America and how special interests control the development of policies.

Plano, Jack C., and Milton Greenberg. *The American Political Dictionary*, 10th ed. Fort Worth, Tex.: Harcourt Brace College, 1997. Provides a source of 1,300 terms used in the study of the political process.

Reed, Ralph. *Active Faith: How Christians Are Changing the Soul of American Politics*. New York: Free Press, 1996. The story of how the Christian Coalition grew from 5,000 members in 1989 to 1.7 million members and supporters in 1995, with almost 2,000 local chapters working to influence legislation from school boards to the United States Congress.

Reed, Sally Gardner. *Making the Case for Your Library: A How-to-Do-It Manual*. New York: Neal-Schuman, 2001.

Reich, Charles A. *Opposing the System*. New York: Crown, 1995. Reich argues "Citizens do not have to choose between "working within the system" and violent revolution. "Regaining control" represents the middle ground of subjecting the system to democratic authority.

Robinson, Judith Schiek. *Tapping the Government Grapevine: The User-Friendly Guide to U.S. Government Information Sources*. 3d. ed. Phoenix: Oryx, 1998. This is a good overall source of how to access information about legislation, regulations, and court decisions. It describes traditional and electronic sources of information as well as what is available through libraries and the depository library program.

Safire, William. *The New Language of Politics: An Anecdotal Dictionary of Catchwords, Slogans & Political Usage*. New York: Random House, 1968. Good source for terms used to describe politics and government.

Schnapper, M. B. *Constraint by Copyright*. Washington, D.C.: Public Affairs Press, 1960.

Sears, Jean L., and Marilyn K. Moody. *Using Government Information Sources Print and Electronic*, 3d. ed. Phoenix: Oryx, 2001.

Seymour, Whitney North Jr., and Elizabeth N. Layne. *For the People: Fighting For Public Libraries*. Garden City, N.Y.: Doubleday, 1979. This book inspired the delegates at the White House conference in 1979 and is still an inspiring book.

Smith, Hedrick. *Power Game, How Washington Works.* New York: Ballantine, 1988. Smith writes about who has power and how they use it in the labyrinth of Washington, D.C., and how insiders use the press to get out their message to increase their power.

Special Library Association Government Information Services Committee and the Committee on Information Hangups. *An Evaluation with Recommendations for Action of the Government Printing Office's Services from the User's Point of View.* New York: Special Library Association, 1978.

Taft Group for the American Library Association. *The Big Book of Library Grant Money 2002–2003: Profiles of Private and Corporate Foundations and Direct Corporate Givers Receptive to Library Grant Proposals.* Chicago: American Library Association, 2001.

Theoharis, Athan G. *A Culture of Secrecy: The Government versus the People's Right to Know.* Lawrence: University Press of Kansas, 1998. Theoharis tells the story of what government information the government is hiding and the fight by many to change the laws and policies to assure that information is made available to the public.

Thomas, Bill. *Club Fed: Power, Money, Sex, and Violence on Capitol Hill.* New York: Scribner's, 1994. Thomas, former reporter for the *Baltimore Sun*, writes about the seamier side of Capitol Hill life and how some people lobby the Congress.

Ward, Geoffrey C., and Ken Burns. *Not for Ourselves Alone: The Story of Elizabeth Cady Stanton and Susan B. Anthony: An Illustrated History.* New York: Knopf, 1999. The story of two of the most effective lobbyists in the history of the United States.

Warner, Robert M. *Diary of a Dream: A History of the National Archives Independence Movement, 1980–1985.* Lanham, Md.: Scarecrow, 1995. The story of the lobbying to establish the National Archives as an independent agency, no longer part of the General Services Administration.

Wellstone, Paul. *The Conscience of a Liberal: Reclaiming the Compassionate Agenda.* New York: Random House, 2001.

Witcover, Jules. *No Way to Pick a President.* New York: Farrar, Straus & Giroux, 1999. Witcover, a newspaperman for over fifty years, covering every election since 1952, discusses how the glut of money and professional paid for campaigners are corrupting American political life.

Wright, Jim. *Balance of Power: Presidents and Congress from the Era of McCarthy to the Age of Gingrich.* Atlanta: Turner, 1996.

Zweig, Michael. *The Working Class Majority: America's Best Kept Secret.* Ithaca, N.Y.: Cornell University Press, 2000. Zweig argues that the majority of people are working class and need to recognize that and organize so they can exercise political power and help shape the world.

Index

About the Author

Bernadine E. Abbott-Hoduski spent twenty years as a professional staff member for the Congressional Joint Committee on Printing. Her primary job was to convince government officials in all three branches of government to provide government information to the public. She spent her previous professional career as a librarian for the Environmental Protection Agency, several universities, and the Kansas City Public Library. She is currently a government information adviser and has consulted with the South Africa and Zimbabwe governments and commercial publishers. She also chairs the ALA Committee on Legislation for 2002 to 2003.